Congress Whispers,
Reservation Nations Endure

D1059851

Congress Whispers,
Reservation Nations Endure
A Century of Public Acts of Aggression, Confusion, & Resolution

B. LEE WILSON

SECOND EDITION

B. L. Wilson & Associates, LLC

CONGRESS WHISPERS, RESERVATION NATIONS ENDURE
A CENTURY OF PUBLIC ACTS OF AGGRESSION, CONFUSION, & RESOLUTION

Second Edition - ISBN: 978-0-692-07685-9
Copyright © 2018 by B. L. Wilson & Associates, LLC
Certain stock imagery © Shutterstock and © Thinkstock.
B. L. Wilson & Associates rev. date: 08/28/18
Cover photo: C. Breeman
All rights reserved.

First Edition - ISBN: 978-1-4582-0596-4 (e)
Copyright ©2012 by B. L. Wilson & Associates, LLC
Abbott Press rev. date: 01/11/13
All rights reserved.

Table of Contents

Legislative Sample, Part III: 1962-1990

Preface

"True patriotism hates injustice in its own land more than anywhere else."

CLARENCE DARROW

TRAVELS INTO FORTY-EIGHT states and dozens of reservation communities amplified my initial interest in reading the public laws that transformed most tribal lands of the Civil War Era into western states, national parks, and public lands. I looked for this legislative collection long before I published it. I looked in bookshops, used book collections, county libraries, and online. Finding astute analyses of each public law featured within this collection, but no corresponding compendium of original transcripts, I rolled up my sleeves and headed for the reading rooms of the National Archives and the Library of Congress.[1] Ten years later, I published a first edition—a sui generis collection of U.S. public law specific to American Indian nations. This second edition represents yet another step in my ongoing quest to comprehend the enduring power of America's fundamental promise to all Americans: Life, Liberty, and the Pursuit of Happiness.

The impact of these laws upon America's past, present, and future is of epic proportions. They affect all Americans and benefit most. This body of law, however, applies most directly to less than 1.5% of our nation's total citizenry—those members of federally recognized tribal nations who live within the geographic boundaries of American Indian or Alaskan Native reservations. While these U.S. citizens are subject to the same public laws as those affecting all other Americans, they must also continuously attune to an abundance of ever-present tribally specific public laws. As an applied anthropologist whose long-term focus remains fixated upon federal policies and related public health outcomes, field experiences redirect me into the cross-referencing of primary source documents at every turn. In this collection, primary sources include samples of more than thirty rarified public laws—quintessential examples of U.S. policies toward American Indian Nations. This collection considers lawmaking of the early eighteenth century, then moves into specific considerations of excerpts and transcripts of the

1885-1990 legislative timeline. Subsequent legislation of this genre resulted in a multitude of amendments of the public laws found herein.[2] Excerpts of transcripts of Senate and House dialogues and orations are also presented as found within various volumes of the official Congressional Record.[3] Every effort has been made to present these varied texts as originally written, keeping their idiosyncrasies of spelling and syntax intact.

A graduate research project introduced me to the analytical works of the most prominent cultural anthropologists, historians, and legal scholars whose writings focused on U.S. policies of this genre. This compendium highlights a selection of in-depth legislative commentaries by such notables in the field as Francis P. Prucha, S. Lyman Tyler, Wilcomb Washburn, Robert M. Utley, Arrell M. Gibson, William T. Hagan, Philleo Nash, Lawrence C. Kelly, and Vine Deloria, Jr.

Other influential publications that influenced the trajectory of this second edition include a Lakota-based mental health curriculum developed collaboratively by Dr. Robin Herman and Gary Neidenthal, the journalistic and creative writings of Harvey Arden, and Dr. Tom Holm's illuminating explanations of the dynamics of the Native American veteran experience. Samples of the Meriam Report of 1928, an oft-referenced Bureau of Indian Affairs analysis of reservation operations and living conditions, appear within several chapters and in Appendix C; some chapters also include key findings of more recent federal inquiries.

Statements made by Will Rogers, as gleaned from his newspaper columns and radio broadcasts about Capitol Hill's "goings-on" between 1925 and 1935 are also included. In my opinion, any review of public lawmaking of these years would be incomplete without savoring some of his brilliant words of compassionate irony and patriotic wisdom.

Ethnographic materials considered during the evolution of this collection derive in large measure from the works of Gregory Gagnon and Karen White Eyes; Severt Young Bear and R. D. Theisz; Elizabeth S. Grobsmith; and Joseph Starita. Reviews of a number of first-person narratives, including those found in the literary works of Chief Arvol Looking Horse, Leonard Peltier, Sherman Alexie, Warren Petoskey, and Michael Dorris, revealed ways in which individual tribal families have been affected by these laws.

Reading room staffs of the Library of Congress and the National Archives in Washington, DC, and the Public Library of Cincinnati and Hamilton County facilitated my collection of Senate and House transcripts. Staff of the Will Rogers Museum in Claremore, Oklahoma, supplied all of the Will Rogers quotations included within this publication.

I wish to thank the many friends and associates who supported this project. Conversations with trusted colleagues—social workers, community advocates, U.S. military combat veterans, college instructors, entrepreneurs, and other tribal community professionals—grounded my considerations of the many ways that generations of reservation families have shouldered the legacy of this set of legislation. I will remain forever indebted to the community leaders of four western reservations who reviewed this volume's initial manuscript prior to its publication.

Residents of contemporary reservation communities know the history, outcomes, and day-to-day responsibilities associated with this American Indian/Alaskan Native-only layer of public law. They also know how it frames the relationships of reservation communities, and their state and federal counterparts. With hopes of expanding such awareness to a wider circle of Americans, and encouraging all Americans to follow public lawmaking with both an open mind and a critical eye, I gratefully conclude this decades-long archival deep dive.

B. Lee Wilson

"In 1830, at the urging of southern and western Congressmen and Senators, the Indian Removal Act was passed ... this act marks the emergence of the legislative branch as the dominant factor in the formation of Indian Policy." [1]

VINE DELORIA, JR.
ANTHROPOLOGIST, AUTHOR, AND LEGAL SCHOLAR

Introduction

"My Country, 'tis of thee, sweet land of Liberty, of thee I sing."

AMERICA'S NATIONAL IDEALS of *Life, Liberty, and the Pursuit of Happiness* function within a legal infrastructure, one comprised of both houses of Congress, the Office of the President, and a national system of federal courts. Collectively, these three federal power centers must set all national policies, administer all federal programs, and uphold the U.S. Constitution. But it is Congress, the repository of the combined intellect of both the House of Representatives and the Senate, which creates all U.S. Public Laws. In this way, Congress expresses the will of the American People—through legislation it proposes, considers, and in some cases, votes into law. These congressional actions provide all Americans a legal architecture from which suspend their individual visions of America's enduring promise: *"… Life, Liberty, and … [opportunities to pursue] … Happiness."*

Congressional Lawmaking

Every federal law is a *Public Law*—a time-stamped legislative action. Public laws constitute the fundamental essence of all U.S. public policy. By casting winning votes to create public laws, congressional legislators collectively assert a measure of stewardship over the U.S. citizenry and the nation's natural resources.

Public lawmaking happens within a congressional whirlwind of conflicting parties, contrasting priorities, and, often, cantankerous mindsets. Special interest groups and other lobbyists promote their own economic and social power agendas to federal legislators and their state/local constituencies. Contemporary lobbyists include forces that President Dwight D. Eisenhower once dubbed "the military industrial complex," along with the insurance

13

industry, energy conglomerates, financial corporations, consumer groups, weapons manufacturers, religious organizations, health advocates, non-governmental organizations, and scores of other small-to-global corporate and nonprofit players.

In spite of the complexity and challenging dynamics of this lawmaking environment, examples of ennobling and enduring historical outcomes abound, e.g., the nation's national parks system, voting rights, child labor laws, safer workplaces, increasingly safer highways and bridges, child protective services, cleaner air, and the eradication of polio in the United States.

In theory, U.S. public lawmaking exists to advance *the public good*. The extent to which any given public law affects individual citizens is weighted by pertinent personal, local, and regional circumstances. For example, laws that fund health services for low-income children may impact families living at the top of the economic ladder less than those dangling from the bottom rung, and laws that create construction jobs in Nevada may never make the news in the Sunshine State.

The public laws enacted by Congress do not always survive the scrutiny of federal courts and state legislatures. Take child labor laws, for example. Early in the twentieth century, when Congress fought to protect children from the dangers of working in coal mines, it met strong opposition within the courts, as explained within this summary of the trajectory of child labor lawmaking, 1916-1938:

> The Keating-Owen Act of 1916, which prevented the interstate shipment of goods produced in factories by children under 14 and in mines by children under 16, was struck down in the Hammer v. Dagenhart (1918) ruling. Likewise, the Pomerane Amendment of 1918, which taxed companies that used child labor, was declared unconstitutional in Bailey v. Drexel Furniture (1922) on the grounds that it was an unwarranted exercise of the commerce power of the federal government and violated states' rights. In 1924, the Senate passed a Constitutional amendment banning child labor, but it was never ratified by enough states. Finally, the Fair Labor Standards Act of 1938 prohibited the full-time employment of those 16 and under (with a few exemptions) and enacted a national minimum wage which made employing most children uneconomical. It received the Supreme Court's blessing.[1]

The purpose of each public law often appears less than transparent at a first reading, as some support multiple or even conflicting objectives. For example, a single legislative proposal might include hundreds of pages detailing ways it could assure cutting-edge upgrades of military equipment—while also including a single paragraph calling for a reduction in community-based services for at-risk children. And although the titles of some public laws align with their intent, other monikers tell little to nothing about the actual purpose of the law. The Indian Employment Act of 1979, for example, never addressed any aspect of "Indian Employment."[2] Even when the purpose of a specific public law is readily apparent, ramifications of its application are often oblique; for example, it is doubtful those legislators who advocated for passage of the "Indian Education Act of 1891" had any way of knowing it would be applied in ways that caused the deaths of many American Indian children.

Whether or not Congress authorizes funding to support its legislative mandates is sometimes left open to question. Indeed, in 2005, the State of Connecticut filed a suit (later dismissed) against the federal government, claiming it had "illegally imposed more than $50 million in unfunded mandates under the No Child Left Behind Act of 2001 ... [cga.ct.gov]." Similarly, on December 8, 1911, Congress set aside a site on Staten Island (New York) for a "Native American Indian Memorial," but when anticipated private funding never materialized, no memorial was constructed. Likewise, Indian Health Service legislation of the 1970s was never applied in a robust manner, as its limited funding filtered through a nationwide competitive system which gave low priority to the delivery of health services in low-population locales (e.g., reservations).

The Congressional Record

Whenever Congress is in session, its proceedings are public. Every public discussion, oration, filibuster, debate, and call for votes is captured as part of a tangible public record. This written record—today's *Congressional Record*—contains verbatim texts of House and Senate discussions, committee reports, proposals, and public laws as read into the official record prior to the call for votes. Members of Congress, their staff, and the general public can access these records through the Library of Congress.[3] Scholars interested in tracking the progress of any pending House bill, for example, can find summaries, updates, and more on the "congress.gov" website. This includes a bill entered into the public record on February 3, 2015 (i.e., H.R. 684) toward the amendment of "... the Trademark Act of 1946 regarding the disparagement of Native American persons or peoples through … [trademarks] … that use … [offensive terms] … and for other purposes."

Congressional Fact-Finding Committees

Congress, if it so chooses, has the authority and the latitude to move with agility from one priority to another. As its collective perspective adjusts to new information and understandings, Congress can, theoretically, attune its lawmaking to changing national circumstances and emerging local, political, regional, or national priorities. Still, its members make decisions within the limits of their individual understandings of national issues, and their personal, regional, and social biases factor into mindsets that may race backwards or shift sideways in time. To bridge gaps in the life experiences and expertise of its members, Congress forms fact-finding committees as needed. Such committees may spend weeks, even years, gathering data to better inform congressional discussions; their findings are then reported to the House and Senate "in Congress assembled." Typically, these committee reports include a historical perspective about the topic of interest, recommendations for specific congressional actions, and provide legislators with unfiltered, bi-partisan, in-depth, primary-source data. Such subcommittee information may not be available from any other verifiable and cohesive source. These reports often identify critical gaps in outcomes-related legislative efficacy.

Public Laws in the Shadows

Legislative actions specific to American Indian nations began with little fanfare with the enactment of the 1819 Civilization Act, and continued with the 1830 passage of the Indian Removal Act.[5] The earliest public laws of those featured within these pages—tribally focused *sui generis* laws—grew out of U.S. attempts to mitigate cross-cultural conflicts and communications between the United States and a broad range of domestic sovereign nations— American Indian tribes.[6] The U.S. Constitution assigned Congress the responsibility of regulating trade with federally recognized tribes through the language of its oft-cited "commerce clause." Legal scholars, including Vine Deloria, Jr (here quoted), identified fundamental expansions of the role of Congress, over time, in its dealings with American Indian nations.

> The commerce clause, Section 8, clause 3 or Article I of the Constitution, gives Congress the power to regulate commerce with foreign nations, and among the several

states, and with the Indian tribes. In theory Congress should have no greater power over Indian nations than it does over states, but in historical practice such has not been the case. The initial tendency of Congress was to establish the rule and regulations under which citizens of the United States could have trade and intercourse with Indian nations. Early statutes reflect this narrow view of the power and responsibilities of the legislative branch. Within two decades of the adoption of the Constitution, however, Congress began to appropriate funds for the civilization of Indians, and the creation of these kinds of funds represented a fundamental shift in Congress' view of its powers under the commerce clause. The goal was wholly humanitarian. Faced with the fictional dilemma of either exterminating or assimilating the Indian tribes, Congress chose the latter course, and began to develop a policy that would accomplish this goal.[7]

Public Laws of this 1885-1990 Legislative Sample

This collection of more than thirty public laws embodies the congressional architecture of America's historic, ongoing, and complicated relationship with its domestic sovereign nations—American Indian nations. Nowhere is the historic will of the American people more transparent than within key passages of the legislation presented within this volume.

The earliest public laws of this collection reflect the confusion and cultural arrogance of the times of their enactment. Their most enduring mandates continue to challenge the resilience of contemporary tribal communities (Legislative Sample, Part I, 1885-1920). Several public laws of this collection demonstrate a convoluted legislative history marked by a series of contrasting "Indian Policy" initiatives, e.g., tribal suppression legislation vs. congressional attempts to assure some measure of human rights for tribal members (Legislative Sample, Part II, 1921-1961). The most recent enactments of this legislative set show Congress granting tribal members U.S. citizenship—and opportunities to tap into the community resources and social service practices common throughout the USA (Legislative Sample, Part III, 1962-1990). The enduring social dichotomy these laws established— still vibrant today—lives in the uniquely American relationship between contemporary American Indian tribal members and their less regulated compatriots.

Most of the public laws presented as part of this legislative collection are quintessential examples of U.S. policies toward tribes. A few are more obscure, yet are included as examples of the broad range of tribally focused topics addressed by Congress during the 1885-1990 time line. Original transcripts of Senate and House sessions, congressional subcommittee reports, and federal commission reports to Congress—i.e., primary source federal documents—inform this volume's discussions of legislative actions, intentions, and outcomes.

Americans most directly affected by this set of legislative actions—with limited exception—meet the following two conditions of legal status: (1) tribal membership within a federally recognized tribe, and (2) residency within the geographic boundaries of a federally designated reservation. While Americans meeting this criteria are subject to the same public laws as those affecting all other U.S. citizens, they must also attune themselves to an abundance of tribally specific public laws.

This genre of Public Law, tribally focused legislation, presents a profusion of intertwined legalistic contradictions. Some of these laws took children away from caring, capable parents and sent them to distant institutions for years of cultural indoctrination, while later laws returned childrearing rights to tribal families and tribal communities. Long after Congress criminalized the speaking of American Indian languages in the nineteenth century, Congress later came to understand indigenous languages as national treasures. Similarly, for decades, Congress prohibited traditional American Indian marriages, religious practices, clothing, and hairstyles, but in time overturned all such prohibitions.

In the context of this legislative set, references to "federal funding" do not equate to general references to "federal tax dollars." Rather, in the context of U.S. Indian Policy discussions, "federal funding" phrasing is a euphemism for the federal distribution of *tribal funds*—those accrued by federal agencies through their rental of reservation lands held "in trust" by the United States. For example, historically and at present, tribal funds collected by federal agencies through their leasing of reservation lands to outside entities—e.g., ranchers, mining companies, and U.S. military bases—have supported the establishment and maintenance of reservation-based initiatives, e.g., food programs, off-reservation boarding schools for tribal children, and Federal Bureau of Investigation (FBI) law enforcement activities on reservations.

Collectively, these laws (legislated 1885-1990) mandated more than fifty often conflicting outcomes. These fifty categories of outcomes trailed along eleven legislative themes, with the top three as follows: (1) transfer of lands away from tribes, (2) economic opportunities for residents of towns bordering reservations and towns wherever distant "Indian boarding schools" were located, and (3) reinstatements of tribal authority. The next most frequent outcomes included adjustments to state/federal jurisdiction over tribes, reductions of tribal power, and economic opportunities for reservation households. Additional themes included the incarceration of tribal adults for violations of culture-specific laws (e.g., speaking indigenous languages), the removal of tribal children from reservations, health services, the return of tribal children to their families, and the granting of U.S. citizenship. Some laws (e.g., the Seven Major Crimes Act of 1885) mandated one outcome, whereas others (e.g., the Indian Reorganization Act) stipulated multiple outcomes. The most significant secondary result of these congressional actions toward tribes was the formation of several western states and the expansion of the landmass of the United States.

Figure 1. This *Sand Creek Massacre Historic Site* sign marks the site of an 1864 massacre. On November 29, 1864, an American flag fluttered in the icy, pre-dawn wind high atop the lodge of Chief Black Kettle; Abraham Lincoln had given the flag to the Cheyenne peace negotiator the one time the two men had met in Washington, D.C. The early morning silence broke as families awoke to the thunder of shod hooves, as a Methodist lay-minister led 645 U.S. soldiers barreling into camp under orders to show no mercy. They killed approximately 230 Cheyenne and Arapaho men, women, and children.[8] News of the fate of the Sand Creek families circulated rapidly from one tribe to another, but it would be many years before members of Congress would learn the true nature of this Civil War Era act of genocide. Four years later (November 27, 1868), survivors of the Sand Creek assault faced another onslaught— at Washita in Oklahoma Territory. This time, it was Colonel Custer and soldiers of the 7th Cavalry who rode in at first light and killed dozens of unsuspecting men, women, and children—Black Kettle and his wife among them. Black Kettle was known for saying *"... although wrongs have been done to me, I live in hope."* Several public laws of the 1885-1920 time line evolved before Congress understood the realities of eighteenth century military post-surrender contacts with American Indian family groups. The *Sand Creek Massacre Historic Site* is one result of a study authorized through passage of Public Law 105-243, in combination with the site authorization mandated by Public Law 106-465, on November 7, 2000. [Photo: NPS (National Park Service)].

Figure 2. George Bent (shown above with Magpie, his wife) knew two women who had survived Custer's daybreak attack of November 28, 1968, at Washita (Oklahoma Territory). These women told Bent about their shared encounter with a U.S. soldier who had found them hiding during the attack; the soldier did not harm them, nor did he disclose their hiding place. Years later, George Bent personally introduced these two survivors to the soldier they had encountered that day in Washita. (Photo: The Denver Public Library, Western History Collection, Call #WH1704).

Figure 3. The Thomas Jefferson Building in Washington, D.C. has housed the Library of Congress archives since 1897. Its elaborate interior staircase features sculpted representations of four cherubic children, each one emblematic of a unique aspect of American's multi-ethnic history, e.g., this representation of a child of Native American descent (Photo: B. L. Wilson).

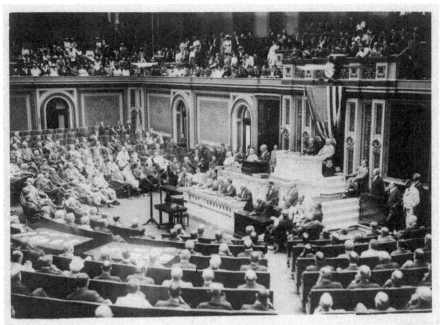

Figure 4. Article I, Section IV of the Constitution of the United States mandates a minimum of one annual meeting of the members of Congress (i.e., the combined membership of the Senate and the House of Representatives). *"Be it enacted by the Senate and the House of Representatives of the United States in Congress assembled,* That..." is the traditional phrasing which follows each legislative action's initial statement of intent, including the public laws of this compendium. This photo, *Congress in session in the Capitol,* taken between 1890 and 1920, remains part of the collections of the Library of Congress. (Photo: Library of Congress).

Figure 5. Congressional power is not without its limits. In 1916, Congress passed legislation designed to end the employment of children under the age of sixteen in coal mines, but it was struck down in the courts. Eight years later, the Senate passed a constitutional amendment to ban all child labor in coal mines, but it was never ratified by enough states to become law. This photograph—titled, "... [a]t the close of the day ... just up from the shaft ..."—shows young boys who worked 5,000 ft. underground in a Pennsylvania coal mine (circa 1911). Unrestrained employment of children in coal mines continued until the Fair Labor Standards Act became law in 1938, i.e., the law that first established a national minimum wage. (Photo: Library of Congress).[8]

Legislated Geographies

AT THE FIRST DAWN of American imaginings, there were no reservations. For thousands of years, hundreds of indigenous populations inhabited their respective traditional North American homelands. As most of these tribal lands morphed into a land base for the United States of America, American Indian reservations came into being.

As of 2018, the Bureau of Indian Affairs acknowledges the USA's official federal recognition of 326 American Indian nations and 229 Alaskan Native tribes. The bureau's 2018 website posts information about 326 American Indian reservations (all located within the continental U.S.), and one Native Alaskan reservation (located within the Annette Island Reserve of southeastern Alaska). The largest of the American Indian reservations is the sixteen million-acre home of the Navajo Nation (located within the combined state boundaries of Arizona, Utah, and New Mexico); this reservation is approximately the size of the state of West Virginia. The smallest American Indian reservation is the 1.32 acre plot in California where the Pit River Tribe maintains a cemetery. Most of the reservations—American Indian and Alaskan Native combined—are less than 1,000 acres in size.

"Some reservations are the remnants of a tribe's original land base. Others were created by the federal government for the resettling of Indian people forcibly relocated from their homelands. Not every federally recognized tribe has a reservation." [1]

The fact that few contemporary American Indian reservations are situated within traditional tribal lands is due, in large part, to the enactment of a tribally focused genre of U.S. legislation that began in the 1800s. During the early 1800s, eastern tribes lived within their respective homelands east of the Mississippi River. In the Southeast, these homelands included the well-established farming communities of the Cherokee. The United States of the time was comprised of just twenty-two states, all located east of the Mississippi River.

During the early 1800s, Thomas Jefferson influenced congressional thinking as to the future of eastern tribes—by promoting the "benefits" of forcing indigenous groups to shed traditional cultural norms (e.g., indigenous languages, religions). Congress responded by enacting the Civilization Act of 1819.[2] Jefferson's expressed intention was to align the economic, religious, linguistic, and other cultural patterns of Native American populations with the cultural norms of the then-idealized American farming lifestyle.[3]

Eleven years into its "civilization" initiative, Congress enacted the Indian Removal Act of 1830. Its passage precipitated the ensuing diaspora faced by most eastern tribes. This act served as a legalistic mechanism for the takeover of eastern tribal farms, farmhouses, livestock, and orchards—and the deportation of eastern American Indian populations to prairie lands west of the Mississippi River. Dozens of tribes, the Creek and the Cherokee among them, were forced to leave the farmlands and woodlands of their ancestors and head westward into the lands of western tribes.[4] All journeyed at the command of mounted U.S. military units; most walked; thousands died along the way. Perhaps as significant as the forced migrations of eastern tribes was the inherent message this 1830 legislation proclaimed to western tribes through its demonstration of an American ideology that favored the destruction of tribal communities.

The Indian Removal Act of 1830

AN ACT[5] to provide for an exchange of lands with the Indians residing in any of the states or territories, and for their removal west of the river Mississippi. *Be it enacted by the Senate and House of Representatives of the United States of America, in Congress assembled,* That it shall and may be lawful for the President of the United States to cause so much of any territory belonging to the United States, west of the river Mississippi, not included in any state or organized territory, and to which the Indian title has been extinguished, as he may judge necessary, to be divided into a suitable number of districts, for the reception of such tribes or nations of Indians as may choose to exchange the lands where they now reside, and remove there; and to cause each of said districts to be so described by natural or artificial marks, as to be easily distinguished from every other.

SEC. 2. *And be it further enacted*, That it shall and may be lawful for the President to exchange any or all of such districts, so to be laid off and described, with any tribe or nation of Indians now residing within the limits of any of the states or territories, and with which the United States have existing treaties, for the whole or any part or portion of the territory claimed and occupied by such tribe or nation, within the bounds of any one or more of the states or territories, where the lands claimed and occupied by the Indians, is owned by the United States, or the United States are bound to the state within which it lies to extinguish the Indian claim thereto.

SEC. 3. *And be it further enacted*, That in the making of any such exchange or exchanges, it shall and may be lawful for the Pres. solemnly to assure the tribe or nation with which the exchange is made, that the United States will forever secure and guaranty to them, and their heirs or successors, the country so exchanged with them; and if made and executed to them for the same: *Provided always*, That such lands shall revert to the United States, if the Indians become extinct, or abandoned the same.

SEC. 4. *And be it further enacted*, That if, upon any of the lands now occupied by the Indians, and to be exchanged for, there should be such improvements as add value to the land claimed by any individual or individuals of such tribes or nations, it shall and may be lawful for the President to cause such value to be ascertained by appraisement or otherwise, and to cause such ascertained value to be paid to the person or persons rightfully claiming such improvements. And upon the payment of such valuation, the improvement so valued and paid for, shall pass to the United States, and possession shall not afterwards be permitted to any of the same tribe.

SEC. 5. *And be it further enacted*, That upon the making of any such exchange as is contemplated by this act, it shall and may be lawful ... [for the U.S.] ... to cause such aid and assistance to be furnished to the emigrants as may be necessary and proper to enable them to remove to, and settle in, the country for which they may have exchanged; and also, to give them such aid and assistance as may be necessary for their support and substance for the first year after their removal.

SEC. 6. *And be it further enacted,* That it shall and may be lawful for ... [for the U.S.] ... to cause such tribe or nation to be protected, at their new residence, against all interruptions or disturbance from any other tribe or nation of Indians, or from any other person or persons whatsoever.

SEC. 7. *And be it further enacted,* That it shall and may be lawful for ... [for the U.S.] ... to have the same superintendence and care over any tribe or nation in the country to which they may remove, as contemplated by this act, that ... [the U.S.]... *Provided,* That nothing in this act contained shall be construed as authorizing or directing the violation of any existing treaty between the United States and any of the Indian tribes.

SEC. 8. *And be it further enacted,* That for the purpose of giving effect to the provisions of this act, the sum of five hundred thousand dollars is hereby appropriated, to be paid out of any money in the treasury, not otherwise appropriated.

Approved May 28, 1830.

Fort Laramie Treaties of 1851 and 1868

During the mid-nineteenth century, federal agents—presidents, military officers, legislators, social advocates, and the judiciary—promoted the notion that most lands west of the Mississippi River should remain forever tribal lands. This concept of western lands as the perpetual homeland of many tribes faded, however, as agriculturists of the Southeast, their soils exhausted through decades of cotton and tobacco mono-cropping, joined in the flow of eastern urbanites moving west. By 1860, the first wave of urban refugees were packing their

"... The Government, by statistics, shows they have got 456 treaties that they have broken with the Indians. That is why the Indians get a kick out of reading the Government's usual remark when some big affair comes up: 'Our honor is at stake ...'"

WILL ROGERS

household goods and leaving Detroit, Chicago, Pittsburgh, Boston, and a host of other eastern cities—their covered wagons rumbling westward into tribal lands. They joined other easterners who followed railroad tracks and the westward trails of miners and cavalry units. The Civil War brought additional urgency to this migration, a phenomenon which would continue throughout the latter nineteenth century and well into the early twentieth century. The ending of the Civil War had politically reunited the South and the North; it could not, however, dissolve the nation's geographic divide. Between the eastern and western states of the geographically disjointed United States stretched the remaining landmass of Indian Territory.

In an apparent attempt to provide clarity as to which portions, if any, of Indian Territory could be readily made available to incoming easterners, two treaties were forged between the U.S. and the tribes of the northern plains. The first was the Fort Laramie Treaty of 1851, also known as the Horse Creek Treaty (see Appendix A); the second was the Fort Laramie Treaty of 1868. The U.S. Senate ratified the 1851 treaty on May 24, 1852.[6]

The Fort Laramie Treaty of 1868 built upon the provisions of the 1851 treaty in establishing an expansive, federally recognized reservation for multiple tribes—primarily the Lakota and their relatives. Enactment of the Great Sioux Reservation Act of 1869 (15 Stat. 635) further formalized the bilateral agreement established between the United States and several western tribes upon the signing of the Fort Laramie Treaty of 1868. Once Congress affirmed this 1868 agreement in the context of Public Law, both the treaty and the resulting legislation clarified the geographic location of an expansive landmass, one sized to accommodate multiple tribal populations, i.e., the Great Sioux Reservation. This public law also specified that this landscape was to remain under the authority of tribal leaders—into perpetuity. At the time of this enactment, February 24, 1869, many tribal populations were struggling to survive their militarily-enforced confinement to small reservations—lands plagued by deplorable conditions—as de facto prisoners of war. With death rates soaring, this legislation carried with it two promises: a return to economic self-sustainability for tribes, and the return of personal liberties for tribal members.

The Great Sioux Reservation Act of 1869

Treaty with the Sioux Indians [established] April 29, 1868 ... Treaty between the United States of America and different Tribes of Sioux Indians; Concluded April 29 at seq., 1868; Ratification advised February 16, 1869; Proclaimed February 24, 1869. ANDREW JOHNSON,

PRESIDENT OF THE UNITED STATES OF AMERICA, To all and singular to who these present shall come, greeting [sic].WHEREAS a treaty was made and concluded at Fort Laramie, in the Territory of Dakota, [now in the Territory of Wyoming,] on the twenty-ninth day of April, and afterwards, in the year of our Lord one thousand eight hundred and sixty-eight, by and between Nathaniel G. Taylor, William T. Sherman, William S. Harney, John B. Sanborn, S. F. Tappan, C. C. Augur, and Alfred H. Terry, commissioners, on the part of the United States, and Ma-za-pon-kaska, Tah-shun-ka-co-qui-pah, Heh-won-ge-chat, Mah-to-non-pah, Little Chief, Makh-pi-ah-lu-tah, Co-cam-i-ya-ya, Con-te-pe-ta, Ma-wa-tau-ni-hav-ska, He-na-pin-wa-ni-ca, Wah-pah-shaw, and other chiefs and headmen of different tribes of Sioux Indians, on the part of said Indians, and duly authorized thereto by them, which treaty is in the words and figures following, to wit: Articles of a treaty made and concluded by and between Lieutenant-General William T. Sherman, General William S. Harney, General Alfred H. Terry, General C C. Augur, J. H. Henderson, Nathaniel G. Taylor, John B. Sanborn, and Samuel F. Tappan, duly appointed commissioners on the part of the United States, and the different bands of the Sioux Nation of Indians, by their chiefs and headmen, whose names are hereto subscribed, they being duly authorized to act in the premises [see Appendix B].

ARTICLE I. From this day forward all war between the parties to this agreement shall forever cease. The government of the United States desires peace, and its honor is hereby pledged to keep it. The Indians desire peace and they now pledge their honor to maintain it. If bad men among the whites, or among other people subject to the authority of the United State, shall commit any wrong upon the person or property of the Indians, the United States will, upon proof made to the agent and forwarded to the Commissioner of Indian Affairs at Washington city, proceed at once to cause the offender to be arrested and punished according to the laws of the United States, and also reimburse the injured person for the loss sustained. If bad men among the Indians shall commit a wrong or depredation upon the person or property of any one, white, black, or Indian, subject to the authority of the United States, and at peace therewith, the Indians herein named solemnly agree that they will, upon proof made to their agent and notice by him, deliver up the wrong-doer to the United States, to be tried and punished according to its laws; and in ease they herefore [*sic*] refuse so to do, the person injured shall be reimbursed for his loss from the annuities or other moneys due or to become due to them under this or other treaties made with the United States. And the President, on advising with the Commissioner of Indian Affairs, shall prescribe such rules and regulations for ascertaining damages under the provisions this ARTICLE as in his judgment may be proper. But no one sustaining loss while violating the provisions of this treaty or the laws of the United States shall be reimbursed herefore [*sic*]. ARTICLE II. The United States agrees that the following district of country, to wit, vis: commencing on

"... ARTICLE II. The United States agrees that the following district ... shall be ... set apart for the absolute and undisturbed use and occupation of the Indians herein named ... and agrees that no ... [other] ... persons ... may ... enter upon ... reservations ... or reside in the territory described in this ARTICLE ..."

the east bank of the Missouri river where the forty-sixth parallel of north latitude crosses the same, thence along low-water mark down said east bank to a point opposite where the northern line of the State of Nebraska strikes the river, thence west across said river, and along the northern line of Nebraska to the one hundred and fourth degree of longitude west from Greenwich, thence north on said meridian to a point where the forty-sixth parallel of north latitude intercepts the same, thence due east along said parallel to the place of beginning; and in addition thereto, all existing reservations on the east bank of said river shall be, and the same is, set apart for the absolute and undisturbed use and occupation of the Indians herein named, and for such other friendly tribes or individual Indians as from time to time they may be willing, with the consent of the United States, to admit amongst them; and the United States now solemnly agrees that no persons except those herein designated and authorized so to do, and except such officers, agents, and employes [*sic*] of the government as may be authorized to enter upon Indian reservations in discharge of duties enjoined by law, shall ever be permitted to pass over, settle upon, or reside in the territory described in this ARTICLE, or in such territory as may be added to this reservation for the use of said Indians, and henceforth they will and do hereby relinquish all claims or right in and to any portion of the United States or Territories, except such as is embraced within the limits aforesaid, and except as hereinafter provided.

ARTICLE III. If it should appear from actual survey or other satisfactory examination of said tract of land that it contains less than one hundred and sixty acres of tillable land for each person who, at the time, may be authorized to reside on it under the provisions of this treaty, and a very considerable number of such persons shall be disposed to commence cultivating the soil as farmers, the United States agrees to set apart, for the use of said Indians, as herein provided, such additional quantity of arable land, adjoining to said reservation, or as near to the same as it can be obtained, as may be required to provide the necessary amount

ARTICLE IV. The United States agrees, at its own proper expense, to construct at some place on the Missouri river, near the center of said reservation, where timber and water may be convenient, the following buildings, to wit; a warehouse, a storeroom for the use of the agent in storing goods belonging to the Indians, to cost not less than twenty-five hundred dollars; an agency building for the residence of the agent, to cost not exceeding three thousand dollars; a residence for the physician, to cost not more than three thousand dollars; and five other buildings, for a carpenter, farmer, blacksmith, miller, and engineer, each to cost not exceeding two thousand dollars; also a school-house or mission building, so soon as a sufficient number of children can be induced by the agent to attend school, which shall not cost exceeding five thousand dollars. The United States agrees further to cause to be erected on said reservation, near the other buildings herein authorized, a good steam circular saw-mill, with a grist-mill and shingle machine attached to the same, to cost not exceeding eight thousand dollars.

ARTICLE V. The United States agrees that the agent for said Indians shall in the future make his home at the agency building; that he shall reside among them, and keep an office open at all times for the purpose of prompt and diligent inquiry into such matters of complaint by and against the Indians as may be presented for investigation under the provisions of their treaty stipulations, as also for the faithful discharge of other duties enjoined on him by law. In all cases of depredation on person or property he shall cause the evidence to be taken in writing and forwarded, together with his findings, to the Commissioner of Indian Affairs, whose decision, subject to the revision of the Secretary of the Interior, shall be binding on the parties to this treaty.

ARTICLE VI. If any individual belonging to said tribes of Indians, or legally incorporated with them, being the head of a family, shall desire to commence farming, he shall have the privilege to select, in the presence and with the assistance of the agent then in charge, a tract of land within said reservation, not exceeding three hundred and twenty acres in extent, which tract when so selected, certified, and recorded in the "landbook [*sic*]," as herein directed, shall cease to be ...

"... ARTICLE VI ... If any ... head of a family, shall desire to commence farming, he shall ... select ... a tract of land within said reservation ... [which] ... shall cease to be held in common, but ... may be ... held in the exclusive possession of the person selecting it, and of his family, so long as he or they may continue to cultivate it ..."

... held in common, but the same may be occupied and held in the exclusive possession of the person selecting it, and of his family, so long as he or they may continue to cultivate it. Any person over eighteen years of age, not being the head of a family, may in like manner select and cause to be certified to him or her, for purpose of cultivation, a quantity of land not exceeding eighty acres in extent, and thereupon be entitled to the exclusive possession of the same as above directed. For each tract of land so selected a certificate, containing a description thereof and the name of the person selecting it, with a certificate endorsed thereon that the same has been recorded, shall be delivered to the party entitled to it, by the agent, after the same shall have been recorded by him in a book to be kept in his office, subject to inspection, which said book shall be known as the "Sioux Land Book" ... [during any subsequent surveys] ... of the reservation ... Congress shall provide for protecting the rights of said settlers in their improvements, and may fix the character of the title held by each. The United States may pass such laws on the subject of alienation and descent of property between the Indians and their descendants as may be thought proper. And it is further stipulated that any male Indians over eighteen years of age, of any hand or tribe that is or shall hereafter become a party to this treaty, who now is or who shall hereafter become a resident or occupant of any reservation or territory not included in the tract of country designated and described in this treaty for the permanent home of the Indians, which is not mineral land, nor reserved by the United States for special purposes other than Indian occupation, and who shalt have made improvements thereon of the value of two hundred dollars or more, and continuously occupied the same as a homestead for the term of three years, shall be entitled to receive from the United States a patent for one hundred and sixty acres of land including his said improvements, the same to be in the form of the legal subdivisions of the surveys of the public lands, Upon [sic] application in writing, sustained by the proof of two disinterested witnesses, made to the register of the local land office when the land sought to be entered is within a land district, and when the tract sought to be entered is not in any land district, then upon said application and proof being made to the commissioner of the general land office. [sic] and the right of such Indian or Indians to enter such tract or tracts of land shall accrue and be perfect from the date of his first improvements thereon, and shall continue as long as he continues his residence and improvements, and no longer. And any Indian or Indians receiving a patent for land under the foregoing provisions shall thereby and from thenceforth become and be a citizen of the United States, and be entitled to all the privileges and immunities of such citizens, and shall, at the same time, retain all his rights to benefits accruing to Indians under this treaty ...

ARTICLE VII. In order to insure the civilization of the Indians entering into this treaty, the necessity of education is admitted, especially, of such of them as are or may be settled on said agricultural reservations, and they therefore pledge themselves to compel their children, male and female, between the ages of six and sixteen years, to attend school; and it is hereby made the duty of the agent for said Indians to see that this stipulation is strictly complied with; and the United States agrees that for every thirty children between said ages who can be induced or compelled to attend school, a house shall be provided and a teacher competent to teach the elementary branches of an English education shall be furnished, who will reside among said Indians, and faithfully discharge his or her duties as a teacher. The provisions of this ARTICLE [*sic*] to continue for not less than twenty years.

"... ARTICLE VII ... the United States agrees that for every thirty children ... who can be induced or compelled to attend school, a house shall be provided and a teacher ... to teach ... English education shall be furnished, who will reside among said Indians ..."

ARTICLE VIII. When the head of a family or lodge shall have selected lands and received his certificate as above directed, and the agent shall be satisfied that he intends in good faith to commence cultivating the soil for a living, he shall be entitled to receive seeds and agricultural implements for the first year, not exceeding in value one hundred dollars, and for each succeeding year he shall continue to farm, for a period of three years more, he shall be entitled to receive seeds and implements as aforesaid, not exceeding in value twenty-five dollars. And it is further stipulated that such persons as commence farming shall receive instruction from the farmer herein provided for, and whenever more than one hundred persons shall enter upon the cultivation of the soil, a second blacksmith shall be provided, with such iron, steel, and other material as may be needed.

ARTICLE IX. At any time after ten years from the making of this treaty, the United States shall have the privilege of withdrawing the physician, farmer, blacksmith, carpenter, engineer, and miller herein provided for, but in ease of such withdrawal, an additional sum thereafter of ten thousand dollars per annum shall be devoted to the education of said Indians, and the Commissioner of Indian Affairs shall, upon careful inquiry into their condition, make such rules and regulations for the expenditure of said sum as will best promote the educational and moral improvement of said tribes.

ARTICLE X. In lieu of all sums of money or other annuities provided to be paid to the Indians herein named, under any treaty or treaties heretofore made, the United States agrees to deliver at the agency house on the reservation herein named, on ... or before* ... [a notation on the bottom of the original page read: *The words "or before" are inserted with black pencil.*] the first day of August of each year, for thirty years, the following Articles, to wit: For each male person over fourteen years of age, a suit of good substantial heref [*sic*] clothing, consisting of coat, pantaloons, flannel shirt, hat, pair of home-made socks. For each female over twelve years of age, a flannel skirt, or the goods necessary to make it, a pair of woolen hose, twelve yards of calico, and twelve yards of cotton domestics. For the boys and girls under the ages named, such flannel and cotton goods as may be needed to make each a suit as aforesaid, together with a pair of heref [*sic*] hose for each. And in order that the Commissioner of Indian Affairs may be able to estimate properly for the Articles herein named, it shall be the duty of the agent each year to forward to him a full and exact census of the Indians, on which the estimate from year to year can be based. And in addition to the clothing herein named, the sum of ten dollars for each person entitled to the beneficial effects of this treaty shall be annually appropriated for a period of thirty years, while such persons roam and hunt, add twenty dollars for each person who engages in farming, to be used by the Secretary of the Interior in the purchase of such Articles as from time to time and the condition and necessities of the Indians may indicate to be proper. And within the thirty years, at any time, it shall appear that the amount of money needed for clothing under this ARTICLE can be appropriated to better uses for the Indians named herein, Congress may, by law, change the appropriation to other purposes; but in no event shall the amount of this appropriation be withdrawn or discontinued for the period named. And the President shall annually detail an officer of the army to be present and attest the delivery of all the goods herein named to the Indians, and he shall inspect and report on the quantity and quality of the goods and the manner of their delivery.

"... an officer of the army ... [will] ... attest the delivery of all the goods herein named to the Indians, and he shall inspect and report on the quantity and quality of the goods and the manner of their delivery..."

And it is hereby expressly stipulated that each Indian over the age of four years, who shall have removed to and settled permanently upon said reservation and complied with the stipulations of this treaty, shall be entitled to receive from the United States, for the period of four years after he shall have settled upon said reservation, one pound of meat and one pound of flour per day, provided the Indians cannot furnish their own subsistence at an earlier date. And it is further stipulated that the United States will furnish and deliver to each lodge of Indians or family of persons legally incorporated with them who shall remove to the reservation herein described and commence farming, one good American cow, and one good well-broken pair of American oxen within sixty days after such lodge or family shall have so settled upon said reservation.

ARTICLE XI. In consideration of the advantages and benefits conferred by this treaty and the many pledges of friendship by the United States, the tribes who are parties to this agreement

"... [Indian Nations] ... reserve the right to hunt on any lands north of North Platte, and on the Republican Fork of the Smoky Hill river, so long as the buffalo may range thereon in such numbers as to justify the chase ..."

hereby stipulate that they will relinquish all right to occupy permanently the territory outside their reservation as herein defined, but yet reserve the right to hunt on any lands north of North Platte, and on the Republican Fork of the Smoky Hill river, so long as the buffalo may range thereon in such numbers as to justify the chase. And they, the said Indians, further expressly agree: 1st. That they will withdraw all opposition to the construction of the railroads now being built on the plains ...

2nd. That they will permit the peaceful construction of an railroad not passing over their reservation as herein defined ... 3rd. That they will not attack any persons at home, or travelling [sic], nor molest or disturb any wagon trains, coaches, mules, or cattle belonging to the people of the United States, or to persons friendly therewith ... 4th. They will never capture, or carry off from the settlements, white women or children ... 5th. They will never kill or scalp white men, nor attempt to do them harm ... 6th. They withdraw all presence of opposition to the construction of the railroad now being built along the Platte river and westward to the Pacific ocean, and they will not in future object to the construction of railroads, wagon roads, mail stations, or other works of utility or necessity, which may be ordered or permitted by the laws of the United States. But should such roads or other works be constructed on the lands of their reservation, the government will pay the tribe whatever amount of damage may be assessed by three disinterested commissioners to be appointed by the President for that purpose, one of said commissioners to be a chief or headman of the tribe ... 7th. They agree to withdraw all opposition to the military posts or roads now established south of the North Platte river, or that may be established, not in violation of treaties heretofore made or hereafter to be made with any of the Indian tribes.

ARTICLE XII. No treaty for the cession of any portion or part of the reservation herein described which may be held in common shall be of any validity or force as against the said Indians, unless executed and signed by at least three fourths of all the adult male Indians, occupying or interested in the same; and no cession by the tribe shall be understood or construed in such manner as to deprive, without his consent, any individual member of the tribe of his rights to any tract of land selected by him, as provided in ARTICLE VI. [sic] of this treaty.

ARTICLE XIII. The United States hereby agrees to furnish annually to the Indians the physician, teachers, carpenter, miner, engineer, farmer, and blacksmiths, as herein contemplated, and that such appropriations shall be made from time to time, on the estimates of the Secretary of the Interior, as will be sufficient to employ such persons.

ARTICLE XIV. It is agreed that the sum of five hundred dollars annually, for three years from date, shall be expended in presents to the ten persons of said tribe who in the judgment of the agent may grow the most valuable crops for the respective year.

ARTICLE XV. The Indians herein named agree that when the agency house and other buildings shall be constructed on the reservation named, they will regard said reservation their permanent home, and they will make no permanent settlement elsewhere; but they shall have the right, subject to the conditions and modifications of this treaty, to hunt, as stipulated in ARTICLE XI. [*sic*] hereof.

ARTICLE XVI. The United States hereby agrees and stipulates that the country north of the North Platte river and east of the summits of the Big Horn mountains shall be held and considered to be unceded Indian territory, and also stipulates and agrees that no white person or persons shall be permitted to settle upon or occupy any portion of the same; or without the consent of the Indians, first had and obtained, to pass through the same; and it is further agreed by the United States, that within ninety days after the conclusion of peace with all the bands of the Sioux nation, the military posts now established in the territory in this ARTICLE named shall be abandoned, and that the road leading to them and by them to the settlements in the Territory of Montana shall be closed.

ARTICLE XVII. It is hereby expressly understood and agreed by and between the respective parties to this treaty that the execution of this treaty and its ratification by the United States Senate shall have the effect, and shall be construed as abrogating and annulling all treaties and agreements heretofore entered into between the respective parties hereto, so far as such treaties and agreements obligate the United States to furnish and provide money, clothing, or other Articles of property to such Indians and bands of Indians as become parties to this treaty, but no further. In testimony of all which, we, the said commissioners, and we, the chiefs and headmen of the Brulé band of the Sioux nation, have hereunto set our hands and seals at Fort Laramie, Dakota Territory, this twenty-ninth day of April, in the year one thousand eight hundred and sixty-eight ... [see Appendix B for complete listing of signatories] ... And whereas, the said treaty having been submitted to the Senate of the United States for its constitutional action thereon, the Senate did, on the sixteenth day of February, one thousand eight hundred and sixty-nine, advice and consent to the ratification of the same, by a resolution in the words and figures following, to wit: In Executive Session, Senate of the United States, February 16, 1869. *Resolved* (two thirds of the senators present concurring), That the Senate advise and consent to the ratification of the treaty between the United States and the different bands of the Sioux nation of Indians, made and concluded on the 29th of April, 1868. Attest: GEO. C. CORHAM, Secretary. Now, therefore let it be known that I, ANDREW JOHNSON, President of the United States of America, do, in pursuance of the advice and consent of the Senate, as expressed in its resolution of the sixteenth of February, one thousand eight hundred and sixty-nine, accept, ratify, and confirm the said treaty. In testimony whereof I have hereto signed my name, and caused the seal of the United States to be affixed. Done at the City of Washington, this twenty-fourth day of February, in the year of our Lord one thousand eight hundred and sixty-nine . . .

[February 24, 1869] ... and of the Independence of the United States of America the ninety-third. ANDREW JOHNSON. By the President: William H. Seward, of State.

[Ratified 2/24/1869]

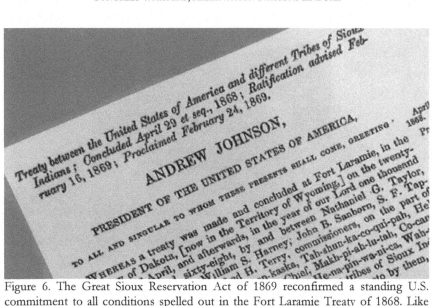

Figure 6. The Great Sioux Reservation Act of 1869 reconfirmed a standing U.S. commitment to all conditions spelled out in the Fort Laramie Treaty of 1868. Like the treaty, the act articulated a U.S. promise to return freedom to western tribes of the northern plains. This photo shows a portion of the first page of this enactment of February 16, 1869 (i.e., 15 Stat. 635); it states: "In Executive Session, Senate of the United States, February 16, 1869. Resolved (two-thirds of the senators present concurring) ... That the Senate advise and consent to the ratification of the treaty between the United States and the different bands of the Sioux ... [Nation] ... made and concluded on the 29th of April, 1868 ..." (Photo: B. L. Wilson).

Figure 7. As of early 1890, the USA was comprised of forty-two states. The nation's eastern and western blocks of states remained separated by expanses of tribal territories (light gray). On July 3, 1890, Idaho emerged out of these tribal lands, becoming the first U.S. state to geographically link the eastern and western states of the USA.

Figure 8. Prior to the mid-1870s, three bison herds traveled the grasslands of the western plains, following ancient north-south grazing routes during seasonal migrations between present-day Texas and Canada. Between 1874 and 1876, federally-contracted bison hunters destroyed all three herds. Several states soon emerged from their pastures. Many of these states later suffered the Great Dustbowl of the 1930s—possibly one cost of the decimation of one of the region's ecological keystone species. This photo (circa 2000) of a lone bison was taken next to a roadside tourist shop in Oklahoma (Photo: B. L. Wilson).

The Uniting of the United States of America

Prior to 1876, close to half the land of today's continental United States remained federally recognized as "Indian Territory." During ensuing years of national expansion, railroad companies lobbied Congress with frequent requests for tribal territories; Congress responded by granting them great expanses of land. Legislative records show that this co-optation of tribal lands took place with little, if any, public discussion. The strips of tribal lands given to railroad companies for their tracks and fueling stations were often 80-100 miles wide.[7]

As railway supply outposts grew into small western towns, citizens of these towns began pressuring Congress for statehood. By 1889, through various acts of Congress, most tribal lands had been redefined as western states.[8] The United States, however, remained a nation comprised of two disjointed blocks of states—those situated to the east of "Indian Territory" and those situated to its west. This reality remained until July 3, 1890, the date Idaho became the forty-third state—and the geographic linchpin linking eastern and western states. By 1912, all forty-eight continental states had emerged, thus fulfilling the "sea to shining sea" ambitions of the expanding United States of America.

American Indian Reservations

In late 1877, the freedom of western tribes ended as the last of the free-roaming bands surrendered at Camp Robinson, Nebraska.[9] By 1889, through multiple congressional actions, western tribes were denied access to most traditional tribal lands—and most reservation lands. Military forts and reservation-based federal agents placed limits on all tribal members' travel to off-reservation destinations. Tribes were restricted to their assigned, shrinking, and isolated reservation lands—or, in the unique case of the Chiricahua Apache, prison.[10]

Figure 9. This Department of the Interior U.S. Geological Survey map of contemporary American Indian reservations shows the location and size of those large enough to be viewed at this scale. Most of the total of 326 reservations—American Indian and Alaskan Native combined—are less than 1,000 acres in size. (Image: Department of the Interior/U.S. Geological Survey).

Figure 10. This contemporary photo shows an often traveled road of a reservation of the American Southwest. (Photo: C. Breeman).

Figure 11. Borderlands of Glacier National Park are part of the rugged terrain of the Blackfeet Nation's reservation and traditional homelands (Photo: B. L. Wilson).

Figure 12. The Yellowstone Act (17 Stat. 32) approved on March 1, 1872, established America's first national park. Yellowstone Falls is one of Yellowstone National Park's many spectacular sites (Photo: B. L. Wilson).

Figure 13. Water conservation is critical to the health and safety of Americans living within reservation communities of the American Southwest. (Photo: C. Breeman).

Figure 14. Nearly half of Badlands National Park (pictured above) lies within the boundaries of the Pine Ridge Reservation of the Oglala Lakota (Photo: B. L. Wilson).

Legislative Sample, Part I
1885-1920

"The utmost good faith shall always be observed towards the Indians ... Their land and property shall never be taken from them without their consent ... they never shall be invaded or disturbed unless in just and lawful wars authorized by Congress ... laws founded in justice and humanity shall from time to time be made, for preventing wrongs being done to them, and for preserving peace and friendship with them."

CONGRESSIONAL RECORD, AUGUST 7, 1789,
NORTHWEST ORDINANCE OF 1789 (1 STAT. 50)

Chapter I

Acts of an Insecure Victor

INDIAN NATIONS did not need, seek, nor invite a cultural revolution, yet by 1885, America's national policy of American Indian cultural suppression was well underway. It challenged the very survival of tribal communities and threatened the continuity of a full spectrum of American Indian cultures. The dominant legislative themes of the 1885-1920 era were the transfer of tribal lands away from tribes and the annihilation of traditional indigenous cultures. Treaty-making had proved futile due to the extreme imbalance in military power—and a climate of deep-seated American ambivalence toward the legal and human rights of indigenous populations.[1] Federal agents readily dismissed treaty provisions, whether due to matters of personal ideology, incompetence, misunderstanding, or simple acquiescence to the demands of railroaders, miners, ranchers, and real estate profiteers.

"Nearly all men can stand adversity, but if you want to test a man's character, give him power."

ABRAHAM LINCOLN[1]

The "Indian Wars" had officially ended in 1876. With western tribes subsequently living in open-air confinement on geographically scattered reservations, Congress had no reason to expect military attacks upon any tribal group. Yet in late December of 1890, a contingent of the Seventh Cavalry intercepted a band of travelers—primarily relatives of the Oglala Lakota of the Pine Ridge Agency—heading south from the Cheyenne River Agency. The group had traveled more than 150 miles through bitter winter weather before camping near the Pine Ridge Agency creek called Wounded Knee. Troops surrounded and then disarmed the band; soon, they killed hundreds of these men, women and children. In press reports and in the military reports sent to government officials, the Seventh Cavalry credited themselves with a "victory" at Wounded Knee. Interviews with survivors, government officials, and military eyewitnesses, as collected in January of 1891, provided evidence that the December massacre had been delivered in revenge for the Seventh Cavalry's defeat at Little Big Horn in 1876.[2] On page twenty of historian Peter Matthiessen's book, In the Spirit of Crazy Horse, the author quotes a physician—Dr. Charles Eastman—who was on-site at the Pine Ridge Agency at the time of the massacre:

> ... three miles from the scene of the massacre ... we found the body of a woman completely covered with a blanket of snow ... from this point on we found them scattered along as they had been relentlessly hunted down and slaughtered while fleeing for their lives. Some of our people discovered relatives or friends among the dead, and there was much wailing and mourning. When we reached the camp where the Indian camp had stood, among the fragments of burned tents and other belongings ... we saw the frozen bodies lying close together and piled one upon another. I counted 80 bodies of men who had been in counsel and who were almost as helpless as the women and babes when the deadly fire began, for nearly all of the guns had been taken from them ... The troops opened fire from all sides, killing not only unarmed men, women, and children, but their own comrades who stood opposite them, for the camp was entirely surrounded.

Eastern news stories celebrated the Seventh Cavalry's massacre as a western-front "victory." This act of genocide—the Wounded Knee Massacre—took place fourteen years after the official ending of all military actions against western tribes—and just two months after the birth of the man who would later become the thirty-fourth President of the United States of America, Dwight David Eisenhower.

Legislative Outcomes, 1885 –1920

REFRAMING TRIBAL LANDS AS STATES

During the 1885-1921 timeline, Congress legislated numerous reductions of tribal lands. Nineteen years after enacting the Great Sioux Reservation Act of 1869, Congress countered it with its passage of the General Allotment Act of

1887, the legislation that distributed most of the lands of the Great Sioux Reservation to outside entities. Repeated constrictions of tribal spaces resulted in a host of new geographic boundaries and social hostilities. These challenges interfered with all traditional means of self-sufficiency and threatened the very survival of tribal communities. With the increasing loss of access to hunting grounds and other natural resources, many western tribal families faced decades of holocaust-like, open-air confinement. Reservation living conditions—abysmal from the outset—deteriorated, as high-ranking officials in Congress, the federal courts, and the Oval Office fragmented tribal communities—through redistributions of tribal territory, possessions (e.g., bison hides, tools, horses, clothing), and even children.

Between 1885 and 1913, ten more western states organized within tribal lands and gained admission into the United States of America: North Dakota, South Dakota, Montana, Washington, Idaho, Wyoming, Utah, Oklahoma, New Mexico, and Arizona. Along with the conversion of almost all remaining tribal lands into western states came the admonition for American Indians to never go "... off reservation."

As railroad corporations, mining companies, and waves of westward-bound settlers claimed more and more reservation lands as their own, tribal families faced starvation epidemics and a labyrinth of lethal social pressures.

DENIALS OF TRIBAL AUTHORITY

Several 1885-1920 laws leveraged authority away from tribes and strengthened state and federal systems of control. Legislation that funded a system of reduced-authority reservation-based courts also served to suppress all indigenous religious, traditional and social practices, and tribal cohesiveness, by prosecuting practitioners of traditional religions. Legislation enacted in 1885 prohibited tribes from pursuing perpetrators of violent crimes, as that aspect of law enforcement was henceforth to be handled by federal law enforcement personnel.

SEPARATION OF FAMILIES

The removal of adults and children from tribal households was another central legislative theme of this era. Several laws enacted between 1885 and 1921 incarcerated tribal adults for actions which, in any other context, would be considered law-abiding. One example is the law that criminalized the speaking of Native American languages—an absurdity of policy by any standard. Then the serial tribal land giveaways enacted in 1887, 1889, 1891, 1894, and 1897 created further systemic political, social, and geographic barriers, all adverse to household-to-household contacts between tribal members. However, the primary cultural conversion legislation of this era (i.e., boarding school legislation) represents an unparalleled maladaptive assault on the fundamental human rights of American Indians.

Numerous "boarding school" laws resulted in the removal of children from their families and communities for indeterminate periods of time, typically years. Enrollment into day or industrial boarding schools often separated parents and their children by hundreds of miles, and in the case of Alaskans, thousands. For instance, the children of the Pine Ridge Reservation, located in present-day South Dakota, were typically sent to schools in Pennsylvania, Virginia, or Nebraska.[3] Curricula at these institutions were designed to supplant the home culture of attending children with a white cultural model. Expressions (verbal or otherwise) indicating any link between children and their families—e.g., clothing, hairstyles, and home languages—were typically forbidden. Punishment for such infractions of school rules often included the withholding of food and solitary confinement.

At their worst, many schools were undeniably nihilistic in intent and outcome. At their best, these boarding schools served as food distribution sites to generations of reservation children, providing food to children who may never have survived the starvation epidemics rampant on reservations during the late nineteenth and early twentieth centuries. Pennsylvania's Carlisle Indian Industrial School operated between 1879 and 1918 and served as a model during the years of expansion of a national network of American Indian boarding schools; during its early years of operation, its child morbidity rates ranged from ten to sixty-five percent.

Although 1885 boarding school legislation served as the initial congressional intrusion into reservation family life, it did not, in fact, call for any forced removal of children. Coercion came later through the misapplication of legislation mandating compulsory schooling for all reservation children. Child death rates at boarding schools remained extreme over the course of ensuing decades.

ECONOMIC BOOSTS TO OFF-RESERVATION COMMUNITIES

Congressional legislation that funded the transfer of tribal children to distant locations to be raised off-reservation proved an economic boon to several eastern and western communities. Brick-and-mortar aspects of these legislative mandates benefited towns through the construction and ongoing maintenance of necessary "boarding school" buildings. Many farmers living near these institutions received stipends for taking Indian children into their homes during summer months. Other locals—many with military backgrounds or other government career histories—staffed the boarding facilities. The following excerpt of a public law approved on July 4, 1885 (22 Stat., 91-92) provides examples of the job opportunities funded through "boarding school" enactments of these years:

For support of Indian day and industrial schools and for other educational purposes not hereinafter provided for, including pay of draughtsman to be employed in the office of the Commissioner of Indian Affairs, one million dollars; for the construction on Indian reservations of school buildings and repair of school buildings, one hundred and twenty-five thousand dollars: *Provided*, That twenty-five thousand dollars of this amount may be used in the erection of building or an industrial school for the Mission Indians near the village of Perris, in California, upon a tract of land to be donated for that purpose of not less than eighty acres; and for purchase of horses, cattle, sheep and swine for schools, fifteen thousand dollars, five thousand dollars of which shall be immediately available; in all, one million one hundred and forty thousand dollars: *Provided*, That the entire cost of any boarding school building, exclusive of outbuildings, to be built from the moneys appropriated hereby, shall not exceed twelve thousand dollars and the entire cost of any day-school building to be built shall not exceed six hundred dollars ... For support and education of Indian pupils at Albuquerque, New Mexico ... Carlisle, Pennsylvania ... Chillocco, Indian Territory...Carson City, Nevada ... Pierre, South Dakota ... Flandreau, South Dakota ... Santa Fe, New Mexico ... Shoshone Indian Reservation, Wyoming ... Grand Junction, Colorado ... Fort Totten, North Dakota ... Hampton, Virginia ... Lawrence, Kansas ... Philadelphia ... Phoenix, Arizona ... Salem, Oregon ... Jocko Reservations, In Montana ... Cherokee, North Carolina ... Minesotá[*sic*] ... Fort Mojave, Arizona ... Renesselaer, Indiana ... Banning, California ... Blackfoot Agency, Montana.

At the time of this enactment (1885), several of the sites the act identifies for boarding school construction were not within any then existent states, but were locations within remaining expanses of tribal territories. North Dakota, South Dakota, and Montana became states in 1889. Arizona and New Mexico, the last two states of the continental USA, both gained statehood in 1912.

HEIGHTENED MILITARY PRESENCE

By 1885, western tribes had been encircled by U.S. military units for more than fourteen years—with tribal members confined to bounded parcels of land (reservations) within the most ecologically barren regions of the West.[4] Tribal populations, many acculturated to nomadic lives of freedom, now faced decades of open-air incarceration. Military forts that sprang up near reservations prevented and/or limited all off-reservation travel.

Continuity of a strong military presence on reservations shows up in legislation passed in 1892, an act that stipulated a preference for the hiring of army officers as "agents" for on-site duty within each reservation.[5] In violation of existent U.S. bilateral agreements with tribes, the army maintained forts in close proximity to Lakota reservations until after World War I.

Chapter II
Federal Agents Only: The Seven Major Crimes Act

IN MOST AMERICAN communities, serious crimes are investigated and prosecuted at the local or state level. Federal agencies occasionally participate in investigations and associated prosecutions, but only when national security, kidnappings, or the crossing of state boundaries are part of a crime scenario. This rule of localized jurisdiction applies throughout the United States with one exception: reservation communities. Prior to 1885, tribal leaders of reservation communities handled all serious transgressions of social norms, including murder. The 1885 Seven Major Crimes Act changed that point of authority by redefining all serious reservation-linked crimes as federal in nature.

"There is little or no monitoring on a national level of the FBI investigative work in Indian country ..."

1981 U.S. DEPARTMENT OF JUSTICE

This legislation mandates federal law enforcement (i.e., in contemporary terms, the Federal Bureau of Investigation) in the case of any major crime committed within reservation boundaries. The range of crimes addressed by this act includes murder, manslaughter, rape, assault with intent to kill, arson, and burglary and larceny, hence the "major crimes" moniker.

The Seven Major Crimes Act of 1885

AN ACT[2] ... Making appropriations for the current and contingent expenses of the Indian Department, and for fulfilling treaty stipulations with various Indian tribes, for the year ending June thirtieth, eighteen hundred and eight-six, and for other purposes. *Be it enacted by the Senate and House of Representatives of the United States of America in Congress Assembled,* That the following sums be, and they are hereby, appropriated, out of any money in the Treasury not otherwise appropriated, for the purpose of paying the current and contingent expenses of the Indian department, and fulfilling treaty stipulations with the various Indian tribes [...]

SEC. 9. That immediately upon and after the date of the passage of this act all Indians, committing against the person or property of another Indian or other person any of the following crimes, namely, murder, manslaughter, rape, assault with the intent to kill, arson, burglary and larceny within any Territory of the United States and either within or without an Indian reservation, shall be subject therefore to the laws of such Territory relating to said crimes and shall be tried therefore in the same courts and in the same manner and shall be subject to the same penalties as are all other persons charged with the commission of said crimes, respectively; and the said courts are hereby given jurisdiction in all such cases; and all such Indians committing any of the above crimes against the person or property of another Indian or other person within the boundaries of any State of the United States and within the limits of any Indian reservation, shall be subject to the same laws, tried in the same courts and in the same manner and subject to the same penalties as are all other persons committing any of the above crimes within the exclusive jurisdiction of the United States.

Approved March 3rd, 1885

The concept of federal (rather than tribal) law enforcement on reservations first appeared three years after the Civil War in the context of a treaty which created the once expansive Great Sioux Reservation and defined adjacent Indian Territories. This Fort Laramie Treaty of 1868 declared:

If bad men among the whites, or among other people subject to the authority of the United States, shall commit any wrong upon the person or property of the Indians, the United States will, upon proof made to the agent and forwarded to the Commissioner of Indian Affairs at Washington City, proceed at once to cause the offender to be arrested and punished according to the laws of the United States, and also reimburse the injured person for the loss sustained. If bad men among the Indians shall commit a wrong or depredation upon anyone, white, black or Indian ... the Indians herein named solemnly agree that they will deliver up the wrongdoer to the United States ... [3]

The Seven Major Crimes Act of 1885 and the Fort Laramie Treaty of 1868 both provide evidence of an historical federal intent to mitigate acts of violence in and around reservation communities. But intentions aside, this legislation set in place systems of state and federal law enforcement which interfered with established tribal peace-keeping practices—and challenged the very survival of law-abiding tribal members.[4] Multiple congressional subcommittees and U.S. Civil Rights commissions have documented the lack of evidence of any consistent enforcement of this law during the many decades since its 1885 enactment.

The Meriam Report of 1928, the congressional subcommittee report completed some forty years after enactment of the Seven Major Crimes Act, found a general state of confusion as to what governmental entity had responsibility for the "... legal jurisdiction over the restricted Indians in such important matters as crimes and misdemeanors and domestic relations."[5] Nearly a century after its enactment, in June of 1981, a U.S. Civil Rights Commission reported a continuing absence of FBI oversight. The 1981 report found no evidence of FBI investigation into any of sixty alleged homicides committed against men, women, and children of one reservation during a single year during the 1970s—as perpetrators operated with impunity.[6] This same civil rights report described how a group of tribal community members tried to gain the attention of Congress in their search for relief from the lawlessness of their reservation:

In February 1973, members of the American Indian Movement...began a 71-day occupation of Wounded Knee, by then a small village, to protest this treatment of tribal people and what they believed was the oppressive leadership of Richard Wilson on the Pine Ridge Reservation. Surrounded by federal troops, the armed activists ... [e.g.,

Vietnam War veterans] ... demanded that the U.S. Senate investigate conditions on the reservation. For weeks the two sides exchanged tens of thousands of rounds of ammunition ... two Ogalala [*sic*] men were killed. After the standoff had ended, 185 tribal people were indicted by Federal grand juries on charges of arson, theft, assault, and '. . . interfering with federal officers.'[7]

Since the Seven Major Crimes Act blocks local, tribal, and state law enforcement, omissions of federal law enforcement between 1885 and the mid-1970s and beyond left reservation communities without even minimal protection from assailants operating from within or beyond reservation boundaries.[8]

Configuration of serious crimes within the purview of federal forces assumes that federal law enforcement agencies will, indeed, conduct investigations and pursue the prosecution of suspected perpetrators of major crimes. Evidence, however, of any reasonable and consistent application of this public law during the century following its enactment is minimal.

"... it is relevant to point out that ... Leonard Peltier has been incarcerated for thirty-three years ... based upon what your own courts have admitted was fabricated evidence ..."[9]

ARCHBISHOP
DESMOND TUTU

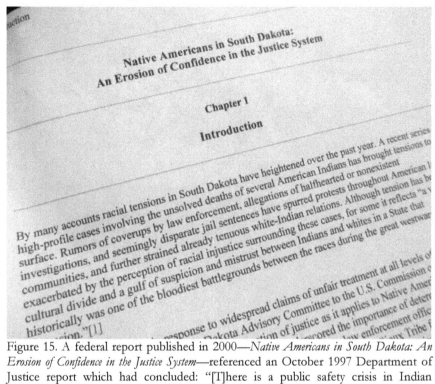

Figure 15. A federal report published in 2000—*Native Americans in South Dakota: An Erosion of Confidence in the Justice System*—referenced an October 1997 Department of Justice report which had concluded: "[T]here is a public safety crisis in Indian Country." Various federal reports attest to the fact that most perpetrators of crimes committed against tribal members are from communities bordering reservations (Photo: B. L. Wilson).

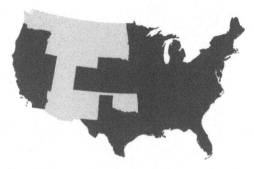

Figure 16. As of May 3, 1885, the date the Major Crimes Act was enacted, the USA was comprised of thirty-eight states. This map depicts the total USA landmass in comparison to the remaining expanses (as of 1885) of tribal lands (light gray).

Chapter III

Checkerboard Shell Game of Gigantic Proportions: General Allotment Act of 1887

THE GENERAL ALLOTMENT Act of 1887 reduced tribal access to water, pastures, wildlife, and hunting grounds—by radically reducing the landmass of most western and mid-western reservations. The act mandated significant opportunities for mining and railroad companies, incoming settlers, and church groups interested in acquiring tribal lands and associated natural resources. This multifaceted act also offered tribal households a measure of U.S. citizenship and title to individual homestead sites, but only if the potential allottee was willing to live "apart" from their tribe. Furthermore, it required states to provide "equal protection" to tribal members, post allotment. The General Allotment Act of 1887 was known by several titles, e.g., the Dawes Allotment Act, the Dawes Act, and the Dawes Severalty Act.

> "*Congress decreed in the General Allotment Act that all Indians would become farmers*
>
> ...
>
> *subsequent agreements and statutes allotting tribal lands were enforced with a frightening efficiency.*" [1]
>
> VINE DELORIA, JR.

The Bureau of Indian Affairs (BIA) determined the size of all individual land parcels (i.e., allotments). Lot sizes varied from one reservation to another; however, individual allotment sizes—typically, 80-160 acres each—remained constant within the context of each reservation. The act required the distribution of land allotments on a one-per-household model, allowing up to four years for each "head of a family" to select an allotment site. Whether a given tract included access to streams and fertile ground, or was judged unsuitable for farming or grazing, the size of each allotted tract remained constant.

BIA agents sized individual land parcels small enough to leave most reservation lands in the balance, post allotment. The act mandated that the Department of the Interior assume and retain control over all such remaining reservation properties. Once un-allotted lands were redefined as "surplus" lands, much of those "surplus" segments of reservations were parceled out to incoming populations (e.g., mining companies, settlers from the East, and railroad companies). A portion of the "surplus lands" were transferred to churches and other outside organizations that had already established a presence within reservation boundaries. Pressures from outside interests influenced priority-setting as to the order in which tribal lands would be redistributed:

> *"In 1871, Congress foreclosed the power to make further treaties with Indian nations, and later, in the General Allotment Act, reopened the treaty process in order to secure massive land cessions and the allotment of Indian lands."*
>
> VINE DELORIA, JR.

> Most of the [tribal] land cessions in this period occurred in the areas of greatest White interest: the Chippewa areas of Wisconsin and Minnesota, the Sioux country of North and South Dakota, and the Indian lands in central and western Oklahoma Territory...allotments made in the period 1900–1921 were principally in Oklahoma, the Dakotas, Minnesota, Montana, Wyoming, Idaho, Washington, Oregon, and Northern California ...[2]

Not all reservations were allotted; several reservations east and west of the Mississippi River were deemed exempt from this law's requirements. The desert lands of the Navajo and Hopi reservations, for example, were exempted and remain geographically cohesive, collectively-managed tribal landscapes to this day. Indeed, this act gave the President authority to pursue the allotment of tribal lands only in cases wherein reservations were judged to be "... advantageous for agricultural and grazing purposes ..."

Early maps of allotted reservations reveal the disjointed, checkerboard patterning of allotments. Natural landscapes and BIA decisions influenced that phenomenon, as some allotments abutted "surplus" parcels, whereas others bordered allotted acreage. The resulting scattering of tribal members was antithetical to the cultural norms of populations with more than 10,000 years of experience functioning within extended family groups acclimated to cooperative economic strategies (e.g., hunting, fishing, irrigation farming).

The General Allotment Act of 1887

AN ACT[3] ... To provide for the allotment of lands in severalty to Indians on the various reservations and to extend the protection of the laws of the United States and the Territories over the Indians and for other purposes. *Be it enacted by the Senate and House of Representatives of the United States of America in Congress Assembled,* That in all cases where any tribe or band of Indians has been, or shall hereafter be, located upon any reservation created for their use, either by treaty stipulation or by virtue of an act of Congress or executive order setting apart the same for their use, the President of the United States be and he hereby is, authorized, whenever in his opinion any reservation or any part thereof of such Indians is advantageous for agricultural and grazing purposes, to cause said reservation, or any part thereof, to be surveyed, or resurveyed if necessary and to allot the lands in said reservation in severalty to any Indian located thereon in quantities as follows: To each head of a family, one-quarter of a section; To each single person over eighteen years of age, one-eighth of a section; To each orphan child under eighteen years of age, one-eighth of a section; and To each other single person under eighteen years now living, or who may be born prior to the date of the order of the President directing an allotment of the lands embraced in any reservation, one-sixteenth of a section: *Provided,* That in case there is not sufficient land in any of said reservations to allot lands to each individual of the classes above named in quantities as above provided, the lands embraced in such reservation or reservations shall be allotted to each individual of each of said classes pro rata in accordance with the provisions of this act: And *provided further,* That where the treaty or act of Congress setting apart such reservation provides the allotment of lands in severalty in quantities in excess of those herein provided, the President, in making allotments upon such reservation, shall allot the lands to each individual Indian belonging thereon in quantity as specified in such treaty or act:

And *provided further,* That when the lands allotted are only valuable for grazing purposes, an additional allotment of such grazing lands, in quantities as above provided, shall be made to each individual.

SEC. 2. That all allotments set apart under the provisions of this act shall be selected by the Indians, heads of families selecting for their minor children and the agents shall select for each orphan child and in such manner as to embrace the improvements of the Indians making the selection. Where the improvements of two or more Indians have been made on the same legal subdivision of land, unless they shall otherwise agree, a provisional line may be run dividing said lands between them and the amount to which each is entitled shall be equalized in the assignment of the remainder of the land to which they are entitled under his act: *Provided,* That if any one [sic] entitled to an allotment shall fail to make a selection within four years after the President shall direct that allotments may be made on a particular reservation, the Secretary of the Interior may direct the agent of such tribe or band, if such there be and if there be no agent, then a special agent appointed for that purpose, to make a selection for such Indian, which selection shall be allotted as in cases where selections are made by the Indians and patents shall issue in like manner.

SEC. 3. That the allotments provided for in this act shall be made by special agents appointed by the President for such purpose and the agents in charge of the respective reservations on which the allotments are directed to be made, under such rules and regulations as the Secretary of the Interior may from time to time prescribe and shall be certified by such agents to the Commissioner of Indian Affairs, in duplicate, one copy to be retained in the Indian Office and the other to be transmitted to the Secretary of the Interior for his action and to be deposited in the General Land Office.

SEC. 4. That where any Indian not residing upon a reservation, or for whose tribe no reservation has been provided by treaty, act of Congress, or executive order, shall make settlement upon any surveyed or unsurveyed lands of the United States not otherwise appropriated, he or she shall be entitled, upon application to the local land-office for the district in which the lands are located, to have the same allotted to him or her and to his or her children, in quantities and manner as provided in this act for Indians residing upon reservations; and when such settlement is made upon unsurveyed lands, the grant to such Indians shall be adjusted upon the survey of the lands so as to conform thereto; and patents shall be issued to them for such lands in the manner and with the restrictions as herein provided. And the fees to which the officers of such local land-office would have been entitled had such lands been entered under the general laws for the disposition of the public lands shall be paid to them, from any moneys in the Treasury of the United States not otherwise appropriated, upon a statement of an account in their behalf for such fees by the Commissioner of the General Land Office and a certification of such account to the Secretary of the Treasury by the Secretary of the Interior.

SEC. 5. That upon the approval of the allotments provided for in this act by the Secretary of the Interior, he shall cause patents to issue therefore in the name of the allottees, which patents shall be of the legal effect and declare that the United

"... SEC. 5 ... the United States does and will hold the land thus allotted, for the period of twenty-five years, in trust for the sole use and benefit of the Indian to whom such allotment shall have been made, or, in case of his decease, of his heirs ..."

States does and will hold the land thus allotted, for the period of twenty-five years, in trust for the sole use and benefit of the Indian to whom such allotment shall have been made, or, in case of his decease, of his heirs according to the laws of the State or Territory where such land is located and that at the expiration of said period the United States will convey the same by patent to said Indian, or his heirs as aforesaid, in fee, discharged of said trust and free of all charge or encumbrance whatsoever: *Provided,* That the President of the United States may in any case in his discretion extend the period. And if any conveyance shall be made of the lands set apart and allotted as herein provided, or any contract made touching the same, before the expiration of the time above mentioned, such conveyance or contract shall be absolutely null and void: *Provided*, That the law of descent and partition in force in the State or Territory where such lands are situate shall apply thereto after patents therefore have been executed and delivered, except as herein otherwise provided; and the laws of the State of Kansas regulating the descent and partition of real estate shall, so far as practicable, apply to all lands in the Indian Territory which may be allotted in severalty under the provisions of this act: And *provided further*, That at any time after lands have been allotted to all the Indians of any tribe as herein provided, or sooner if in the opinion of the President it shall be for the best interests of said tribe, it shall be lawful for the Secretary of the Interior to negotiate with such Indian tribe for the purchase and release by said tribe, in conformity with the treaty or statute under which such reservation is held, of such portions of its reservation not allotted as such tribe shall, from time to time, consent to sell, on such terms and conditions as shall be considered just and equitable between the United States and said tribe of Indians, which purchase shall not be complete until ratified by Congress and the form and manner of executing such release prescribed by Congress: *Provided however*, That all lands adapted to agriculture, with or without irrigation so sold or released to the United States by any Indian tribe shall be held by the United States for the sole purpose of securing homes to actual settlers and shall be disposed of by the United States to actual and bona fide settlers only tracts not exceeding one hundred and sixty acres to any one person, on such terms as Congress shall prescribe, subject to grants which Congress may make in aid of education: And *provided further*, That no patents shall issue therefore except to the person so taking the same as and for a homestead, or his heirs and after the expiration of five years occupancy thereof as such homestead; and any conveyance of said lands taken as a homestead, or any contract touching the same, or lieu thereon, created prior to the date of such patent, shall be null and void. And the sums agreed to be paid by the United States as purchase money for any portion of any such reservation shall be held in the Treasury of the United States for the sole use of the tribe or tribes Indians; to whom such reservations belonged; and the same, with interest thereon at three per cent per annum, shall be at all times subject to appropriation by Congress for the education and civilization of such tribe or tribes of Indians or the members thereof. The patents aforesaid shall be recorded in the General Land Office and afterward delivered, free of charge, to the allottee entitled thereto. And if any religious society or other organization is now occupying any of the public lands to which this act is applicable, for religious or educational work among the Indians, the Secretary of the Interior is hereby authorized to confirm such occupation to such society or organization, in quantity not exceeding one hundred and sixty acres in any one tract, so long as the same shall be so occupied, on such terms as he shall deem just; but nothing herein contained shall change or alter any claim of such society for religious or educational purposes heretofore granted by law. And hereafter in the employment of Indian police, or any other employees in the public service among any of the Indian tribes or bands affected by this act and where Indians can perform the duties required, those Indians who have availed themselves of the provisions of this act and become citizens of the United States shall be preferred.

"... lands adapted to agriculture, with or without irrigation so sold or released to the United States by any Indian tribe ... shall be held by the United States for the sole purpose of securing homes to actual settlers ..."

SEC. 6. That upon the completion of said allotments and the patenting of the lands to said allottees, each and every member of the respective bands or tribes of Indians to whom allotments have been made shall have the benefit of and be subject to the laws, both civil and criminal, of the State or Territory in which they may reside; and no Territory shall pass or enforce any law denying any such Indian within its jurisdiction the equal protection of the law. And every Indian born within the territorial limits of the United States to whom allotments shall have been made under the provisions of this act, or under any law or treaty and every Indian born within the territorial limits of the United States who has voluntarily taken up, within said limits, his residence separate and apart from any tribe of Indians therein and has adopted the habits of civilized life, is hereby declared to be a citizen of the United States and is entitled to all the rights, privileges and immunities of such citizens, whether said Indian has been or not, by birth or otherwise, a member of any tribe of Indians within the territorial limits of the United States without in any manner affecting the right of any such Indian to tribal or other property.

SEC. 7. That in cases where the use of water for irrigation is necessary to render the lands within any Indian reservation available for agricultural purposes, the Secretary of the Interior be and he is hereby, authorized to prescribe such rules and regulations as he may deem necessary to secure a just and equal distribution thereof among the Indians residing upon any such reservation; and no other appropriation or grant of water by any riparian proprietor shall be permitted to the damage of any other riparian proprietor.

SEC. 8. That the provisions of this act shall not extend to the territory occupied by the Cherokees, Creeks, Choctaws, Chickasaws, Seminoles and Osage, Miamis and Peorias and Sacs and Foxes, in the Indian Territory, nor to any of the reservations of the Seneca Nation of New York Indians in the State of New York, nor to that strip of territory in the State of Nebraska adjoining the Lakota Nation on the south added by executive order.

SEC. 9. That for the purpose of making the surveys and resurveys mentioned in section two of this act, there be and hereby is, appropriated, out of any moneys [*sic*] in the Treasury not otherwise appropriated, the sum of one hundred thousand dollars, to be repaid proportionately out of the proceeds of the sales of such land as may be acquired from the Indians under the provisions of this act.

"... SEC. 10 ... That nothing in this act ... shall be so construed to affect the ... power of Congress to grant the right of way through any lands granted to an Indian, or a tribes of Indians, for railroads or other highways, or telegraph lines, for the public use ..."

SEC. 10. That nothing in this act contained shall be so construed to affect the right and power of Congress to grant the right of way through any lands granted to an Indian, or a tribe of Indians, for railroads or other highways, or telegraph lines, for the public use, or condemn such lands to public uses, upon making just compensation.

SEC. 11. That nothing in this act shall be so construed as to prevent the removal of the Southern Ute Indians from their present reservation in Southwestern Colorado to a new reservation by and with consent of a majority of the adult male members of said tribe.

Approved February, 8, 1887.

In 1928, a congressional subcommittee reported on the fundamental failure of this legislation to live up to its stated objectives: "... in some instances Indians have not only never lived on their allotments, they have never seen them and have no desire to go to the place where their land is ... In such cases the land should, if possible, be sold and the proceeds used to purchase land for the Indian in the neighborhood where he desires to live ..."[4]

Noted American historian Stephan Dow Beckman, in an article appearing in the Handbook of North American Indians (Vol. 12), summarized this public act as follows:

The Dawes Severalty Act of 1887 became the means for the most significant assault on tribal land tenure of any measure since the ratification of treaties and cessions of aboriginal homelands in the 1850s and 1860s. Allotment was another variant on the scheme of consolidating Indians, reducing their land base, and increasing government control and oversight over their activities. The guise of gaining citizenship at the termination of trust over their lands was not explained in the terms of the tax responsibility that befell the holder of the fee-patented allotment.[5]

Two weeks after Congress enacted the General Allotment Act of 1887, what appears to be the most critical message of a front page newspaper article— "Indian Ponies," published on February 23, 1887, in the DC newspaper, *The Bee*— is tucked into its last line, as follows:

The Indians' war ponies are always the best of the herd ... buffalo pony ranks next ... [and] . . knows how to elude the charge of a mad bull as well as I know how to skin an antelope ... take a green horse and hunt a buffalo, and you'll find the affair isn't so tame ... I'd like to see some attention paid to raising good Sioux ponies ... They are apt to shy badly, but that's because they've stepped into prairie dog or fox holes occasionally ... every tuft of long grass or ... gravel created suspicion ... *It is thought that the great Sioux Indian reservation of 33,000 square miles will soon be thrown open to settlement ...*

Subsequent amendments (e.g., the Sioux Dawes Act) tailored the provisions of the General Allotment Act to the landscapes and circumstances of individual reservations.

Figure 17. In his 1985 book, *American Indian Policy in the Twentieth Century*, anthropologist, author, and attorney Vine Deloria, Jr., quoted President Theodore Roosevelt's summation of the Dawes legislation. Roosevelt (shown above in 1907) called it a "mighty pulverizing engine ... to break up the tribal mass ..." (Photo: Underwood & Underwood, Publisher, *Teddy Roosevelt speaking at the back of a railroad car*, ca. 1907. May 25. Photograph. Retrieved from the Library of Congress, item #2009633760).

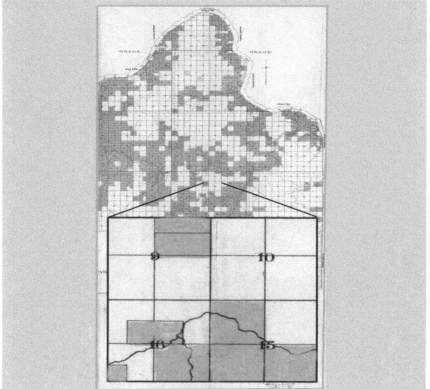

Figure 18. This image is an approximation of two sections (one, the close-up) of a post-allotment 1893 map of one Nebraska reservation. It represents lands allotted to members of the Pawnee Nation (darker blocks) in contrast to those redefined by the General Allotment (Dawes) legislation as "surplus" reservation lands. This representation is based upon the highly detailed map produced by the Hudson-Kimberly Pub. Co. and now archived within the collections of the Library of Congress Geography and Map Division. Names of the owners (circa 1893) of individual allotments shown on the original map have been blurred out to protect the privacy of their descendants.

Chapter IV
Erasing Tribal Spaces: The 1888 Dawes Amendment to Reduce Lakota Lands

THE FORT LARAMIE Treaty of 1868 had been ratified by Congress in 1869. Theoretically, this ratification had further assured the continuity of the expansive Great Sioux Reservation into perpetuity.[1] However, twenty years later, a single Dawes (i.e., General Allotment) amendment reduced the landmass of the Great Sioux Reservation by approximately 88.5%.

Congress enacted multiple amendments to the General Allotment Act of 1887. This 1888 amendment adapted provisions of the original General Allotment Act to congressional visions of the lands and circumstances of the Lakota—and thus dissolved the 1868 vision of a permanent and collective Lakota homeland.

"Liberty doesn't work as good in practice as it does in speeches."

WILL ROGERS

Members of Congress understood the ethical compromise this legislation represented; many voted against it. Congressional opponents of this amendment perceived it as an illegality, given its obvious contradiction of congressional actions of 1869. Referenced by various titles (e.g., the Sioux Dawes Act) this legalistic device served to fragment the Great Sioux Reservation by parceling out most of its land to miners, railroad companies, churches, border towns, ranchers, settlers, and other off-reservation beneficiaries. This amendment mandated the selection of separate sites for various Lakota groups, and prescribed the subdivision of each of these separate land masses—all located within the original boundaries of the Great Sioux Reservation—into 160-acre allotments. Each Lakota household was required to select one land allotment within the first five years following enactment of this public law; if none was selected by any given household, a reservation agent was required to select an allotment for that household. This divide-and-distribute strategy resulted in the allocation of approximately 11.5% of the Great Sioux Reservation to tribal members.

This amendment further stipulated the distribution of twenty dollars, garden seed enough for two years of planting, two milk cows, and either a pair of oxen with yoke and chain, or a pair of mares with harnesses, to each tribal household. It assigned to agents of the Secretary of the Interior the role of decision-makers in all determinations of which, if any, farming implements individual tribal households might receive.

Assignments of individual land parcels for the Lakota resulted in a checker-boarding of legal, social, and economic landscapes. For example, federal agents at the Pine Ridge Agency assigned to the Oglala Lakota restricted all travel (e.g., walking) from one allotment site to another—unless a reservation agent had given prior permission for such travel. Such onerous prohibitions were not stipulated within this act, nor within the 1887 General Allotment Act (i.e., the 1887 Dawes Act). These locally defined restrictions, given the disjointed configuration of allotment sites, separated family members from even their closest kin—and precluded any pooling of resources (e.g., cooperative farming strategies). Since permission to cross allotment boundaries at the Pine Ridge Agency could only be granted by an agent of the Office of Indian Affairs, any contact between family members living on non-adjacent allotments, if occurring without federal permission, could be interpreted locally as a violation of federal law.[2]

Within the revised geographic limits of Lakota lands, most un-allotted lands of the Great Sioux Reservation were relabeled as "federal trust lands." As such, although situated within reservation boundaries, these lands fell under the absolute control of the Department of the Interior—not tribes. This 1888 amendment gave the Secretary of the Interior the political authority and the legalistic mandates needed to offer most of the lands of the Great Sioux Reservation to waves of settlers, corporations, and border towns. Railroad companies, churches, cattle ranchers, and homesteaders pursued the most desirable sites, leaving limited arable land for the Lakota.

The 1888 Amendment to Reduce Lakota Lands

> AN ACT[3] ... To divide a portion of the reservation of the Sioux Nation of Indians in Dakota into separate reservations and to secure the relinquishment of the Indian title to the remainder. *Be it enacted by the Senate and House of Representatives of the United States of America in Congress Assembled,* That the following tract of land,

being a part of the Great Reservation of the Sioux Nation, in the Territory of Dakota, is hereby set apart for a permanent reservation for the Indians receiving rations and annuities at the Pine Ridge Agency, will in the Territory of Dakota, namely: beginning at the intersection of the one hundred and third meridian of longitude with the northern boundary of the State of Nebraska; thence west on said north line to the place beginning. Also, the following

"... AN ACT ... To divide a portion of the reservation of the Sioux Nation of Indians ... into separate reservations ... and to secure the relinquishment of the Indian title to the remainder ..."

tract of land situate in the State of Nebraska, namely: beginning at a point on the boundary line between the State of Nebraska and the Territory of Dakota where the range line between ranges forty-four and forty-five west of the six principal Meridian, in the Territory of Dakota, intersects said boundary line; thence east along said boundary line five miles; thence due south five miles; thence due west ten miles; thence due north to said boundary line; thence due east along said boundary line to the place of beginning: *Provided,* That the said tract of land in the State of Nebraska shall be reserved, by executive order, only so long as it may be needed for the use and protection of the Indians receiving rations and annuities at the Pine Ridge Agency.

SEC. 2. That the following tract of land, being a part of the said Great Reservation of the Sioux Nation, in the Territory of Dakota, is hereby set apart for a permanent reservation for the Indians receiving rations and annuities at the Rosebud Agency, in said Territory of Dakota, namely: commencing in the middle of the main channel of the Missouri River, at the intersection of the South line of Brulé County; thence down said middle of the main channel of said river to the intersection of the ninety-ninth degree of west latitude from Greenwich; thence due south to the forty-third parallel of latitude; thence west along said parallel to a point due south from the source of the principal branch of Pass Creek; thence due north to the said source of the said principal branch of Pass Creek; thence down Pass Creek to White River; thence down White River to a point intersecting the west line of Gregory County extended north; thence south on said extended west line of Gregory County to the intersection of the south line of Brulé County extended west; thence due east on said south line of Brulé County extended to the point of beginning in the Missouri River, including entirely within said reservation all islands, if any, in said river.

SEC. 3. That the following tract of land, being a part of the said Great Reservation of the Sioux Nation, in the Territory of Dakota, is hereby set apart for a permanent reservation for the Indians receiving rations and annuities at the Standing Rock Agency, in the said Territory of Dakota, namely: beginning at the point in the center of the main channel of the Missouri River, opposite the mouth of Cannon Ball River; thence down said center of the main channel to a point ten miles north of the mouth of the Moreau River, including also within said reservation all islands, if any, in said river; thence due west to the hundred and second degree of west longitude from Greenwich; thence north along said meridian to its intersection with the South Branch of Cannon Ball River, also known as Cedar Creek; thence down said South Branch of Cannon Ball River, to its intersection with the main Cannon Ball River, and down said main cannonball River to the center of the main channel of the Missouri River at the place of beginning SEC. 4. Following tract of land, being a part of the said Great Reservation of the Sioux Nation, in the Territory of Dakota, is hereby set apart for permanent reservation for the Indians receiving rations and annuities at the Cheyenne River Agency, in the said Territory of Dakota, namely: Beginning at a point in the center of the main channel of the Missouri River, ten miles north of the mouth of the Moreau River, said point being the southeasterly corner of the Standing Rock Reservation; thence down said center of the main channel of the Missouri River, including also entirely within said reservation all islands, if any, in said river, to a point opposite the mouth of the Cheyenne River; thence west to said Cheyenne River, and up the same to its intersection with the hundred and second meridian of longitude; thence north long said meridian to its intersection with the line due west from a point in the Missouri River ten miles north of the mouth of the Moreau River; thence due east to the point of beginning.

SEC. 5. That the following tract of land, being a part of the said Great Reservation of the Sioux Nation, in the Territory of Dakota, is hereby set apart for permanent reservation for the Indians receiving rations and annuities at the Lower Brulé agency, in said Territory of Dakota, namely: Beginning on the Missouri River at old Fort George; thence running due west to the western boundary of Presho County; thence unning south on said western boundary to a forty-fourth degree of latitude; thence on said forty-fourth degree of latitude to western boundary of township number seventy-two; thence south on said township western line to an intersecting line running due west from Fort Lookout; thence eastwardly on said line to the center of the main channel of the Missouri River at Fort Lookout; thence north in the center of the main channel of the said river to the original starting point.

SEC. 6. That the following tract of land, being a part of the Great Reservation of the Sioux Nation, in the Territory of Dakota, is hereby set apart for a permanent reservation for the Indians receiving rations and annuities at the Crow Creek Agency, in said Territory of Dakota, namely: The whole township one hundred and six, range seventy; township one hundred and seven, range seventy-one; township one hundred and eight, range seventy-one; township one hundred and eight, range seventy-two; township one hundred and nine, range seventy-two, and the south half of township one hundred and nine, range seventy-one, and all except sections one, two, three, four, nine, ten, eleven, and twelve of township one hundred and seven, range seventy, and such parts as lie on the east or left bank of the Missouri River, of the following townships, to wit: Township one hundred and six, range seventy-one; township one hundred and seven, range seventy-two; township one hundred and eight, range seventy-three; township one hundred and eight, range seventy-four; township one hundred and eight, range seventy-five; Township one hundred and eight, range seventy-six; township one hundred and nine, range seventy-three; township one hundred and nine, range seventy-four; south half of township one hundred and nine, range seventy-five, and township one hundred and seven, range seventy-three; also the west half of township one hundred and six, range sixty-nine and sections sixteen, seventeen, eighteen, nineteen, twenty, twenty-one, twenty-eight, twenty-nine, thirty, thirty-one, thirty-two, and thirty-three of township one hundred and seven, range sixty-nine.

SEC. 7. That each member of the Santee Sioux tribe of Indians now occupying a reservation in the State of Nebraska shall be entitled to allotment upon said reserve and Nebraska as follows: To each head of a family one quarter of a section; to each single person over eighteen years of age, one-eighth of a section; to each orphan child under eighteen years, one-eighth of a section; to each other person under eighteen years of age now living, one-sixteenth of a section; with title thereto, in accordance with the provisions of article six of the treaty concluded April twenty-ninth, eighteen hundred and sixty-eight, and the agreement with said Santee Sioux approved February twenty-eight, eighteen hundred and seventy-seven, and rights under the same in all other respects conforming to this act. And said Santee Sioux shall be entitled to all other benefits under this act in the same manner, and with the same conditions as if they were residents upon said Sioux Reservation, receiving rations at one of the agencies here in named: *Provided,* That all allotments heretofore made to said Santee Sioux in Nebraska are hereby ratified and confirmed; and each member of the Flandreau Band of Sioux Indians is hereby authorized to take allotments on the Great Sioux Reservation, or in lieu therefore shall be paid at the rate of fifty cents per acre for the land to which they would be entitled to be paid out of the proceeds of land relinquished under this act, which shall be used under the direction of the Secretary of the Interior; and said Flandreau band of Sioux Indians is in all other respects entitled to the benefits of this act, the same as if receiving rations and annuities at any of the agencies aforesaid.

SEC. 8. That the President is hereby authorized and required, whenever in his opinion any reservation of such Indians or any part thereof, is advantageous for agricultural grazing purposes, and the progress and civilization of the Indians receiving rations on either or any of said reservations shall be such as to encourage the belief that an allotment in severalty to such Indians, or any of them, could be for the best interest of said Indians, to cause said reservation, or so much thereof as is necessary, to be surveyed, or resurveyed, and to allot the lands in said reservation in severalty to the Indians located thereon as aforesaid, in quantities as follows: To each head of a family, one quarter of a section; to each single person over eighteen years of age, one-fourth of a section; to each orphan child under eighteen years of age, one-fourth of a section; and to each other person under eighteen years now living, or who may be born prior to the date of the order of the President directing allotment of the lands embraced in any reservation, one-eighth of a section. In case there is not sufficient land in either of said reservations to allot lands to each individual of the classes above named in quantities as above provided, the lands embraced in such reservation or reservations shall be allotted to each individual of each of said classes pro rata in accordance with the provisions of this act: *Provided*, That where the lands on any reservation are mainly valuable for grazing purposes, and additional allotment of such grazing lands, in quantities as above provided, shall be made to each individual; or in case any two or more Indians who may be entitled to allotment shall so agree, the President may assign the grazing lands to which they may be entitled to them in one tract, and to be held and used in common.

SEC. 9. That all allotments set apart under the provisions of this act shall be selected by the Indians, heads of families selecting for their minor children, and the agency shall select for each orphan child, and in such manner as to embrace the improvements of the Indians making the selection. Where the improvements of two or more Indians have been made on the same legal subdivision of land, unless they shall otherwise agree, a provisional line may be run dividing said lands between them, and the amount to which each is entitled shall be equalized in the assignment of the remainder of the land to which they are entitled under this act: *Provided*, That if anyone entitled to an allotment shall fail to make a selection within five years after the President shall direct that allotments may be made on a particular reservation, the Secretary of the Interior may direct the agent of such tribe or band, if there be, and if there be no agent, then a special agent appointed for that purpose, to make a selection for such Indian, which selection shall be allotted as in cases where selections are made by the Indians, and patents shall issue in like manner.

SEC. 10. That the allotments provided for in this act shall be made by special agents appointed by the President for such purpose, and the agency in charge of the respective reservations in which the allotments are directed to be made, under such rules and regulations as the Secretary of the Interior may from time to time prescribe, and shall be certified by such agents to the Commissioner of Indian Affairs, in duplicate, one copy to be retained in the Indian office and the other to be transmitted to the Secretary of the Interior for his action, and to be deposited in the General Land Office.

"... SEC. 11. That upon the approval of the allotments ... by the Secretary of the Interior, he shall cause patents to issue ... and declare that the United States does and will hold the lands ... for ... twenty-five years, in trust for the sole use and benefit of the Indian to whom such allotment shall have been made ..."

SEC. 11. That upon the approval of the allotments provided for in this act by the Secretary of the Interior, he shall cause patents to issue therefore in the name of the allottee, which patent shall be of the legal effect, and declare that the United States does and will hold the lands thus allotted, for the period of twenty-five years, in trust for the sole use and benefit of the Indian to whom such allotment shall have been made, or, in case of his decease, of his heirs according to the laws of the State or Territory where such land is allotted, and that at the expiration of said period the United States will convey the same by patent to said Indian, or his heirs as aforesaid, in fee, discharged of said trust and free of all charge or encumbrance whatsoever, and patents shall issue accordingly: *Provided,* That the President of the United States may in any case, in his discretion, extend the period by a term not exceeding ten years; and if any lease or conveyance shall be made by the land set apart and allotted as herein provided, or any contract made touching the same, before the expiration of the time above mentioned, such lease or conveyance or contract shall be absolutely null and void: *Provided, further,* that the law of dissent and partition in force in the State or Territory where the lands may be situated shall apply thereto after patents therefore have been executed and delivered. Each of the patents aforesaid shall be recorded in the General Land Office, and afterward delivered, free of charge, to the herefor [*sic*] entitled thereto.

SEC. 12. That at any time after lands have been allotted to all the Indians of any tribe as herein provided, or sooner, if in the opinion of the President it shall be for the best interests of said tribe, it shall be lawful for the Secretary of the Interior to negotiate with such Indian tribe for the purchase and release by said tribe, in conformity with the treaty or statute under which such reservation is held, of such portions of its reservation not allotted as such tribe shall, from time to time, consent to sell on terms and conditions as shall be considered just and equitable between United States and said tribe of Indians, which purchase shall not be complete until ratified by Congress: *Provided, however,* that all lands adapted to agriculture, with or without irrigation, so sold or released to the United States by any Indian tribe shall be held by the United States for the sole purpose of securing homes to actual settlers, and shall be disposed of by the United States to actual and bona fide settlers only in tracts not exceeding one hundred and sixty acres to any one person on such terms as Congress shall prescribe, subject to grants which Congress may make in aid of education: *And provided further,* that no patents shall issue therefore except to the person so taking the same as and for a homestead, or his

"... SEC. 12 ... And the sums agreed to be paid ... for any portion of any such reservation shall be held in the Treasury of the United States for the sole use of the tribe or tribes of Indians to whom such reservation belonged ..."

heirs and after the expiration of five years occupancy there of as such homestead; and any conveyance of said land so taken as a homestead, or any contract touching the same, or lien thereon, created prior to the date of such patent, shall be null and void And the sums agreed to be paid by the United States as purchase money for any portion of any such reservation shall be held in the Treasury of the United States for the sole use of the tribe or tribes of Indians to whom such reservation belonged; and the same, with interest thereon at five per centum per annum, shall be at all times subject to appropriation by Congress for the education and civilization of such tribe or tribes of Indians or the members thereof. The patents aforesaid shall be recorded in the General Land Office, and afterward delivered, free of charge, to the herefor [*sic*] titled thereto.

SEC. 13. That any Indian receiving and entitled to rations and annuities that either of the agencies mentioned in this act at the time the same shall take effect, but residing upon any portion of said Great Reservation not included in either of the separate reservations herein established, may, at his option, within one year from the time when this act shall take effect, and within one year after he has been notified of his said right of option in such manner as the Secretary of the Interior shall direct by recording a selection with the proper agent at the agency to which he belongs, have the allotment to which he would be otherwise entitled on one of said separate reservations upon the land where such Indian may reside, such allotment in all other respects to conform to the allotments herein before provided. Each member of the Ponca Tribe of Indians now occupying a part of the old Ponca Reservation, within the limits of the said Great Sioux Reservation, shall be entitled to allotments upon said old Ponca reservation as follows: To each head of a family, one quarter of the section; to each single person over eighteen years of age, one-eighth of a section; to each orphan child under eighteen years of age, one-eighth of a section; and to each other person under eighteen years now living, one-sixteenth of a section, with title hereto and rights under the same in all other respects conforming to this act. And said Poncas shall be entitled to all benefits under this act in the same manner and with the same conditions as if they were a part of the Sioux Nation receiving rations at one of the agencies herein named. When the allotments to the Ponca tribe of Indians and to such other Indians as allotments are provided for by this act shall have been made upon that portion of said reservation which is described in the act entitled "AN ACT To extend the northern boundary of the State of Nebraska," approved March twenty-eighth, eighteen hundred and eighty-two, the President shall, in pursuance of said act, declare that the Indian title is extinguished to all lands described in said act not so allotted hereunder, and thereupon all of said lands not allotted and included in said act of March twenty-eighth, eighteen hundred and eight-two shall be open to settlement, as provided in this act: *Provided,* That the allotments to Ponca and other Indians authorized by this act be made upon the land described in the said act entitled "AN ACT To extend the northern boundary of the State of Nebraska," shall be made within six months from the time this act shall take effect.

SEC. 14. That in cases where the use of water for irrigation is necessary to render the lands within any Indian reservation created by this act available for agricultural purposes the Secretary of the Interior be, and he is hereby, authorized to prescribe such rules and regulations as he may deem necessary to secure a just and equal distribution thereof among the Indians residing upon any such Indian reservation created by this act; and no other appropriation or grant of water by any riparian proprietor shall be authorized or permitted to the damage of any other riparian proprietor.

SEC. 15. That if any Indian has, under and in conformity with the provisions of the treaty with the great Sioux nation concluded April twenty-ninth, eighteen hundred and sixty-eight, and proclaimed by the President February twenty-fourth, eighteen hundred and sixty-nine, will or any existing law, taken allotments of land within or without the limits of any of the separate reservations established by this act, such allotments are hereby ratified and make valid, and such Indian is entitled to a patent therefore in conformity with the provisions of said treaty and existing law and of the provisions of this act in relation to patents for individual allotments.

"... the acceptance of this act by the Indians ... shall be taken and held to be a release of all title on the part of the Indians receiving rations and annuities on each of the said separate reservations ... to the lands described ..."

SEC. 16. That the acceptance of this act by the Indians in manner and form as required by the said treaty concluded between the different bands of the Sioux Nation of Indians and the United States, April twenty-ninth, eighteen hundred and sixty-eight, and proclaimed by the President February twenty-fourth, eighteen hundred and sixty-nine, as herein provided, shall be taken and held to be a release of all title on the part of the Indians receiving rations and annuities on each of the said separate reservations, to the lands described in each of the other separate reservations so created, and shall be held to confirm in the Indians, entitled to receive rations, and each of said separate reservations respectively, to their separate and exclusive use and benefit, all in the title and interest of every name in nature secured therein to the different bands of the Sioux Nation by said treaty of April twenty-ninth, eighteen hundred and sixty-eight. This release shall not affect the title of any individual Indian to his separate allotment on land not included in any of said separate reservations provided for in this act, which title is hereby confirmed, nor any agreement heretofore made with the Chicago, Milwaukee and Saint Paul Railroad Company, or the Dakota Central Railroad for a right of way through said reservation; and for any lands required by any such agreement to be used in connection therewith, except as here in after provided; but the Chicago, Milwaukee and Saint Paul Railroad Company or the Dakota Central Railroad Company shall, respectively, have the right to take and use, prior to any white person, and to any corporation, the right-of-way provided for in said agreements, with not to exceed twenty acres of land, in addition to the right-of-way, for stations for every ten miles of road; and said companies shall also, respectively, have the right to take in use for right of way, side-track, depot and station privileges, machine-shop, freight-house, round-house, and yard facilities, prior to any white person, and to any corporation or association, so much of the two separate sections of land embraced in said agreements; also, the former company so much of the one hundred and eighty-eight acres and the latter company so much of the seventy-five, on the east side of the Missouri River, likewise embraced in said agreements, as the Secretary of the Interior shall decide to have been agreed upon and paid for by said railroads and to be reasonably necessary upon each side of said river for approaches to the bridge of each of said companies to be constructed across the river, for the right of way, side-track, depot and station privileges, machine-shop, freight-house, round-house, and yard facilities, and no more: *Provided,* That the said railway company shall have made the payments according to the terms of said agreements for each mile of right of way and each acre of land for railway purposes, which said companies take and use under the provisions of this act, and shall satisfy the

Secretary of the Interior to that effect: *Provided further*, That no part of the lands here in authorized to be taken shall be sold or conveyed except by way of sale of, or mortgage of, the railway itself. Nor shall any of said lands be used directly or indirectly for town-site purposes, it being the intention hereof that said lands shall be held for general railway uses and purposes only, including stock-yards, warehouses, elevators, terminal and other facilities of and for said railways; but nothing herein contained shall be construed to prevent any such railroad company from building upon such lands, houses for the accommodation or residents of their employees, or leasing grounds contiguous to its tracks for warehouse or elevator purposes connected with said railways: *And provided further*, that said payment shall be made and said conditions performed within six months after this act shall take effect: *And provided further*, that said railway companies and each of them shall within nine months after this act takes effect, definitely locate their respective lines of road, including all station grounds and terminals across and upon the lands of said reservation designated in said agreements, and shall also within the said period of nine months, file with the Secretary of the Interior, a map of such definite location, specifying clearly the line of road, the several station grounds, any amount of land required for railway purposes, as herein specified, of the said separate sections of land in said tracts of one hundred and eighty-eight acres and seventy-five acres; and the Secretary of the Interior shall, within three months after the filing of such map, designate the particular portions of said sections and of said tracts of land which the said railway companies respectively may take and hold under the provisions of this act for railway purposes. And the said railway companies and each of them shall, within three years after this act takes effect, construct, complete, and put in operation there said lines of road; and in cases the said lines of road are not definitely located and maps of the location filed within the periods hereinbefore provided, or in case the said lines of road are not constructed, completed, and put in operation within the time herein provided, then, and in either case, the lands granted for right of way station grounds, or other real way purposes as in this act provided, shall, without any further act or ceremony, be declared by proclamation of the President forfeited, and shall, without entry or further action on the part of the United States, revert to the United States and be subject to entry under the other provisions of this act; and whenever such forfeiture occurs the Secretary of the Interior shall ascertain the fact and give due notice thereof to the local land officers, and thereupon the lands so forfeited shall be open to homestead entry under the provisions of this act.

SEC. 17. That it is hereby enacted that the seventh article of the said treaty of April twenty-ninth, eighteen hundred and sixty-ht, securing to said Indians the benefits of education, subject to such modifications as Congress shall deem most effective to secure to said Indians equivalent benefits of such education, shall continue in force for twenty years from and after the time this act shall take effect; and the Secretary of the Interior is hereby authorized and directed to purchase, from time to time, for the use of said Indians, such and so many American breeding cows of good quality, not exceeding twenty-five thousand in number, and bulls of like quality, not exceeding one thousand in number, as in his judgment can be, under regulations furnished by him, cared for and preserved, with their increase, by said Indians: *Provided* That each head of family or single person over the age of eighteen years, who shall have or may hereafter take his or her allotment of land in severalty, shall be provided with two Milch [*sic*] cows, one pair of oxen, with yoke and chain, one plow, one wagon, one harrow, one hoe, one axe, and one pitchfork, all suitable to the work they may have to do and also twenty dollars in cash. That for two years the necessary seed shall be provided to plant five acres of ground into different crops, if so much can be used, and provided that in the purchase of such seed preference shall be given to Indians who may have raised the same for sale, and so much money as shall be necessary for this purpose is hereby appropriated out of any money in the Treasury not otherwise appropriated; and in addition thereto there shall be set apart, out of any money in the Treasury not otherwise appropriated, the sum of one million dollars, which said sum shall be deposited in the Treasury of the United States to the credit of the Sioux Nation of Indians as a permanent fund, the interest of which, at five per centum per annum, shall be appropriated, under the direction of the Secretary of the Interior, to the use of the Indians receiving rations and annuities upon the reservations created by this act, in proportion to the numbers that shall so receive rations and annuities at the time this act shall take effect, as follows: One-half of said interest shall be so expended for the promotion of industrial and other suitable education among said

Indians, and the other half thereof in such manner and for such purposes, including reasonable cash payment per capita as, in the judgment of said Secretary, shall, from time to time, most contribute to the advancement of said Indians in civilization and self-support: *Provided,* That after the government has been reimbursed for the money expended for said Indians under the provisions of this act, the Secretary of the Interior, may, in his discretion, expend, in addition to the interest of the permanent fund, not to exceed ten per centum per annum of the principle of said fund in the employment of farmers, and in the purchase of agricultural implements, teams, seeds, including reasonable cash payments per capita, and other articles necessary to assist them in agricultural pursuits, and he shall report to Congress in detail each year his doing hereunder.

SEC. 18. That if any land in said Great Sioux Reservation is now occupied and used by any religious society for the purpose of missionary or educational work among said Indians, whether situate outside of or within the lines of any reservation constituted by this act, or if any such land is so occupied upon the Santee Sioux Reservation, in Nebraska, the exclusive occupation and use of said land, not exceeding one hundred and sixty acres on any one tract, is hereby, with the approval of the Secretary of the Interior, granted to any such society so long as the same shall be occupied and used by such society for educational and missionary work among said Indians; and the Secretary of the Interior is hereby authorized and directed to give to such religious society a patent of such tract of land to the legal effect aforesaid; and purpose of such educational or missionary work any such society may purchase, upon any of the reservations herein are created, in a tract of land not exceeding in any one tract one hundred and sixty acres, not interfering with the title in severalty of any Indian, and with the approval of and upon such terms, not exceeding fifty cents an acre, as shall be prescribed by the Secretary of the Interior. And the Santee Normal Training School may, in like manner, purchase for such educational or missionary work on the Santee Reservation, in addition to the foregoing, in such location and quality, not exceeding three hundred and twenty acres, as shall be approved by the Secretary of the Interior.

SEC. 19. That all the provisions of the said treaty with the different bands of the Sioux Nation of Indians concluded April twenty-ninth, eighteen hundred and sixty-eight, and the ...

"... SEC. 19. That all the provisions of the said treaty with the different bands of the Sioux Nation of Indians concluded ... [April 29, 1868] ... and the agreement with the same approved ... [February 28, 1877] ... not in conflict with the provisions and requirements of this act, are hereby continued in force according to their tenor and limitation, anything in this act to the contrary notwithstanding ..."

agreement with the same approved February twenty-eighth, eighteen hundred and seventy-seven, not in conflict with the provisions and requirements of this act, are hereby continued in force according to their tenor and limitation, anything in this act to the contrary notwithstanding.

SEC. 20. The Secretary of the Interior shall cause to be erected not less than thirty school-houses, and more, if found necessary, on the different reservations, at such points as he shall think for the best interest of the Indians, but at such distance only as will enable as many as possible attending schools to return home nights, as white children to attending district schools: *And Provided,* That any white children residing in the neighborhood are entitled to attend the said school on such terms as the Secretary of the Interior may prescribe.

SEC. 21. That all the lands in the Great Sioux Reservation outside of the separate reservations herein described are hereby restored to the public domain, except American Island, Farm Island, and Niobrara Island, and shall be disposed of by the United States to actual settlers only, under the provisions of the homestead law (except section two thousand three hundred and one thereof) and under the law relating to town-sites: *Provided,* That each settler, under and in accordance with the provisions of said homestead acts, shall pay to the United States, for the land so taken by him, in addition to the fees provided by law, the sum of fifty cents for each and every acre, and shall be entitled to a patent therefore, according to said homestead laws, and after the full payment of said some of fifty cents per acre therefore; but the rights of soldiers, as defined and described in sections two thousand three hundred and four and two thousand three hundred and five of the Revised Statutes of the United States, shall not be abridged, except as to said fifty cents per acre; and any conveyance of said lands so taken as a homestead, or any contract touching the same, or lien thereon, created prior to the date of final entry, shall be null and void: *And Provided,* That lands entered for town-site purposes shall be paid for at the rate of one dollar and twenty-five cents per acre: *And provided further,* That nothing in this act contained shall be so construed as to affect the right of Congress or of the Territorial government of Dakota to establish public highways or to grant to railroad companies the right of way through said lands, or to exclude the said lands, or any thereof, from the operation of the general laws of the United States now in force granting to rail way companies the right of way and depot grounds over and upon the public lands. American Island, an island in the Missouri River, near Chamberlain, in the Territory of Dakota, and now part of the Sioux Reservation, is hereby donated to the said city of Chamberlain: *Provided further,* That said city of Chamberlain shall formally accept the same within one year from the passage of this act, upon the express condition that the same shall be preserved and used for all time entire as a public park, and for no other purpose, to which all persons shall have free access; and said city shall have authority to adopt all proper rules and regulations for the improvement and care of said park; and upon the failure of any of said conditions the said island shall revert to the United States, to be disposed of by future legislation only. Farm Island, an island in the Missouri River near Pierre, in the Territory of Dakota, and now part of the Sioux Reservation, is hereby donated to the said city of Pierre: *Provided further,* That the said city of Pierre shall formally accept the same within one year from the passage of this act, upon the express condition that this same shall be preserved and used for all time entire the public park, and for no other purpose, to which all persons shall have free access; and said city shall have authority to adopt all proper rules and regulations for the improvement in care of said park; and upon the failure of any of the said conditions the said islands shall revert to the United States, to be disposed of by the future legislation only. Niobrara Island, an island in the Niobrara River, near Niobrara, and now part of the Sioux Reservation, is hereby donated to the said city of Niobrara: *Provided further*, That the said city of Niobrara shall formally accept the same within one year from the passage of this act, upon the express condition that the same shall be preserved and used for all time entire as a public park, and for no other purpose, to which all persons shall have free access; and said city shall have authority to adopt all proper rules and regulations for the improvement and care of said park; and upon the failure of any of said conditions the said islands shall revert to the United States, to be disposed of by future legislation only: *And provided further*, That if any full or mixed blood Indian of the Sioux Nation shall have located on Farm Island, American Island, or Niobrara Island before the date of the passage of this act, it shall be the duty of the Secretary of the Interior, within three months from the time this act shall have taken effect, to cause all improvements made by any such Indian so located upon either of these said islands, and all damage that may accrue to him by a removal therefrom [*sic*], to be appraised, and upon the payment of the sum so determined within six months after the notice thereof, by the city to which the island is here to donated to such Indian, said Indian shall be required to remove from said island, and shall be entitled to select instead of such location his allotment according to the provisions of this act upon any of the reservations here in established, or upon any land opened to settlement by this act not already located upon.

SEC. 22. That all money accruing from the disposal of lands in conformity with the foregoing section shall, after deducting the necessary expenses attending such disposition thereof, be paid into the Treasury of the United States and be applied solely as follows: First, to the reimbursement of the United States for all necessary and actual expenditures provided; and after such reimbursement to the increase of said permanent fund for the purposes therein before provided.

SEC. 23. That all persons who, between the twenty-seventh day of February, eighteen hundred and eighty-five, and the seventeenth day of April, eighteen hundred and eighty-five, in good faith, entered upon our made settlements with intent to enter the same under the homestead or pre-emption laws of the United States upon any part of the Great Sioux Reservation lying east of the Missouri River, and known as the Creek Crow Creek and Winnebago Reservation, which by the President's proclamation of date February twenty-five, was declared to be open to settlement, and not included the new reservation established by section six of this act, and who, being otherwise legally entitled to make such entries, located or attempted to locate thereon homestead, pre-emption, or town-site claims, by actual settlement and improvement of any portion of such lands, shall, for a period of ninety days after the proclamation of the President required to be made by this act, have a right to re-enter upon said claims and shall procure title thereto under the homestead or pre-emption laws of the United States, and complete the same as required therein, and their said claim shall, for such time, have a preference over later entries; and when they shall have in other respects shown themselves entitled and shall have complied with the law regarding such entries, and, as to homestead, with the special provisions of this act, they shall be entitled to have said lands, and patents therefore shall be issued as in like cases: *Provided,* That pre-emption claimants shall reside on their lands the same length of time before procuring title as homestead claimants under this act. The price to be paid for town-site entries shall be such as is required by law in other cases, and shall be paid into the general fund provided for by this act.

SEC. 24. That this act shall take effect only upon the acceptance thereof and consent thereto by the different bands of the Sioux Nation of Indians, in manner and form prescribed by the twelfth article of the said treaty between the United States and said Indians, concluded April twenty-ninth, eighteen hundred and sixty-eight, which said acceptance and consent shall be made known by proclamation thereof by the President of the United States, upon satisfactory proof presented to him that the same had has been obtained in the manner and form required by said twelfth article of said treaty, which proof shall be presented to him within one year from the passage of this act; and upon failure of such proof and proclamation this act becomes of no effect, and null and void.

SEC. 25. That section sixteen and thirty-six of each township of the lands open to settlement under the provisions of this act, whether surveyed or unsurveyed, are hereby reserved for the use and benefit of the public schools as provided by the act organizing the Territory of Dakota, and whether surveyed or unsurveyed said sections shall not be subject to claim, settlement, or entry under the provision of this act or any of the land laws of the United States: *Provided however*, that the United States shall pay to said Indians, out of any moneys in the Treasury not otherwise appropriated, the sum of fifty cents per acre for all lands reserved under the provisions of this section.

SEC. 26. That there is hereby appropriated, out of any money in the Treasury not otherwise appropriated, the sum of eighteen thousand dollars, which sum shall be expended, under the direction of the Secretary of the Interior, for procuring the assent of the Sioux Indians to this act provided in section twenty-four.

Approved April 30, 1888.

Figure 19. This bullet-riddled sign (photographed in 1989 along the southern border of the Pine Ridge Reservation, a remnant of the former Great Sioux Reservation) features a hand-painted narrative about the legendary Oglala Lakota leader, Crazy Horse. After leading 13,000 starving followers into Fort Robinson during the bitter winter of 1877, Crazy Horse was killed by his captors. The Pine Ridge Reservation was one result of land allotment legislation enacted in 1888 (Photo: B. L. Wilson).

Figure 20. By 1890, towns bordering western reservations were loading cattle onto railroad cars bound for Chicago meat-packing plants. Indian children of four years and older—and sometimes younger—were loaded onto railcars for transport to off-reservation cultural conversion programs, i.e., education programs designed to force tribal children into conforming to the cultural norms of English-speaking farmers, farm wives, and factory workers. This photograph (circa 1992) was taken near the southern boundary of a western reservation (Photo: B. L. Wilson).

Chapter V
The Spoils of Soil:
The Leasing of Indian Lands Act of 1891

THE LEASING OF INDIAN LANDS Act evolved as westward bound settlers, miners, and railroad companies sought increased access to western reservation lands. Starvation epidemics, commonplace on many western reservations by the 1870s, complicated the leasing environment—as did the controversial dealings of several reservation agents.[1] Prior to this enactment, questions as to whether or not reservation lands could be leased to any entity, tribal or otherwise, could not, in any legal sense, be definitively answered. Clarification came by way of this amendment's dramatic expansion of the reach of the General Allotment Act of 1887.

This act mandated that tribal land leasing could proceed only after a Bureau of Indian Affairs agent determined relevant "disability" or "age" factors specific to individual tribal landowners; three years later, a subsequent amendment added "inability" to this leasing rationale. The act permitted leasing—only if by reason of "... age or other disability ..." the landowner was not able to prosper from a property in any other way.[2] This use of the word "disability"—as descriptor of a person's economic options—appears as a linguistic anomaly unparalleled in American Discourse.

"They say: 'You can have this ground as long as the grass grows and the water flows' ... Now they have moved the Indians and they settled the whole thing by putting them on land where the grass won't grow and the water won't flow, so now they have it all set."

WILL ROGERS

99

This act placed time limits on the duration of leases, the longest being the ten-year leasing term focused on mining operations. And although this legislation provided a legalistic framework for the distribution of reservation lands and associated natural resources to off-reservation parties, albeit on a time-limited basis, it did assert the legal rights of ownership to individual tribal landowners.

The Leasing of Indian Lands Act of 1891

AN ACT[3] ... To amend and further extend the benefits of the act approved February eighth, eighteen hundred and eighty-seven [the Dawes Act of 1887], entitled "An act to provide for the allotment of land in severalty to Indians on the various reservations, and to extend the protection of the laws of the United States over the Indians, and for other purposes. *Be it enacted by the Senate and House of Representatives of the United States of America in Congress Assembled,* That section one of the act entitled 'AN ACT To provide for the allotment of lands in severalty to Indians on the various reservations and to extend the protection of the laws of the United States and the Territories over the Indians and for other purposes,'" approved February eight, eighteen hundred and eight-seven, be and the same is hereby, amended so as to read as follows:

SEC. 1. That in all cases where any tribe or band of Indians has been, or shall hereafter be, located upon any reservation created for their use, either by treaty stipulation or by virtue of an Act of Congress or Executive order setting apart the same for their use, the President of the United States be and hereby is, authorized, whenever in his opinion any reservation, or any part thereof, of such Indians is advantageous for agricultural or grazing purposes, to cause said reservation, or any part thereof, to be surveyed, or resurveyed, if necessary, and to allot to each Indian located thereon one-eighth of a section of land: *Provided,* That in case there is not sufficient land in any of said reservations to allot lands to each individual in quantity as above provided the and in such reservation or reservations shall be allotted to each individual pro rata, as near as may be, according to legal subdivisions: *Provided further,* That where the treaty or act of Congress setting apart such reservation provides for the allotment of lands in severalty to certain classes in quantity in excess of that herein provided the President, in making allotments upon such reservation, shall allot the land to each individual Indian of said classes belonging thereon in quantity as specified in such treaty or act, and to other Indians belonging thereon in quantity as herein provided: *Provided further,* That where existing agreements or laws provide for allotments in accordance with the provisions of said act of February eighth, eighteen hundred and eighty-seven, or in quantities substantially as therein provided, allotments may be made in quantity as specified in this act, with the consent of the Indians, expressed in such manner as the President, in his discretion, may require: *And provided further,* That when the lands allotted, or any legal subdivision thereof, are only valuable for grazing purposes, such lands shall be allotted in double quantities.

SEC. 2. That where allotments have been made in whole or in part upon any reservation under the provisions of said act of February eighth, eighteen hundred and eighty-seven and the quantity of land in such reservation is sufficient to give each member of the tribe eighty acres, such allotments shall be revised and equalized under the provisions of this act: *Provided,* That no allotment heretofore provided by the Secretary of the Interior shall be reduced in quantity.

SEC. 3. That whenever it shall be made to appear to the Secretary of the Interior that, by reason of age or other disability, any allotted under the provisions of said act, or any other act or treaty cannot personally and with benefit to himself occupy or improve his allotment or any part thereof the same may be leased upon such terms, regulations and conditions as shall be prescribed by such Secretary, for a term not exceeding three years for farming or grazing, or ten years for mining purposes: *Provided,* That where lands are occupied by Indians who have bought and paid for the same and which lands are not needed for farming or agricultural purposes and are not desired for individual allotments, the same may be leased by authority of the Council speaking for such Indians, for a period not to exceed five years for grazing, or ten years for mining purposes in such quantities and upon such terms and conditions as the agent in charge of such reservation may recommend, subject to the approval of the Secretary of the Interior.

SEC. 4. That where any Indian entitled to allotment under existing laws shall make settlement upon any surveyed or unsurveyed lands of the United State not otherwise appropriated, he or she shall be entitled, upon application to the local lands office for the district in which the lands are located, to have the same allotted to him or her and to his or her children, in quantities and manner as provided in the foregoing section of this amending act for the Indians residing upon reservations; and when such settlement is made upon unsurveyed lands the grant to such Indians shall be adjusted upon the survey of the lands so as to confirm thereto; and patents shall be issued to them for such lands in the manner and with the restrictions provided in the act to which this is an amendment and the fees to which the officers of such local land office would have been entitled had such lands been entered under the general laws for the disposition of the public lands shall be paid to them from any moneys in the Treasury of the United States not otherwise appropriated, upon a statement of an account in their behalf for such fees by the commissioner of the General Land Office and a certification of such account to the Secretary of the Treasury by the Secretary of the Interior.

SEC. 5. That for the purpose of determining the descent of land to the heirs of any deceased Indian under the provisions of the fifth section of said act, whenever any male and female Indian shall have cohabitated together as husband and wife according to the custom and manner of Indian life the issue of such co-habitation shall be, for the purpose aforesaid, taken and deemed to be the legitimate issue of the Indians so living together, and every Indian child, otherwise illegitimate, shall for such purpose be taken and deemed to be the legitimate issue of the father of such child: *Provided,* That the provisions of this act shall not be held or construed as to apply to the lands commonly called and known as the "Cherokee Outlet": *And provided further,* That no allotment of lands shall be made or annuities of money paid to any of the Sac and Fox of the Missouri Indians who were not enrolled as members of said tribe on January first, eighteen hundred and ninety; but this shall not be held to impair or otherwise affect the rights or equities of any person whose claim to membership in said tribe is now pending and being investigated.

Approved February 28, 1891.

Figure 21. This map compares the growing landmass of the USA—forty-four states as of February 28, 1891, the date of the passage of the Leasing of Indian Lands Act— with the remaining expanses of tribal lands (light gray).

Chapter VI
Take the Children Away:
The Indian Education Act of 1891

THE INDIAN EDUCATION Act of 1891 gave the U.S. Commissioner of Indian Affairs authority to control the whereabouts, activities, and treatment of all tribal children. This act provided off-reservation housing for reservation children by mandating the collection and transportation of tribal children to Indian boarding schools, and then placing them—with the consent of their parents—under the care and control of "... suitable white ..." families.

This 1891 act resulted in a sizeable expansion of a national system of boarding schools for children of reservation populations. Initially, these institutions enjoyed substantial political support, in part because of the jobs the legislation created during the nation's first depression (e.g., gainful employment for retired generals). This act did not overturn a standing policy, enacted in 1886, which required parental consent prior to the enrollment of reservation children in schools located out-of-state or in other territories.[1] However, starvation epidemics being common within most reservation communities at the time of its enactment, if consent was given, it often came within the context of unfathomable family life and death circumstances.

"Grown men may learn from very little children for the hearts of little children are pure. Therefore, the Great Spirit may show to them many things which older people miss ..."

BLACK ELK

The Indian Education Act of 1891

AN ACT[2] ... Making appropriations for the current and contingent expense of the Indian Department, and for fulfilling treaty stipulations with various Indian tribes, for the year ending June thirtieth, eighteen hundred and ninety-two, and for other purposes. *Be it enacted by the Senate and House of Representatives of the United States of America in Congress assembled,* That the following sums be, and they are hereby, appropriated, out of any money in the Treasury not otherwise appropriated, for the purpose of paying the current and contingent expenses of the Indian Department for the year ending June thirtieth, eighteen hundred and ninety-two, and fulfilling treaty stipulations with the various Indian tribes, namely: [...] For support of Indian day and industrial schools, and for other educational purposes not hereinafter provided for, including pay of draughtsman to be employed in the office of the Commissioner of Indian Affairs, one million dollars; for the construction on Indian reservations of school buildings and repair of school buildings, one hundred and twenty-five thousand dollars: *Provided,* That twenty-five thousand dollars of this amount may be used in the erection of buildings for an industrial school for the Mission Indians near the village of Perris, in California, upon a tract of land to be donated for that purpose of not less than eighty acres; and for purchase of horses, cattle, sheep, and swine for schools, fifteen thousand dollars, five thousand dollars of which shall be immediately available; in all, one million one hundred and forty thousand dollars: *Provided,* That the entire cost of any boarding school building, exclusive of outbuildings, to be built from the moneys appropriated hereby, shall not exceed twelve thousand dollars, and the entire cost of any day-school building to be so built shall not exceed six hundred dollars. For support and education of Indian pupils at Albuquerque, New Mexico, at one hundred and seventy-five dollars per annum for each pupil, and for the erection and repairs of buildings, and pay superintendent, at one thousand eight hundred dollars per annum, sixty-six thousand dollars. For support of Indian industrial school at Carlisle, Pennsylvania, at not exceeding one hundred and sixty-seven dollars for each pupil, for transportation of pupils to and from Carlisle school, and for the erection and repair of buildings, one hundred and ten thousand dollars, and five thousand dollars of this amount to be used in the erection of a new dormitory for girls. For annual allowance to Captain R. H. Pratt in charge of said school, one thousand dollars; in all, one hundred and eleven thousand dollars. For support of Indian pupils, at one hundred and sixty seven dollars per annum each; purchase of material, erection of buildings, shops, barns, and necessary outbuildings, and of repairs of same at Indian school at Chilloeco, Indian Territory (formerly near Arkansas City, Kansas), and for pay of superintendent of said school, at two thousand dollars per annum, one hundred thousand dollars. For support of Indian pupils, at one hundred and seventy-five dollars per annum each; necessary outbuildings, repairs, and fencing at the Indian school at Carson City, Nevada, and for pay of superintendent of said school, at one thousand five hundred dollars per annum, twenty-five thousand dollars and improving buildings, necessary outbuildings, repairs, and fencing at the Indian school at Pierre, South Dakota, and for pay of superintendent of said school, at one thousand five hundred dollars per annum, thirty-five thousand dollars. For the purpose of erecting, constructing, and completing suitable school buildings and for the support of an Indian industrial school near the village of Flandreau, South Dakota, twenty-five thousand dollars. *Provided* any unexpended balance of former appropriations are hereby re-appropriated not to exceed twenty-five thousand dollars. For support of Indian pupils, at one hundred and seventy-five dollars per annum each; necessary buildings, repairs, and fencing, and irrigation at the Indian school at Santa Fe, New Mexico, and for pay of superintendent of said school, at one thousand five hundred dollars per annum, forty thousand dollars. For support of Indian pupils at one hundred and sixty-seven dollars per annum each; pay of superintendent, at two thousand dollars per annum repairs and erection of buildings at Indian school, Genoa, Nebraska, minding heating apparatus, sixty thousand dollars. For the erection and completion of buildings and for the support of an Indian industrial school at the Shoshone Indian Reservation, Wyoming, twenty-five thousand dollars. For support of Indian pupils, at one hundred and seventy-five dollars per annum each; for necessary repairs, furnishings, tools, and farm implements; and for pay of superintendent at the Indian school, Grand Junction, Colorado, at one thousand five hundred dollars per annum, twenty-five thousand dollars. For support of Indian pupils at one hundred and sixty-seven dollars per annum each and repairs of buildings at the Indian school, Fort Totten, North Dakota, and for pay of superintendent of said school, at one thousand eight hundred dollars per annum, forty thousand dollars. For support and education of one hundred and twenty Indian pupils at the school at Hampton, Virginia, twenty thousand and forty dollars. For support of Indian pupils, at one hundred and sixty-seven dollars per annum each; necessary buildings, repairs at the Indian school at Lawrence, Kansas, and for pay of superintendent of said school, at two thousand dollars per annum one hundred thousand dollars. For support and education of two hundred Indian pupils at Lincoln Institution, Philadelphia at one hundred and sixty-seven dollars per annum each, thirty-three thousand four hundred dollars. For support of pupils at one hundred and seventy-five dollars per annum. Each, erection of buildings, purchase of lands or improvements, not to exceed six thousand dollars and pay of superintendent at Phoenix, Arizona., at one thousand eight hundred dollars per annum, fifty thousand dollars. For support of Indian pupils at one hundred and seventy-five dollars per annum each; necessary out-buildings, repairs, and fencing at the Indian school at Salem, Oregon (formerly Forest Grove school), and for pay of the superintendent of said school, at two thousand dollars per annum, fifty-four thousand five hundred dollars. For support of three hundred Indian pupils at the Saint Ignatius Mission school, on the Jocko Reservations, in Montana, at one hundred and fifty dollars per annum each, forty-five thousand dollars. For support of sixty Indian pupils at White's Manual Labor Institute, of Wabash, Indiana, ten thousand and twenty dollars. For support of eighty pupils at the Cherokee Training School at Cherokee, North Carolina, at one hundred and sixty-seven dollars per annum each, thirteen thousand three hundred and sixty dollars. For education and support of one hundred Chippewa boys and girls at Saint John's University, and at Saint Benedict's Academy in Stearns County, State of Minnesota, at one hundred and fifty dollars each per annum, and for the education and support of one hundred Indian pupils at Saint Paul's Industrial School at Clontarf, in the State of Minnesota, thirty thousand dollars. For support of Indian pupils, at one hundred and sixty-seven dollars per annum each; necessary buildings, repairs, fencing, and irrigation at the Indian school at Fort Mojave, Arizona, and for pay of superintendent of said school, at one thousand five hundred dollars per annum, twenty thousand dollars, For care, support, and education of Indian pupils at industrial, agricultural, mechanical, and other schools, other than those herein provided for, in any of the States or Territories of the United States, at a rate not to exceed one hundred and sixty-seven dollars for each pupil, seventy-five thousand dollars. For support and education of sixty Indian pupils at Saint Joseph's Normal School at Rensselaer, Indiana, eight thousand three hundred and thirty dollars. For support and education of one hundred Indian pupils at Saint Boniface's Industrial School at Banning, California, twelve thousand five hundred dollars.

"... also for the transportation of Indian pupils from all the Indian schools and placing of them ... under the care and control of such suitable white families as may in all respects be qualified to give such pupils [sic] moral, industrial, and educational training ... in exchange for their labor ..."

For the education and support of one hundred Indian children at the Holy Family Indian School, at Blackfoot Agency, Montana, twelve thousand five hundred dollars. For collecting and transportation of pupils to and from Indian schools, and also for the transportation of Indian pupils from all the Indian schools and placing of them, with the consent of their parents, under the care and control of such suitable white families as may in all respects be qualified to give such pupils moral; industrial, and educational training, under arrangements in which their proper care, supports and education shall be in exchange for their labor; forty thousand dollars. *Provided,* That at least five hundred and thirty-five thousand dollars of the money appropriated for the support of schools by this act shall be used exclusively for the support and education of Indian industrial and day schools in operation under contracts with the Indian Bureau. That the expenditure of money appropriated for any of the purposes of education of Indian children, those children of Indians who have taken lands in severalty under any existing law, shall not, by reason thereof, be excluded from the benefits of such appropriation. And the Commissioner of Indian Affairs, subject to the direction of the Secretary of the Interior, is hereby authorized and directed to make and enforce by proper means such rules and regulations as will secure the attendance of Indian children of suitable age and health schools established and maintained for their benefit. That the expenditure of the money appropriated for school purposes in this act shall be at all time under the supervision and direction of the Secretary of the Interior, and in all respects in conformity with such conditions, rules, and regulations as to the conduct and methods of instruction and expenditure of money as may from time to time be prescribed by him ...

INTEREST ON TRUST FUND STOCKS ...

SEC. 2. That ... for payment of interest on certain abstracted and non-paying State stocks belonging to the various Indian tribes. And held in trust by the Secretary of the Interior, for the year ending June thirtieth, eighteen hundred and ninety one, namely: For trust-fund interest due Cherokee national fund, twenty five thousand six hundred and forty dollars; For trust fund interest due Cherokee school fund one thousand six hundred and thirty dollars; For trust fund interest due Chickasaw national fund, nineteen thousand eight hundred and twenty dollars; For trust fund interest due Choctaw general fund, twenty seven thousand dollars; For trust fund interest due Iowas, three thousand two hundred and eighty dollars; For trust fund interest due Kaskaskias, Peorias, Weas, and Plankeshaws, two thousand four hundred and one dollars; For trust-fund interest due Kaskaskia, Wea, Peoria, and Piankesham school-fund, one thousand four hundred and forty-nine dollars; For trust-fund interest due Delaware general fund, four thousand one hundred and thirty dollars. For trust fund interest due Menominees, nine hundred and fifty dollars; in all eighty-six thousand three hundred dollars ...

SEC. 3. That no purchase of supplies for which appropriations are herein made, exceeding in the aggregate five hundred dollars in value.

Approved ... [sic] ... 1891.

Figure 22. This exterior photograph, taken at Pennsylvania's Carlisle Indian Industrial School during the 1920s, shows the boarding school's entire student body—and the facility's manicured lawns and well-maintained buildings. This boarding school served as the national model for communities nationwide, i.e., those developing their first American Indian boarding schools. (Photo courtesy of the Cumberland County Historical Society).

ART STUDIO.

Figure 23. This interior photograph shows well-dressed young men and women of the Carlisle Indian School in Pennsylvania engaged in lofty activities more indicative of elite collegiate environments than institutions of cultural conversion and confinement. Greek sculptures, Baroque paintings—the wealth of the world's classical arts appears to surround them. But idyllic photographic imagery aside, this type of coercive, military-styled institution had more in common with youth lockdown facilities—yet lacked the child safety and child health aspects of today's juvenile justice norms. (Photo courtesy of the Carlisle Indian School Digital Resource Center).

Figure 24. These two photographs show of a group of children sent from Alaska to Pennsylvania to attend the Carlisle Indian Boarding School. The top photo shows them upon arrival; the second shows them in school attire. (Photo courtesy of the Carlisle Indian School Digital Resource Center).

Chapter VII

Fair Play in the Balance:
The Burke Act of 1906

THE BURKE ACT appears as a probable congressional attempt to ameliorate complexities inherent within the implementation of the General Allotment Act of 1887.[1] In response to the legally ambiguous real estate atmosphere surrounding reservation locales of the era, this act—one of several amendments to the General Allotment Act—shifted oversight of all sales of tribal lands away from states and into the purview of federal agents. Furthermore, it limited the term of federal control of tribal land allotments to twenty-five years, and required completion of the twenty-five year "trust" period prior to any consideration of an individual tribal member's application for U.S. citizenship. In this convoluted way, this amendment blocked sales of individual tribal land parcels for the first twenty-five years following allotment. This act also authorized the President of the United States to extend "trust" periods in limited cases, and to remove restrictions on allotments in other instances—given the approval of the U.S. Secretary of the Interior—once the legal "competence" of the requester had been established.[2]

"We the people are the rightful masters of both Congress and the Courts ... not to overthrow the Constitution ... but to overthrow the men who pervert the Constitution."

ABRAHAM LINCOLN[1]

115

The Burke Act of 1906

AN ACT[3] ... To amend section six of an Act approved February eighth, eighteen hundred and eight-seven, entitled "AN ACT To provide for the allotment of lands in severalty to Indians on the various reservations and to extend the protection of the laws of the United States and the Territories over the Indians and for other purposes. *Be it enacted by the Senate and House of Representatives of the United States of America in Congress assembled ...*" be amended to read as follows:

SEC. 6. [*sic*] That at the expiration of the trust period and when the lands have been conveyed to the Indians by patent in fee, as provided in section five of this Act, then each and every allottee shall have the benefit of and be subject to the laws, both civil and criminal, of the State or Territory in which they may reside; and no Territory shall pass or enforce any law denying any such Indian within its jurisdiction the equal protection of the law. And every Indian born within the territorial limits of the United States to whom allotments shall have been made and who has received a patent in fee simple under the provisions of this Act, or under any law or treaty and every Indian born within the territorial limits of the United States who has voluntarily taken up within said limits his residence, separate and apart from any tribe of Indians therein and has adopted the habits of civilized life, is hereby declared to be a citizen of the United States and is entitled to all the rights, privileges and immunities of such citizens, whether said Indian has been or not, by birth or otherwise, a member of any tribe of Indians within the territorial limits of the United States without in any manner impairing or otherwise affecting the right of any such Indian to tribal or other property: *Provided,* That the Secretary of the Interior may, in his discretion and he is hereby authorized, whenever he shall be satisfied that any Indian allottee is competent and capable of managing his or her affairs at any time to cause to be issue to such allottee a patent in fee simple and thereafter all restrictions as to sale, encumbrance, or taxation of said land shall be removed and said land shall not be liable to the satisfaction of any debt contracted prior to the issuing of such patent: *Provided further,* That until the issuance of fee simple patents all allottees to who trust patents shall hereafter be issued shall be subject to the exclusive jurisdiction of the United States: And *provided further*, That the provisions of this act shall not extend to any Indians in the Indian Territory. That hereafter when an allotment of land is made to any Indian and any such Indian dies before the expiration of the trust period, said allotment shall be cancelled and the land shall revert to the United States and the Secretary of the Interior shall ascertain the legal heirs of such Indian and shall cause to be issue to said heirs and in their names, a patent in fee simple for said land, or he may cause the land to be sold as provided by law and issue a patent therefore to the purchaser or purchasers and pay the net proceeds to their heirs, or their legal representatives, of such deceased Indian. The action of the Secretary of the Interior in determining the legal heirs of any decreased Indian, as provided herein, shall in all respects be conclusive and final.

Approved May 8, 1906.

Chapter VIII

Thirty Years in Coming: The Sioux Pony Act of 1906

OFTEN REFERENCED AS the "Sioux Pony Act," this public law, enacted on June 21, 1906, served as a mechanism for the symbolic return of tribal property—i.e., horses confiscated in 1876 by members of the U.S. Seventh Cavalry.

The Sioux Pony Act of 1906

AN ACT[1] ... Making appropriations for the current and contingent expenses of the Indian Department, for fulfilling treaty stipulations with various Indian tribes, and for other purposes, for the fiscal year ending June thirtieth, nineteen hundred and seven. *Be it enacted by the Senate and House of Representatives of the United States of America in Congress assembled,* That the following sums be, and they are hereby, appropriated, out of any money in the Treasury not otherwise appropriated, for the purpose of paying the current and contingent expenses of the Indian Department, for fulfilling treaty stipulations with various Indian tribes, and in full compensation for all offices the salaries for which are specially provided for herein for the service of the fiscal year ending June thirtieth, nineteen hundred and seven ... namely

"Remember, write to your Congressman. Even if he can't read, write to him."

WILL ROGERS

119

... For payment to fifteen Sioux Indians of Pine Ridge Agency, South Dakota, for property taken from them in the year eighteen hundred and seventy-six by the United States military ...

"... For payment to fifteen Sioux Indians ... for property taken from them in the year eighteen hundred and seventy-six by the United States military authorities for reasons of military expediency ..."

... authorities for reasons of military expediency, while they were in amity with the Government, the names of the Indians and mounts to be paid to each having heretofore been found by the Department of the Interior and reported in estimates for appropriations required for the service of the fiscal year ending June thirtieth, nineteen hundred and five, and prior years, by the Indian Service, the sum of six thousand three hundred and twenty dollars. [...]

Approved June 21, 1906.

Chapter IX

Witness to Economic Barriers: Buy Indian Act of 1910

THE BUY INDIAN ACT required agents of the federal government to consider purchasing necessary goods and services from American Indian sources—just as they might from any other source. But whether or not American Indian goods and services would ever actually be purchased by any government agency remained at the discretion of the sitting U.S. Secretary of the Interior.[1] Therefore, although the title suggests a preference for American Indian sources, no such preference was mandated.

"The trouble with you politicians is you see, but you don't see far. You wear your reading glasses when you are looking into the future. You got your putter in your hand when you ought to have your driver."

WILL ROGERS

Buy Indian Act of 1910

AN ACT[2] ... To provide for determining the heirs of deceased Indians, for the disposition and sale of the allotments of deceased Indians, for the leasing of allotments, and for other purposes. *Be it enacted by the Senate and House of Representatives of the United States of America in Congress assembled,* That ...

SEC. 23. That hereafter the purchase of Indian supplies shall be made in conformity with the requirements of section thirty-seven hundred and nine of the Revised Statutes of the United States: *Provided,* That so far as may be practicable Indian labor shall be employed, and purchases of the products of Indian industry may be made in open market in the discretion of the Secretary of the Interior. All Acts and parts of Acts in conflict with the provisions of this section are hereby repealed.

Approved June 25, 1910.

Legislative Sample, Part II
1921-1961

"... The powers of this Bureau ... over the property, the persons, the daily lives and affaires of the Indians have in the past been almost unlimited. It has been an extraordinary example of political absolutism in the midst of a free democracy—absolutism built upon the most rigid bureaucratic lines, irresponsible to the Indians and to the public ... shackled by obsolete laws ... resistant to change, reform or progress ... which over a century, has handled the Indians without understanding or sympathy, which has used methods of repression and suppression unparalleled in the modern world outside of Czarist Russia and the Belgian Congo ..."

REPRESENTATIVE EDGAR HOWARD,
AS QUOTED IN THE CONGRESSIONAL RECORD OF JUNE 15, 1934

Chapter X

Public Acts of Mixed Intent

WHEREAS THE PREDOMINATING theme of the preceding legislative era was the intentional suppression of American Indian cultures, legislation enacted during the 1920s, 1930s, 1940s, 1950s, and early 1960s demonstrated a more complex congressional intent. This era marked a significant shift in federal policies, as "... Cultural Pluralism, with its emphasis upon the preservation and intensification of Indian heritage, replaced assimilation as the goal of federal policy ..."[2] Cultural suppression continued, as did the transfer of tribal lands and natural resources away from tribes, but Congress also introduced a modicum of human rights into its cacophony of conflicting legislative priorities.

"I have said that the greatest tragedy is not the loss of one's freedom, but the loss of the knowledge of what true freedom really is." [1]

WARREN PETOSKEY

Legislation enacted between 1921 and 1961 reflected a growing congressional acceptance—and apparent appreciation—of the American Indian and Alaskan Native cultures. Public laws Congress enacted during these years amplified a steady waning of earlier congressional supports of the forced assimilation of American Indians into mainstream American Culture. Jousting, however, between federal and state legislatures, those fighting for jurisdictional powers over tribal nations and reservation resources, continued throughout this 1921-1961 timeline.

Philleo Nash (anthropologist, federal official) credited an American attorney, Felix Cohen, with altering the direction of U.S. policies during the 1940s, by creating an exhaustive reference tool, one that proved useful to tribal leaders, legislators, anthropologists, and others. Nash asserted that a "... milestone in Indian Affairs was reached ... [in 1942] ... with the compilation of The Handbook of Federal Indian Law by Felix S. Cohen."[3]

125

Legislative Outcomes, 1921-1961

Decade by decade, the mandated outcomes of 1921-1961 legislation reflected the complexity of the congressional intent of the era. Actions offering adaptive approaches to reservation challenges included: emergency funding to end starvation epidemics, easing of severe shortages of medical professionals available to reservation populations, granting of U.S. citizenship to all tribal members, and modest expansions of economic opportunities available to tribal members. Conversely, mandates counter to the well-being of reservation populations fostered multiple problematic results: the ongoing removal of tribal children from their families and communities, the continuous geographic distancing of tribal households, the continuation of the reduction of reservation lands, and the ongoing incarceration of tribal members for non-criminal behaviors. Adding to this policy-based social complexity, congressional actions of this 1921-1961 timeline also further limited tribal authority and ended the federal recognition of dozens of American Indian nations.[4] Simultaneously, populations of the towns and farm communities bordering reservations—and boarding school communities—all benefited from employment opportunities provided by way of this era's program-based legislation (e.g., boarding schools). Other outside beneficiaries included those corporations and individuals who profited from mandated increases in opportunities for outsiders to own or otherwise access tribal lands and land-based tribal resources (e.g., uranium, water ...).

WITHDRAWALS OF THE FEDERAL RECOGNITION OF TRIBES

The Bureau of Indian Affairs defines the interplay of American Indian nations and the United States as follows: "The relationship ... is one between sovereigns, i.e., between a government and a government. This government-to-government principle, which is grounded in the United States Constitution, has helped to shape the long history of relations between the federal government and these tribal nations." However, as one major result of the series of "termination" policies Congress legislated between 1953 and the early 1960s, more than 100 tribes lost all federal recognition of their status as tribal nations, i.e., domestic sovereign nations.

U.S. CITIZENSHIP ACKNOWLEDGED

By 1920, the long history of American Indian U.S. military service was part of the historical record. Perhaps in recognition of this history of sacrifice, Congress legislated that U.S. citizenship become a reality for all American Indians at birth. Furthermore, in 1928, when a riveting subcommittee report slammed members of Congress into a heightened awareness of the disastrous outcomes of previous "boarding school" mandates, legal control over the education of tribal children was returned—during the 1930s—to tribal parents and American Indian nations.

ECONOMIC BOOSTS TO STATES AND OFF-RESERVATION COMMUNITIES

Economic benefits to several states and towns bordering reservations came primarily through: (1) opportunities to acquire tribal lands and associated natural resources, and (2) opportunities to bid on lucrative federal contracts for the delivery of various mandated services to tribal communities. States and towns bordering reservations also benefited from federally managed funds that Congress allocated to states in exchange for state administration of reservation-based social service programs. Border towns gained social service positions along with opportunities to compete for federal contracts that were to be awarded for the design and development of vocational training programs for tribal job seekers—i.e., programs typically delivered within border towns and/or distant, large city locations (e.g., Minneapolis). Furthermore, since policies of this era terminated the federal recognition of more than 100 tribes, outsiders gained opportunities to access tribal lands and associated natural resources. The Menominee lands, rich in timber reserves, were the first reservation lands affected by the termination policies of the 1950s.

HIGH CHILD MORBIDITY RATES

Throughout the 1921-1961 time line, the enrollment of tribal children in off-reservation boarding schools was commonplace. Child death rates in most boarding schools were extreme by any standard. During its early years, morbidity rates reported for the Carlisle Indian Industrial School in Pennsylvania ranged from ten to sixty-five percent; of one group of fifteen children sent to Carlisle from the Shoshone Agency, eleven died. Reported child morbidity rates at Nebraska institutions were similar. Most deaths resulted from crowding children into small rooms for sleeping, in rows of beds crowded one against another—and often with four children in each bed. William J. McConnell, an Interior Department Indian Inspector for fourteen years, used the word "murder" when referring to the housing of healthy tribal children with sick children. This once common practice was further exacerbated whenever terminally ill children were sent home to die, thus carrying boarding-school disease outbreaks into reservation communities.

Federal Inquiry

The most significant federal inquiry report of the 1921-1961 timeline, the Meriam Subcommittee Report, surfaced in response to mounting rumors of systemic abuses of children and adults in tribal communities. Congress formed this subcommittee to investigate management systems and living conditions on reservations and in boarding school communities. This subcommittee conducted field interviews with, among others, members of the military, tribal leaders, humanitarians, survivors of massacres, and the staff of various boarding schools. Their purpose was to stand and bear witness, so as to either substantiate, or dismiss, rumors of substandard living conditions and the pervasive, ongoing abuse of tribal populations. The 1928 release of their pivotal findings provided Congress with proof of disturbing, systemic, debilitating conditions as commonplace within reservations and boarding schools.

The Meriam Report (i.e., the Meriam Subcommittee Report) also cast a first light upon the relentless cycle of vicious assaults upon tribal members—perpetrated by murderers and rapists operating with impunity along the outer edges of reservation borders. The veracity of the report shattered social myths that had influenced congressional actions toward tribes for decades. It provided irrefutable evidence that many of the routine field updates Congress had relied upon whenever drafting tribe-related legislative proposals—reports submitted by key federal agents (military and civilian)—had been unreliable.

Prior to the revelations of the game-changing Meriam Report, few members of Congress could have known the fate of tribal children who died as a result of their boarding school sojourns. Few could have learned about the boarding schools that routinely sent sick children home, thus bringing devastating outbreaks of boarding school diseases (e.g., tuberculosis, influenza) to reservations. Few could have imagined the cultural complexity and isolation faced by surviving children who, upon returning home—often as young adults—were no longer able to speak the language of their parents.[5]

Congressional reactions to the Meriam Report findings suggest that most members of Congress never intended to project such hardships onto tribal children, their families, or tribal communities in general. The report alerted Congress to earlier legislative errors by demonstrating how ill-informed public lawmaking had contributed to the decades of untold suffering for tribally affiliated Americans. This was the first congressional report which proved beyond a doubt that in many regions, these American citizens were living in conditions akin to the open-air incarceration of Japanese-Americans during World War II—but without the adequate access to food, water, and safety measures present within internment camps.

The Meriam Report revealed the simple fact that many congressional actions resulted in public laws that were applied—at local, state, and federal levels—in ways Congress never intended. Furthermore, the findings of the Meriam Report inspired Congress to lift many restrictions upon tribal freedoms, most of which had been enacted during the early 1920s.[6]

Figure 25. Will Rogers, popular radio commentator, newspaper columnist, and actor (seen here standing to the right of Charles Lindbergh), was well known for his cutting wit, honesty, and insightful all-American candor. Speaking from his Cherokee roots, he came onto the public scene during the 1920s, leveling a message of commonsense governance through his good-natured jabs at both parties and a range of Senate and House proceedings. One of his children later served in the House of Representatives. The wisdom of his commentary is timeless, as is apparent in this excerpt from Rogers' radio broadcast of March 30, 1931: *"When this senator read my offering, the other senator said, after all the yielding was all over, the other senator said, 'I object. I object to the remarks of a professional joke maker being put into the Congressional Record.' You know, meaning me. See? Taking a dig at me, see? They didn't want any outside fellow contributing. Well, he had me wrong. Compared to them, I'm an amateur ... and the thing about my jokes is they don't hurt anybody."* [7] (Photo courtesy of the Will Rogers Museum of Claremore, Oklahoma).

Figure 26. This circa 1925 photo shows members of the staff of the Carlisle boarding school in Pennsylvania. Boarding school communities and towns bordering reservations gained jobs and profited from the sale of goods and services needed to fulfill mandated requirements of tribally-focused federal projects of the 1921-1961 era. (Photo courtesy of the Carlisle Indian School Digital Resource Center).

Chapter XI

Keeping the Wheels Turning: Administration Act of 1921

THE CONTINUITY and general operations of the Bureau of Indian Affairs gained funding through passage of this untitled act in late 1921. It was enacted as observers attested to "... [an] ... army of entrepreneurs ... making fortunes funneling bad food, shoddy blankets, and poisonous whiskey to the thousands of Indians trapped on reservations ..."[1]

Two decades after this enactment, the administrative scope of the bureau's responsibilities expanded to include Japanese-American internment camps. Dillon S. Myer (Indian Affairs Commissioner during Truman's presidency, 1945-1953) ran the World War II Japanese-American internment camps (e.g., the Tule Lake Relocation Center of Newell, California) where thousands of U.S. citizens of all ages were confined throughout the war years.

The Administration Act of 1921

AN ACT[2] --- Authorizing appropriations and ... expenditures for the administration of Indian affairs, and for other purposes. *Be it enacted by the Senate and House of Representatives of the United States of America in Congress assembled,* That the Bureau of Indian Affairs, under the supervision of the Secretary of the Interior, shall direct, supervise, and expend such moneys as Congress may from time to time appropriate, for the benefit, care, and assistance of the Indians throughout the United States for the following purposes: General support and civilization, including education. For relief of distress and conservation of health. For industrial assistance and advancement and general administration of Indian property. For extension, improvement, operation, and maintenance of existing Indian irrigation systems and for development of water supplies. For the enlargement, extension, improvement, and repair of the buildings and grounds of existing plants and projects For the employment of inspectors, supervisors, superintendents, clerks, field matrons, farmers, physicians, Indian police, Indian judges, and for other employees. For the suppression of traffic in intoxicating liquor and deleterious drugs. For the purchase of horse-drawn and motor-propelled passenger-carrying vehicles for official use. And for general and incidental expenses in connection with the administration of Indian affairs.

Approved November 2, 1921

Figure 27. This 1921 photo shows American Indian children digging onions for a Pennsylvania farmer. For decades, it was common practice for children taken from western reservation communities to work for farmers of boarding school locales during the summer months. This photo shows students assigned to the boarding school in Carlisle, PA. (Photo courtesy of the Carlisle Indian School Digital Resource Center).

Chapter XII

Closing the Loopholes:
Indian Citizenship Act of 1924

BY THE EARLY 1920s, the vast majority of tribal members had become U.S. citizens through various legal devices, including military service, land allotments, and multiple legislative mandates specific to individual tribes—yet no generalized rule for American Indian citizenship existed in the U.S. until 1924.[1] Congress closed all remaining loopholes of U.S. citizenship with passage of the Indian Citizenship Act on June 2, 1924. This public law brought American Indians, theoretically, under the protection of the rights of U.S. citizenship— as guaranteed by the Fourteenth Amendment. Henceforth, tribal members were to be federally recognized as citizens the United States and of their respective states of residence, while still retaining their rights of tribal citizenship. Consequently, from June of 1924 forward, tribally-enrolled citizens living on reservations became subject to three sets of legal rights and responsibilities: federal, state, and tribal.[2]

With the June 1924 passage of the Indian Citizenship Act, the U.S. citizenship of American Indians became a condition of birth. The clarity of this law notwithstanding, several states refused to recognize the U.S. citizenship of American Indians for decades following its enactment.

Waves of earlier voting rights legislation preceded this 1924 enactment, as America's universal suffrage evolved over the course of centuries. Starting in the seventeenth century, landowners made up the first

"Fourscore and seven years ago, our fathers brought forth upon this continent, a new nation, conceived in Liberty and dedicated to the proposition that all men are created equal."

ABRAHAM LINCOLN

wave of eligible American voters. By the late eighteenth century, all white men, regardless of social status, held voting rights. Congress further extended voting rights through passage of the Fifteen Amendment to the U.S. Constitution in 1869 and its ratification in 1870, thus granting African American men the right to vote. Passage of the Nineteen Amendment in 1920 granted voting rights to American women. Four years later, the Indian Citizenship Act of 1924 clarified the legal status and voting rights of tribally affiliated Americans.

"... Returning Indian war veterans . . . [of WWII] ... found themselves barred from registering to vote ... [and] ... began to pressure the Bureau of Indian Affairs to help them secure the vote in Arizona and New Mexico, two of the last states to bar Indians." [3]

The Indian Citizenship Act of 1924

AN ACT[4] ... To authorize the Secretary of the Interior to issue certificates of citizenship to Indians. *Be it enacted by the Senate and House of Representatives of the United States of America in Congress assembled,* That all non-citizen Indians born within the territorial limits of the United States be and they are hereby, declared to be citizens of the United States: *Provided,* That the granting of such citizenship shall not in any manner impair or otherwise affect the right of any Indian to tribal or other property.

Approved June 2, 1924.

Figure 28. "We the People" references all citizens of the United States, but few American Indians were recognized as U.S. citizens prior to Congress's passage, in 1924, of a single paragraph of citizenship legislation (Photo: B. L. Wilson).

Figure 29. Prior to the 1924 enactment of the American Indian Citizenship legislation, approximately 10,000 American Indians enlisted into the military and served during World War I. Prior to his WWI military service, this soldier, Fred Blythe, graduated from the Carlisle Indian School in Carlisle, Pennsylvania. (Photo, circa 1918, courtesy of the Carlisle Indian School Digital Resource Center).

Figure 30. Two U.S. Olympic champions—Louis Tewanima, 'first place Olympic medal winner, and his teammate, Mitchell Arquette who placed fifth—were photographed after finishing their marathon runs in New York City on May 6, 1911. These U.S. Olympians were also both members of the Carlisle Indian School's cross-country team. (Photo courtesy of the Carlisle Indian School Digital Resource Center).

Chapter XIII

Good News at Last:
The Johnson-O'Malley Act of 1934

THE JOHNSON-O'MALLEY Act of 1934 increased tribal access to medical services, educational opportunities, and social service programming. This legislation authorized the Secretary of the Department of the Interior to contract with individual states or territories to provide social and educational services within reservation communities. In 2000, the U.S. Commission on Civil Rights referenced this act's historic role in creating linkages between American Indian nations and state and federal social service programs.

> Recognizing the poor administration of Indian affairs by the Indian Service of the Department of the Interior, Collier ... [sociologist, Commissioner of Indian Affairs during Roosevelt presidency] ... promoted a new policy ... making the new Indian citizens beneficiaries of State and Federal social services programs. A principal piece of legislation to accomplish this ... was the Johnson-O'Malley Act.[1]

The Johnson-O'Malley Act of 1934

> AN ACT[2] ... Authorizing the Secretary of the Interior to arrange with States or Territories for the education, medical attention, relief of distress, and social welfare of Indians, and for other purposes. *Be it enacted by the Senate and House of Representatives of the United States of America in Congress assembled,* That the Secretary of the Interior is hereby authorized, in his discretion, to enter into a contract or contracts with any State or Territory having legal authority so to do, for the education, medical attention, agri-

cultural assistance and social welfare, including relief of distress, of Indians in such State or Territory, through the qualified agencies of such State or Territory and to expand under such contract or contracts money appropriated by Congress for the education, medical attention, agricultural assistance and social welfare, including relief of distress, of Indians in such State.

SEC. 2. That the Secretary of the Interior, in making any contract herein authorized with any State or Territory, may permit such State or Territory to utilize for the purpose of this Act, existing school buildings, hospitals and other facilities and all equipment therein or appertaining thereto, including livestock and other personal property owned by the Government, under such terms and conditions as may be agreed upon for their use and maintenance.

SEC. 3. That the Secretary of the Interior is hereby authorized to perform any and all acts and to make such rules and regulations, including minimum standards of service, as may be necessary and proper for the purpose of carrying the provisions of this Act into effect: *Provided,* That such minimum standards of services are not less than the highest maintained by the States or Territories with which said contract or contracts, as herein provided, are executed.

SEC. 4. That the Secretary of the Interior shall report annually to the Congress any contract or contracts made under the provisions of this Act and the moneys expended thereunder

SEC. 5. That the provisions of this Act shall not apply to the State of Oklahoma.

Approved April 16, 1934.

Chapter XIV

Mixed Intentions: The Indian Reorganization Act of 1934

THE INDIAN REORGANIZATION Act (IRA) of 1934 capitalized on several of the recommendations of the Meriam Report of 1928. Its passage brought significant remedial changes in U.S. relations with tribes. This act, also known as the Wheeler-Howard Act, addressed matters foundational to basic economic opportunity, primarily by curtailing the systemic, policy-driven reductions of reservation lands—as by the early thirties, "... two-thirds of the tribal lands had passed into outside populations' ownership."[1]

This act restored to tribal ownership a measure of "surplus" reservation lands and provided for the acquisition of additional lands for tribes seeking to maintain tribal land bases. The IRA also included a provision for the preferential Bureau of Indian Affairs

> *"Congress didn't vote on the bills, they just wave at them as they go by."*
>
> WILL ROGERS

(BIA) hiring of qualified Indian job applicants, and established tribal governments and courts.[2] Furthermore, it authorized a financial development program, a credit system designed for certain tribal organizations.[3] Enactment of the IRA inspired passage of the Indian Arts and Crafts Board Act the following year—to further enhance reservation-based economies.[4]

By 1934, reservations established fifty and more years earlier had been severely diminished in size. Residents had limited or no access to lands suitable for hunting or agriculture. In discussions on the House floor just prior to the voting on the bill which would soon become the Indian Reorganization Act (IRA), a congressional representative, Edgar Howard, commented on the disastrous impact of previous congressional actions,

143

primarily the General Allotment Act (aka *Dawes Act*) of 1887:

> A few comparisons may be helpful in understanding the conditions which this bill is designed to correct. In making these comparisons I shall not turn back a single page of history. I shall only return to a period within the memory of most of us here today, to the year 1887, when the last major Indian policy, the general allotment law, was enacted. Indian statistics are somewhat incomplete and may not always be entirely accurate, but I believe those I shall now present are approximately correct ... In 1887 our Indian wards numbered 243,000. They owned 137,000,000 acres of land, more than one-third good farming land, and considerable portion valuable timberlands. Today they number about 200,000. Their land holding has shrunk to a mere 47,000,000 acres. Of this remnant only 3,500,000 acres may be classed as farming lands, 8,000,000 acres as timberlands of any value, 16,000,000 acres as good grazing lands and 19,000,000 acres, almost one-half the Indian land remaining, as desert or semi-arid lands of limited use or value ... In 1887 there were less than 5,000 landless Indians. Today, there are more than 100,000 ... In 1887 Indian trust funds, which are administered by the Government, aggregated $29,000,000 Notwithstanding the subsequent addition of more than $500,000,000, derived largely from the sale of Indians lands and assets, these funds today amount to but $13,500,000. A factor in the dissipation of these funds has been their use to pay the salaries of employees, generally whites, in the Indians Service. Although greatly reduced in recent years, the amount so used is still in excess of $2,000,000 per annum ... In 1887 the average Indian was self-supporting. Today nearly one-half are virtual paupers. The number of such is steadily increasing. A recent survey among typical Indian families by the Indian Office shows the average per capita income to be but $48 per annum in money and in produce raised and consumed ... The annual death rate among the Indian population in 1887 is given as 18 per thousand. Today it is 26 per thousand, more than twice that of the general population ... These comparisons tell a tragic story. They reveal a lamentable lowering of the social and economic status of the Indians. They show a startling loss of assets and

an income diminished to the point where the burden of Indian care is becoming a heavy one upon the local and Federal Governments. It is not my purpose at this time to dwell upon the responsibility for this sad state of affairs. In all fairness, it may be said that it is due in part to well-intentioned but mistaken policies and in part to improper administration. The failure of their governmental guardian to conserve the Indians' lands and assets and the consequent loss of income or earning power, has been the principal cause of the present plight of the average Indians. The loss of land is primarily due to the Allotment Act of 1887 and the manner in which it has been administered. Often against their wishes, allotments were forced upon Indians who were not prepared to manage their property. They have since sold their lands or had it sold at tax sale. A large acreage of inherited allotted land has also been lost to the Indians through partition sales. Much so-called "ceded" or "surplus" Indian land has been sold to whites. Immense sums derived from the sale of Indian lands, timber, oil, and minerals have been squandered by the guardians. Whether these funds were disbursed to the Indians in per capita payments or whether they were paid as salaries to Indian Bureau employees, the result is now the same. The prevailing living conditions among the great majority of the Indians are conducive to the development and spread of disease. With comparatively few exceptions, the diet of the Indians is bad. It is generally insufficient in quantity, lacking in variety...The deplorable conditions I have outlined were clearly developed in extensive hearings before the committee over a period of 3 months. Every interested person and organization, and especially the Indians themselves, were given opportunity to express their views. The hearings have been published in nine parts and are now available...The housing conditions are likewise conducive to bad health...there is great overcrowding, so that all members of the family are exposed to any disease that develops and it is virtually impossible in any way even partially to isolate a person suffering from a communicable disease. In certain jurisdictions, notably the Osage and the Kiowa, the government has stimulated the building of modern homes, bungalows, or even more pretentious dwellings, but most of the permanent houses...are small shacks...with inadequate provision for ventilation…Water is ordinarily carried considerable distances from natural springs or streams, or occasionally from wells. In many sections the supply is inadequate, although in some jurisdictions, notably in the desert country of the Southwest, the government has materially improved the situation, an activity that is appreciated by the Indians. John Collier, Commissioner of the Bureau of Indian Affairs at the time of this legislation's passage, said the original bill was fifty-five pages long, but became the much shorter Public Law 383. Enacted as the Indian Reorganization Act (IRA) on June 18, 1934, this public law was purportedly crafted to "… conserve and develop Indian lands and resources; to extend to Indians the right to form business and other organizations; to establish a credit system for Indians; to grant certain rights of home rule to Indians … and to afford U.S. citizens residing within reservations rights similar to those enjoyed by other citizens." With passage of the Indian Reorganization Act, the BIA officially ceased efforts to suppress indigenous languages and traditional cultural practices. However, since indigenous languages had been banned throughout the 1920s and into the early 1930s, by 1934, many tribal children spoke only English.

The Indian Reorganization Act of 1934

AN ACT[5] … To conserve and develop Indian lands and resources; to extend to Indians the right to form business and other organizations; to establish a credit system for Indians; to grant certain rights of home rule to Indians; and for other purposes. *Be it enacted by the Senate and House of Representatives of the United States of America in Congress assembled,* That hereafter no land of any Indian reservation, created or set apart by treaty of agreement with the Indians, Act of Congress, Executive order, purchase or otherwise shall be allotted in severalty to any Indian.

SEC. 2. The existing periods of trust placed upon any Indian lands and any restriction on alienation thereof are hereby extended and continued until otherwise directed by Congress.

SEC. 3. The Secretary of the Interior, if he shall find it to be in the public interest, is hereby authorized to restore to tribal ownership the remaining surplus lands of any Indian reservation heretofore opened, or authorized to be open to sale, or any other form of disposal by Presidential proclamation, or by any of the public-land laws of the United States: *Provided however*, That valid rights or claims of any person to any lands so withdrawn existing on the date of the withdrawal shall not be affected by this Act:*Provided further*, That this section shall not apply to lands within any reclamation project heretofore authorized in any Indian reservation: *Provided further*, that the order of the Department of the Interior signed, dated and approved Honorable Ray Lyman Wilbur, as Secretary of the Interior on October 28, 1932, temporarily withdrawing land of the Papago Indian reservation in Arizona from all forms of mineral entry or claim under the public land mining laws, is hereby revoked and rescinded and the lands of said Papago Indian Reservation are hereby restored to exploration and location under the existing mining laws of the United States, in accordance with the express terms and provisions declared and set forth in the Executive orders establishing said Papago Indian Reservation: *Provided further*, That damages shall be paid to the Papago Tribe for loss of any improvements on any land located for mining in such a sum as may be determined by the Secretary of the Interior but not to exceed the cost of said improvements: *Provided further*, That a yearly rental not to exceed five cents per acre shall be paid to the Papago Tribe for loss of the use or occupancy of any land withdrawn by the requirements of mining operations and payments derived from damages or rentals shall be deposited in the Treasury of the United States to the credit of the Papago tribe: *Provided further*, That in the event any person or persons, partnership, corporation, or association desires a mineral patent, according to the mining laws of the United States. He or they shall first deposit in the Treasury of the United States to the credit of the Papago Tribe the sum of $1.00 per acre in lieu of annual rental, as hereinbefore provided, to compensate for the loss or occupancy of the lands withdrawn by the requirements of mining operations: *Provided further*, That patentee shall also pay into the Treasury of the United States to the credit of the Papago Tribe damages for the loss of improvements not heretofore paid in such a sum as may be determined by the Secretary of the Interior, but not to exceed the cost thereof; the payment of $1.00 per acre for surface use to be refunded to patentee in the event that patent is not acquired. Nothing herein contained shall restrict the granting or use of permits for easements or rights-of-way; or ingress or egress over the lands for all proper and lawful purposes; and, nothing contained herein, except as expressly provided, shall be construed as authority for the Secretary of the Interior, or any other person, to issue or promulgate a rule or regulation in conflict with the Executive order of February 1, 1917, creating the Papago Indian Reservation in Arizona or the Act of February 21, 1931 (46 Stat. 1202).

SEC. 4. *Except as herein provided,* no sale, devise, gift, exchange or other transfer of restricted Indian lands or of shares in the assets of any Indian tribe or corporation organized hereunder, shall be made or approved: *Provided, however,* That such lands or interests may, with the approval of the Secretary of the Interior, be sold, devised, or otherwise transferred to the Indian tribe in which the lands or shares are located or from which the shares were derived or to a successor corporation; and in all instances such lands or interests shall descend or be devised, in accordance with the then existing laws of the Stare, or Federal laws where applicable; in which said lands are located or in which the subject matter of the corporation is located, to any member of such tribe or of such corporation or any heirs of such member: *Provided further,* That the Secretary of the Interior may authorize voluntary exchanges of lands of equal value and the voluntary exchange of shares of equal value whenever such exchange, in his judgment, is expedient and beneficial for or compatible with the proper consolidation of Indian lands and for the benefit of cooperative organizations.

SEC. 5. The Secretary of the Interior is hereby authorized, in his discretion, to acquire through purchase, relinquishment, gift, exchange, or assignment, any interest in lands, water rights or surface rights to lands, within or without existing reservations, including trust or otherwise restricted allotments whether the allottee be living or deceased, for the purpose of providing land for Indians. For the acquisition of such lands, interests in land, water rights and surface rights and for expenses incident to such acquisition, there is hereby authorized to be appropriated, out of any funds in the Treasury not otherwise appropriated, a sum not to exceed $2,000,000 in any one fiscal year: *Provided,* That no part of such funds shall be used to acquire additional land, outside of the exterior boundaries of Navajo Indian Reservation for the Navajo Indians in Arizona and New Mexico, in the event that the proposed Navajo boundary extension measures now pending in Congress and embodied in the bills (S.2499 and H.R. 8927) to define the exterior boundaries of the Navajo Indian Reservation in Arizona and for other purposes and the bills (S. 2531 and H.R. 8982) to define the exterior boundaries of the Navajo Indian Reservation in New Mexico and for other purposes, or similar legislation, become law. The unexpended balances of any appropriations made pursuant to this section shall remain available until expended. Title to any lands or rights acquired pursuant to this Act shall be taken in the name of the United States in trust for the Indian tribe or individual Indian for which the land is acquired and such lands or rights shall be exempt from State and local taxation.

SEC. 6. The Secretary of the Interior is directed to make rules and regulations for the operation and management of Indian forestry units on the principle of sustained-yield management, to restrict the number of livestock grazed on Indian range units to the estimated carrying capacity of such ranges and to promulgate such other rules and regulations as may be necessary to protect the range from deterioration, to prevent soil erosion, to assure full utilization of the range and like purposes.

"... SEC. 7 ... lands added to existing reservations shall be designated for the exclusive use of Indians entitled by enrollment or by tribal membership to residence at such reservations ..."

SEC. 7. The Secretary of the Interior is hereby authorized to proclaim new Indian reservations on lands acquired pursuant to any authority conferred by this Act, or to add such lands to existing reservations: *Provided*, That lands added to existing reservations shall be designated for the exclusive use of Indians entitled by enrollment or by tribal membership to residence at such reservations.

SEC. 8. Nothing contained in this Act shall be construed to

relate to Indian holdings of allotments or homesteads upon the public domain outside of the geographic boundaries of any Indian reservation now existing or established hereafter.

SEC. 9. There is hereby authorized to be appropriated, out of any funds in the Treasury not otherwise appropriated, such sums as may be necessary, but not to exceed $250,000 in any fiscal year, to be expended at the order of the Secretary of the Interior, in defraying the expenses of organizing Indian chartered corporations or other organizations created under this Act.

SEC. 10. There is hereby authorized to be appropriated, out of any funds in the Treasury not otherwise appropriated, the sum of $10, 000,000 to be established as a revolving fund from which the Secretary of the Interior, under such rules and regulations as he may prescribe, may make loans to Indian chartered corporations for the purpose of promoting the economic development of such tribes and of their members and may defray the expenses of administering such loans. Repayment of amounts loaned under this authorization shall be credited to the revolving fund and shall be available for the purposes for which the fund is established. A report shall be made annually to Congress of transactions under this authorization.

SEC. 11. There is hereby authorized to be appropriated, out of any funds in the United States Treasury not otherwise appropriated, a sum not to exceed $250,000 annually, together with any unexpended balances of previous appropriations made pursuant to this section, for loans to Indians for the payment of tuition and other expenses in recognized vocational and trade schools: *Provided*, That not more than $50,000 of such sum shall be available for loans to Indian students in high schools and colleges. Such loans shall be reimbursable under rules established by the Commissioner of Indian Affairs.

SEC. 12. The Secretary of the Interior is directed to establish standards of health, age, character, experience, knowledge and ability for Indians, who may be appointed, without regard to civil-service laws, to the various positions maintained, now or hereafter, by the Indian Office, in the administration of functions or services affecting any Indian tribe. Such qualified Indians shall hereafter have the preference to appointment to vacancies in any such positions.

SEC. 13. The provisions of this Act shall not apply to any of the Territories, colonies, or insular possessions of the United States, except that sections 9, 10, 11, 12 and 16, shall apply to the Territory of Alaska: *Provided*, That Sections 2, 4, 7, 16, 17 and 18 of this Act shall not apply to the following-named Indian tribes, the members of such Indian tribes, together with members of other, tribes affiliated with such named tribes located in the State of Oklahoma, as follows: Cheyenne, Arapaho, Apache, Comanche, Kiowa, Caddo, Delaware, Wichita, Osage, Kaw, Otoe, Tonkawa, Pawnee, Ponca, Shawnee, Ottawa, Quapaw, Seneca, Wyandotte, Iowa, Sac and Fox, Kickapoo, Pottawatomi, Cherokee, Chickasaw, Choctaw, Creek and Seminole. Section 4 of this Act shall not apply to the Indians of the Klamath Reservation in Oregon.

SEC. 14. The Secretary of the Interior is hereby directed to continue the allowance of the articles enumerated in Section 17 of the Act of March 2, 1889 (23 Stat. L. 894), or their commuted cash value under the Act of June 10, 1896 (29 Stat. L. 334), to all Lakota Indians who would be eligible, but for the provisions of this Act, to receive allotments of lands in severalty under Section 19 of the Act of May 29, 1908 (25 Stat. L, 451), or under any prior Act and who have the prescribed status of the head of a family or single person over the age of eighteen years and his approval shall be final and conclusive, claims therefore to be paid as formerly from the permanent appropriation made by said Section 17 and carried on the books of the Treasury for this purpose. No person shall receive in his own right more than one allowance of the benefits and application must be made and approved during the lifetime of the allottee or the right shall lapse. Such benefits shall continue to be paid upon such reservation until such time as the lands available therein for allotment at the time of the passage of this Act would have been exhausted by the award to each person receiving such benefits of an allotment of eighty acres of such land.

SEC. 15. Nothing in this Act shall be construed to impair or prejudice any claim or suit of any Indian tribe against the United States. It is hereby declared to be the intent of Congress that no expenditures for the benefit of Indians made out of appropriations authorized by this Act shall be considered as offsets in any suit brought to recover upon any claim of such Indians against the United States.

SEC. 16. Any Indian tribe or tribes, residing on the same reservation, shall have the right to organize for its common welfare and may adopt an appropriate constitution and bylaws, which shall become effective when ratified by a majority vote of the adult members of the tribe, or of the adult Indians residing on such reservation; as the case may be, at a special election authorized and called by the Secretary of the Interior under such rules and regulations as he may prescribe. Such constitution and bylaws when ratified as aforesaid and approved by the Secretary of the Interior shall be revocable by an election open to the same voters and conducted in the same manner as hereinabove provided. Amendments to the constitution and bylaws may be ratified and approved by the Secretary in the same manner as the original constitution and bylaws. In addition to all powers vested in any Indian tribe or tribal council by existing law, the constitution adopted by said tribe shall also vest in such tribe or its tribal council the following rights and powers: To employ legal counsel, the choice of counsel and fixing of fees to be subject to the approval of the Secretary of the Interior; to prevent the sale, disposition, lease, or encumbrance of tribal lands, interests in lands, or other tribal assets without the consent of the tribe; and to negotiate with the Federal, State and local Governments. The Secretary of the Interior shall advise such tribe or its tribal council of all appropriation estimates or Federal projects for the benefit of the tribe prior to the submission of such estimates to the Bureau of the Budget and the Congress.

SEC. 17. The Secretary of the Interior may, upon petition by at least one-third of the adult Indians, issue a charter of incorporation to such tribe: *Provided*, That such charter shall not become operative until ratified at a special election by a majority vote of: the adult Indians living on the reservation. Such charter may convey to the incorporated tribe the power to purchase, take by gift, or bequest, or otherwise, own, hold, manage, operate and dispose of property of every description, real and personal, including the power to purchase restricted Indian lands and to issue in exchange therefore interests in corporate property and such further powers as may be incidental interests in corporate property and such further powers as may be incidental to the conduct of corporate business, not inconsistent with law, but no authority shall be granted to sell, mortgage, or lease for a period exceeding ten years any of the land included in the limits of the reservation. Any charter so issued shall not be revoked or surrendered except by Act of Congress.

SEC. 18. This Act shall not apply to any reservation wherein a majority of the adult Indians, voting at a special election duly called by the Secretary of the Interior, shall vote against its application. It shall be the duty of the Secretary of the Interior, within one year after the passage and approval of this Act, to call such an election, which election shall be held by secret ballot upon thirty days' notice.

"SEC. 19 ... For the purposes of this Act, Eskimos and other aboriginal peoples of Alaska shall be considered Indians."

SEC. 19. The term "Indian" as used in this Act shall include all persons of Indian descent who are members of any recognized Indian tribe now under Federal jurisdiction and all persons who are descendants of such members who were, on June 1, 1934, residing within the present boundaries of any Indian reservation and shall further include all other persons of one-half or more Indian blood. For the purposes of this Act, Eskimos and other aboriginal peoples of Alaska shall be considered Indians. The term "tribe" wherever used in this Act shall be construed to refer to any Indian tribe, organized band, pueblo, or the Indians residing on one reservation. The word "adult Indians" wherever used in this Act shall be construed to refer to Indians who have attained the age of twenty-one years.

Approved June 18, 1934.

Figure 31. John Collier, then Commissioner of the Bureau of Indian Affairs, spoke to members of Congress about the Indian Reorganization Act in 1934, stating: "Some people ridiculed this bill [the initial proposal] because it contained 52 [*sic*] printed pages. They forgot that it was offered as a successor to the greater part of several thousand pages of Indian law ..." This photo was taken as Collier appeared before the Senate Indian Affairs Committee on June 10, 1940, in Washington D.C. (Photo: Library of Congress).

Chapter XV

An Economic Boost: The Arts & Crafts Board Act of 1935

THE ARTS AND CRAFTS Board Act, approved August 27, 1935, mandated an extension of economic opportunities available to reservation communities. This legislation appeared as an outgrowth of Meriam Report recommendations presented before Congress in 1928. The Meriam Report had recommended immediate action be taken to identify income streams for reservation households—and had identified the potential economic opportunities inherent within the national popularity of American Indian arts and crafts.[1] The Arts and Crafts Board Act began as a U.S. Senate bill (S. 2203). Brought to the Senate floor by "Mr. Thomas of Oklahoma," Senator Thomas introduced the bill as follows:

"Everybody in America has been good to me and I love you all, even critics and Congressmen."

WILL ROGERS

Mr. President. We have in the United States something like 350,000 Indians. These Indians are found in 20 states. There are something like 200 different tribes. These Indians in times past have made their living in their native original way. In some reservations they make their living by the manufacture of pottery, at other points by the manufacture of baskets, at other points by the manufacture of silverware ... So popular has the handiwork of the Indian tribes become that certain companies are imitating it and placing the imitations

155

on the market as if they were genuine. For several years past, the Interior Department has made and tried to devise a plan to give the Indians protection in the matter of wares and merchandise which they themselves make. The bill is the result of the recommendations of the department. It provides for the creation of a commission consisting of five men who are to serve without pay, save for their expenses. The commission[ers] are to make a study of the situation, and investigation and study of the articles made by the several Indian tribes; and, when they find an Indian tribe in good faith making some article, they would be authorized to stamp that article as having been made by the Indians or to provide a plan of stamping. The bill provides a system of protection and assistance for the Indians who are trying to make the original goods. I hope this bill will receive the favorable consideration of the Senate.[2]

The Arts and Crafts Board Act of 1935

AN ACT[3] ... To promote the development of Indian arts and crafts and to create a board to assist therein and for other purposes. *Be it enacted by the Senate and House of Representatives of the United States of America in Congress assembled,* That a board is hereby created in the Department of the Interior to be known as "Indian Arts and Crafts Board," and hereinafter referred to as the Board. The Board shall be composed of five commissioners who shall be appointed by the Secretary of the interior as soon as possible after the passage of this Act ...The commissioners shall serve without compensation: *Provided,* That each Commissioner shall be reimbursed for all actual expenses, including travel expenses, subsistence and office overhead, which the Board shall certify to have been incurred as properly incidental to the performance of his duties as a member of the Board.

SEC. 2. It shall be the function and the duty of the Board to promote the economic welfare of the Indian tribes and the Indian wards of the government through the development of

Indian arts and crafts and the expansion of the market for the products of Indian art and craftsmanship. In the execution of this function the Board shall have the following powers: (a) To undertake market research to determine the best opportunity for the sale of various products; (b) to engage in technical research and give technical advice and assistance; (c) to engage in experimentation directly or through selected agencies; (d) to correlate and encourage the activities of the various governmental and private agencies in the field; (e) to offer assistance in the management of operating groups for the furtherance of specific projects; (f) to make recommendations to appropriate agencies for loans in furtherance of the production and sale of Indian products; (g) to create Government trademarks of genuineness and quality for Indian products and the products of particular Indian tribes or groups; to establish standards and regulations for the use of such trademarks; to license corporations, associations, or individuals to use them; and to charge a fee for their use; to register them in the United States Patent Office without charge; (h) to employ executive officers, including a general manager and such other permanent and temporary personnel as may be found necessary and prescribe the authorities, duties, responsibilities and tenure and fix the compensation of such officers and other employees: *Provided*, That the classification Act of 1923, as amended, shall be applicable to all permanent employees except executive officers and that all employees other than executive officers shall be appointed in accordance with the civil-service laws from lists of eligibles to be supplied by the Civil Service Commission; (i) as a Government agency to negotiate and execute in its own name contracts with operating groups to supply management, personnel and supervision at cost and to negotiate and execute in its own name such other contracts and to carry on such other business as may be necessary for the accomplishment of the duties and purposes of the board: *Provided*, That nothing in the foregoing enumeration of powers shall be construed to authorize the Board to borrow or lend money or to deal in Indian goods.

SEC. 3. The Board shall prescribe from time to time rules and regulations governing the conduct of its business and containing such provisions as it may deem appropriate for the effective execution and administration of the powers conferred upon it by this Act: *Provided*, That before prescribing any procedure for the disbursement of money the Board shall advise and consult with the General Accounting Office: *Provided further,* That all rules and regulations proposed by the Board shall be submitted to the Secretary of the Interior and shall become effective upon his approval.

> *"... SEC. 3 ... before ... [distributing] ... money the Board shall advise and consult with the General Accounting Office ... all rules and regulations proposed by the Board shall be submitted to the Secretary of the Interior and shall become effective upon his approval ..."*

SEC. 4. There is hereby authorized to be appropriated out of any sums in the Treasury not otherwise appropriated such sums as may be necessary to defray the expenses of the Board and carry out the purposes and provisions of this Act. All Income derived by the Board from any Source shall be covered into the Treasury of the United States and shall constitute a special fund which is hereby appropriated and made available until expended for carrying out the purposes and provisions of this Act. Out of the funds available to it at any time the Board may authorize such expenditures consistent with the provisions of this Act, as it may determine to be necessary for the accomplishment of the purposes and objectives of this Act.

SEC. 5. Any person who shall counterfeit or colorably imitate any Government trade mark used or devised by the Board as provided in section 2 of this Act, or shall, except as authorized by the Board, affix any such Government trade mark, or shall knowingly, willfully and corruptly affix any reproduction, counterfeit, copy, or colorable imitation thereof upon any products, Indian or otherwise, or to any labels, signs, prints, packages, wrappers, or receptacles intended to be used upon or in connection with the sale of such products, or any person who shall knowingly make any false statement for the purpose of obtaining the use of any such Government trade mark, shall be guilty of a misdemeanor and upon conviction thereof shall be enjoined from further carrying on the act or acts complained of and shall be subject to a fine not exceeding six months, or both such fine and imprisonment.

SEC. 6. Any person who shall willfully offer or display for sale any goods, with or without any Government trade mark [sic], as Indian products or Indian products of a particular Indian tribe or group, resident within the United States or the Territory of Alaska, when such person knows such goods are not Indian products or are not Indian products of the particular Indian tribes or group, shall be guilty of a misdemeanor and be subject to a fine not exceeding $2,000 or imprisonment not exceeding six months, or both such fine and imprisonment. It shall be the duty of each district attorney, to who the Board shall report in writing any violation of the provisions of this section which has occurred within his jurisdiction, to cause appropriate proceedings to be commenced and prosecuted in the proper courts of the United States for the enforcement of the penalties herein provided.

Approved August 27, 1935.

Figure 32. The Arts and Crafts Board Act proposal and enactment came in response to the national popularity of tribal arts, such as this wool rug purchased at an off-reservation tourist shop in Arizona. Passage of this public law activated the following legislative intent: "... to devise a plan to give the Indians protection in the matter of wares and merchandise which they themselves make ..." (Photo: B. L. Wilson).

Chapter XVI

An Honorable Move: U.S. Indian Claims Commission Act of 1946

THE INDIAN CLAIMS Commission Act of 1946 provided the mechanism by which Indian tribal claims against the U.S. federal government could be leveraged. This act offered a way tribes could pursue reimbursement for lands, horses, personal belongings, and other resources taken by U.S. military and civilian service personnel in violation of treaty agreements. This act essentially reestablished, under a different name, the Court of Indian Affairs which had been dismantled twelve years earlier through passage of the Indian Reorganization Act in 1934.[1]

"If the present Congress errs in too much talking, how can it be otherwise ... in a body to which the people send one hundred and fifty lawyers ... whose trade it is to question everything, yield nothing, and talk by the hour?"

THOMAS JEFFERSON

Indian Claims Commission Act of 1946

AN ACT[2] ... To create an Indian Claim Commission, to provide for the powers, duties, and funtions thereof, and for other purposes. *Be it enacted by the Senate and House of Representatives of the United States of America in Congress assembled,* That there is hereby created and established an Indian Claims Commission, hereafter referred to as the Commission.

JURISDICTION

SEC. 2. The Commission shall hear and determine the following claims against the United States on behalf of any Indian tribe, band, or other identifiable group of American Indians residing within the territorial limits of the United States or Alaska: (1) claims in law or equity arising under the Constitution, laws, treaties of the United States, and Executive orders of the President; (2) all other claims in law or equity, including those sounding in tort, with respect to which the claimant would have been entitled to sue in a court of the United States if the United States was subject to suit; (3) claims which would result if the treaties, contracts, and agreements between the claimant and the United States were revised on the ground of fraud, duress, unconscionable consideration, mutual or unilateral mistake, whether of law or fact, or any other ground cognizable by a court of equity; (4) claims arising from the taking by the United States, whether as the result of a treaty of cession or otherwise, of lands owned or occupied by the claimant without the payment for such lands of compensation agreed to by the claimant; and (5) claims based upon fair and honorable dealings that are not recognized by any existing rule of law or equity. No claim accruing after the date of the approval of This Act shall be considered by the Commission. All claims hereunder may be heard and determined by the Commission notwithstanding any statute of limitations or laches, but all other defenses shall be available to the United States. In determining the quantum of relief the Commission shall make appropriate deductions for all payments made by the United States on the claim, and for all other offsets, counterclaims, and demands that would be allowable in a suit brought in the Court of Claims under section 145 of the Judicial Code (36 Stat. 1136; 28 U. S. C. SEC. 250), as amended; the Commission may also inquire into and consider all money or property given to or funds expended gratuitously for the benefit of the claimant and if it finds that the nature of the claim and the entire course of dealings and accounts between the United States and the claimant in good conscience warrants such action, may set off all or part of such expenditures against any award made to the claimant, except that it is hereby declared to be the policy of Congress that monies spent for the removal of the claimant from one place to another at the request of the United States, or for agency or other administrative, educational, health or highway purposes, or for expenditures made prior to the date of the law, treaty or Executive Order under which the claim arise or for expenditures made pursuant to the Act of June 18, 1934 (48 Stat. 984), save expenditures made under section 5 of that Act, or for expenditures under any emergency appropriation or allotment made subsequent to March 4, 1933, and generally applicable throughout the United States for relief in stricken agricultural areas, relief from distress caused by unemployment and conditions resulting therefrom [*sic*], the prosecution of public work and public projects for the relief of unemployment or to increase employment, and for work relief (including the Civil Works Program) shall not be a proper offset against any award.

> *"... SEC. 3 ... at least two members of the Commission shall be members of the bar of the Supreme Court of the United States ... not more than two of the members shall be of the same political party ... Each ... shall take an oath to support the Constitution of the United States ..."*

MEMBERSHIP APPOINTMENT; OATH; SALARY

SEC. 3. (a) The Commission shall consist of a Chief Commissioner and two Associate Commissioners, who shall be appointed by the President, by and with the advice and consent of the Senate, and each of whom shall receive a salary of $10,000 per year. At all times at least two members of the Commission shall be members of the bar of the Supreme Court of the United States in good standing: *Provided further*, That not more than two of the members shall be of the same political party. Each of them shall take an oath to support the Constitution of the United States and to discharge faithfully the duties of his office.

TERM OF OFFICE; VACANCIES; REMOVAL

(b) The Commissioners shall hold office during their good behavior until the dissolution of the Commission as hereinafter provided. Vacancies shall be filled in the same manner as the original appointments. Members of the Commission may be removed by the President for cause after notice and opportunity to be heard.

NOT TO ENGAGE IN OTHER VOCATIONS OR REPRESENT TRIBES

(c) No Commissioner shall engage in any other business, vocation, or employment during his term of office nor shall he, during his term of office or for a period of two years thereafter, represent any Indian tribe, band, or group in any matter whatsoever, or have any financial interest in the outcome of any tribal claim. Any person violating the provisions of this subdivision shall be fined not more than $10,000 or imprisoned not more than two years, or both.

QUORUM

(d) Two members shall constitute a quorum, and the agreement of two members shall be necessary to any and all determinations for the transaction of the business of the Commission, and, if there be a quorum, no vacancy shall impair or affect the business of the Commission, or its determinations.

STAFF OF COMMISSION

SEC. 4. The Commission shall appoint a clerk and such other employees as shall be requisite to conduct the business of the Commission. All such employees shall take oath for the faithful discharge of their duties and shall be under the direction of the Commission in the performance thereof OFFICES

SEC. 5. The principal office of the Commission shall be in the District of Columbia.

EXPENSES OF COMMISSION

SEC. 6. All necessary expenses of the Commission shall be paid on the presentation of itemized vouchers therefore approved by the Chief Commissioner or other member or officer designated by the Commission.

TIME OF MEETINGS

SEC. 7. The time of the meetings of the Commission shall be prescribed by the Commission.

RECORD

SEC. 8. A full written record shall be kept of all hearings and proceedings of the Commission and shall be open to public inspection.

CONTROL OF PROCEDURES

SEC. 9. The Commission shall have power to establish its own rules of procedure.

PRESENTATION OF CLAIMS

SEC. 10. Any claim within the provisions of this Act may be presented to the Commission by any member of an Indian tribe, band, or other identifiable group of Indians as the representative of all its members; but wherever any tribal organization exists, recognized by the Secretary of the Interior as having authority to represent such tribe, band, or group, such organization shall be accorded the exclusive privilege of representing such Indians, unless fraud collusion, or lathes on the part of such organization be shown to tie satisfaction of the Commission.

TRANSFER OF SUITS FROM COURT OF CLAIMS

SEC. 11. Any suit pending in the Court of Claims or the Supreme Court of the United States or which shall be filed in the Court of Claims under existing legislation, shall not be transferred to the Commission: *Provided,* That the provisions of section 2 of this Act with respect to the deduction of payments, offsets, counterclaims and demands, shall supersede the provisions of the particular jurisdictional Act under which any pending or authorized suit in the Court of Claims has been or will be authorized: *Provided further,* That the Court of Claims in any suit pending before it at the time of the approval of this Act shall have exclusive jurisdiction to hear and determine any claim based upon fair and honorable dealings arising out of the subject matter of any such suit.

LIMITATIONS

SEC. 12. The Commission shall receive claims for a period of five years after the date of the approval of this Act and no claim existing before such date but not presented within such period may thereafter be submitted to any court or administrative agency or consideration, nor will such claim thereafter be entertained by the Congress.

"... SEC. 12. The Commission shall receive claims for a period of five years after the date of the approval of this Act ... no claim existing before ... but not presented within such period may ... be submitted to any court or administrative agency for consideration, nor will such claim thereafter be entertained by the Congress ..."

NOTICE AND INVESTIGATION

SEC. 13. (a) As soon as practicable the Commission shall send a written explanation of the provisions of this Act to the recognized head of each Indian tribe and band, and to any other identifiable groups of American Indians existing as distinct entities, residing within the territorial limits of the United States and Alaska, and to the superintendents of all Indian agencies, who shall promulgate the same, and shall request that a detailed statement of all claims be sent to the Commission, together with the names of aged or invalid Indians from whom depositions should be taken immediately and a summary of their proposed testimonies. (b) The Commission shall establish an Investigation Division to investigate all claims referred to it by the Commission for the purpose of discovering the facts relating thereto. The Division shall make a complete and thorough search for all evidence affecting each claim, utilizing all documents and records in the possession of the Court of Claims and the several Government departments, and shall submit such evidence to the Commission. The Division shall make available to the Indians concerned and to any interested Federal agency any data in its possession relating to the rights and claims of any Indian.

CALLS UPON DEPARTMENTS FOR INFORMATION

SEC. 14. The Commission shall have the power to call upon any of the departments of the Government for any information it may deem necessary, and shall have the use of all records, hearings, and reports made by the committees of each House of Congress, when deemed necessary in the prosecution of its business. At any hearing held hereunder, any official letter, paper, document, map, or record in the possession of any officer or department, or court of the United States or committee of Congress (or a certified copy thereof), may be used in evidence insofar as relevant and material, including any deposition or other testimony of record in any suit or proceeding in any court of the United States to which an Indian or Indian tribe or group was a party, and the appropriate department of the Government of the United States shall give to the attorneys for all tribes or groups full and free access to such letters, papers, documents, maps, or records as may be useful to said attorneys in the preparation of any claim instituted hereunder, and shall afford facilities for the examination of the same and, upon written request by said attorneys, shall furnish certified copies thereof.

REPRESENTATION BY ATTORNEYS

SEC. 15. Each such tribe, band, or other identifiable group of Indians may retain to represent its interests in the presentation of claims before the Commission an attorney or attorneys at law, of its own selection, whose practice before the Commission shall be regulated by its adopted procedure. The fees of such attorney or attorneys for all services rendered in prosecuting the claim in question, whether before the Commission or otherwise, shall, unless the amount of such fees is stipulated in the approved contract between the attorney or attorneys and the claimant, be fixed by the Commission at such amount as the Commission, in accordance with standards obtaining for prosecuting similar contingent claims in courts of law, finds to be adequate compensation for services rendered and results obtained, considering the contingent nature of the case, plus all reasonable expenses incurred in the prosecution of the claim; but the amount so fixed by the Commission, exclusive of reimbursements for actual expenses, shall not exceed 10 per centum of the amount recovered in any case. The attorney or attorneys for any such tribe, band, or group as shall have been organized pursuant to section 16 of the Act of June 18, 1934 (48 Stat. 987; 25 U. S. C., SEC. 476) shall be selected pursuant to the constitution and bylaws of such tribe, band, or group. The employment of attorneys for all other claimants shall be subject to the provisions of sections 2103 to 2106, inclusive, of the Revised Statutes (25 U. S. C. SECs. 81, 82-84). The Attorney General or his assistants shall represent the United States in all claims presented to the Commission, and shall have authority, with the approval of the Commission, to compromise any claim presented to the Commission. Any such compromise shall be submitted by the Commission to the Congress as a part of its report as provided in section 21 hereof in the same manner as final determinations of the Commission, and shall be subject to the provisions of section 22 hereof.

NO MEMBERS OF CONGRESS TO PRACTICE BEFORE COMMISSION

SEC. 16. No Senator or Member of or Delegate to Congress shall, during his continuance in office, practice before the Commission.

HEARING

SEC. 17. The Commission shall give reasonable notice to the interested parties and an opportunity for them to be heard and to present evidence before making any final determination upon any claim. Hearings may be held in any part of the United States or in the Territory of Alaska.

TESTIMONY

SEC. 18. Any member of the Commission or any employee of the Commission, designated in writing for the purpose by the Chief Commissioner, may administer oaths and examine witnesses. Any member of the Commission may require by subpoena (I) the attendance and testimony of witnesses, and the production of all necessary books, papers, documents, correspondence, and other evidence, from any place in the United States or Alaska at any designated place of hearing; or (2) the taking of depositions before any designated individual competent to administer oaths under the laws of the United States or of any State or Territory. In the case of a deposition, the testimony shall be reduced to writing by the individual taking the deposition or under his direction and shall be subscribed by the deponent. In taking testimony, opportunity shall be given for cross-examination, under such regulations as the Commission may prescribe. Witnesses subpoenaed to testify or whose depositions are taken pursuant to this Act, and the officers or persons taking the same, shall severally be entitled to do the same fees and mileage as are paid for like services in the courts of the United States.

FINAL DETERMINATIONS

SEC. 19. The final determination of the Commission shall be in writing, shall be filed with its clerk, and shall include (1) its findings of the facts upon which its conclusions are based; (2) a statement (a) whether there are any just ground for relief of the claimant and, if so, the amount thereof; (b) whether there are any allowable offsets, counterclaims, or other deductions and, if so, the amount thereof; and (3) a statement of its reasons for its findings and conclusions.

REVIEW BY COURT OF CLAIMS

SEC. 20. (a) In considering any claim the Commission at any time may certify to the Court of Claims any definite and distinct questions of law concerning which instructions are desired for the proper disposition of the claim; and thereupon the Court of Claims may give appropriate instructions on the questions certified and transmit the same to the Commission for its guidance in the further consideration of the claim. (b) When the final determination of the Commission has been filed with the clerk of said Commission the clerk shall give notice of the filing of such determination to the parties to the proceeding in manner and form as directed by the Commission. At any time within three months from the date of the filing of the determination of the Commission with the clerk either Party may appeal from the determination of the Commission to the Court of Claims, which Court shall have exclusive jurisdiction to affirm, modify, or set aside such final determination. On said appeal the Court shall determine whether the findings of fact of the Commission are supported by substantial evidence, in which event the shall be conclusive, and also whether the conclusions of law, including any conclusions respecting "fair and honorable dealings," where applicable, stated by the Commission as a basis for its final determination, are valid and supported by the Commission's findings of fact. In making the foregoing determinations, the Court shall review the whole record or such portions thereof as may be cited by any party, and due account shall be taken of the rule of prejudicial error. The Court may at any time remand the cause to the Commission for such further proceedings as it may direct, not inconsistent with the foregoing provisions of this section. The Court shall promulgate such rules of practice as it may find necessary to out the foregoing provisions of this section. (c) Determinations of questions of law by the Court of Claims under Court under this section shall be subject to review by the Supreme Court of the United States in the manner prescribed by section 3 of the Act of February 13, 1925 (43 Stat. 939; 28 U. S. C., SEC. 288), as amended.

REPORT OF COMMISSION TO CONGRESS

SEC. 21. In each claim, after the proceedings have been finally concluded, the Commission shall promptly submit its report to Congress. The report to Congress shall contain (1) the final determination of the Commission; (2) a transcript of the proceedings or judgment upon review, if any, with the instructions of the Court of Claims; and (3) a statement of how each Commissioner voted upon the final determination of the claim.

EFFECT OF FINAL DETERMINATION OF COMMISSION

SEC. 22. (a) When the report of the Commission determining any claimant to be entitled to recover has been filed with Congress, such report shall have the effect of a final judgment of the Court of Claims, and there is hereby authorized to be appropriated such sums as are necessary to pay the final determination of the Commission. The payment of any claim, after its determination in accordance with this Act, shall be a full discharge of the United States of all claims and demands touching any of the matters involved in the controversy. Further claim (b) A final determination against a claimant made and reported barred, in accordance with this Act shall forever bar any further claim or demand against the United States arising out of the matter involved in the controversy.

"... SEC. 23. The existence of the Commission shall terminate at the end of ten years after the first meeting of the Commission or at such earlier time after the expiration of the five-year period of limitation set forth in section 12 ..."

DISSOLUTION OF THE COMMISSION

SEC. 23. The existence of the Commission shall terminate at the end of ten years after the first meeting of the Commission or at such earlier time after the expiration of the five-year period of limitation set forth in section 12 hereof as the Commission shall have made its final report to Congress on all claims filed with it. Upon its dissolution the records of the Commission shall be delivered to the Archivist of the United States.

FUTURE INDIAN CLAIMS

SEC. 24. The jurisdiction of the Court of Claims is hereby extended to any claim against the United States accruing after the date of the approval of this Act in favor of any Indian tribe, band, or other identifiable group of American Indians residing within the territorial limits of the United States or Alaska whenever such claim is one arising under the Constitution, laws, treaties of the United States, or Executive orders of the President, or is one which otherwise would be cognizable in the Court of Claims if the claimant were not an Indian tribe, band, or group. In any suit brought under the jurisdiction conferred by this section the claimant shall be entitled to recover in the same manner, to the same extent, and subject to the same conditions and limitations, and the United States shall be entitled to the same defenses, both at law and in equity, and to the same offsets, counterclaims, and demands, as in cases brought in the Court of Claims under section 145 of the Judicial Code (36 Stat. 1136E 28 U. S. C., SEC. 250), as amended: *Provided, however,* That nothing contained in this section shall be construed as altering the SEC. 25. All provisions of law inconsistent with this Act are hereby repealed to the extent of such inconsistency, except that existing provisions of law authorizing suits in the Court of Claims by particular tribes, bands, or groups of Indians and governing the conduct or determination of such suits shall continue to apply to any case heretofore or hereafter instituted thereunder [*sic*] save as provided by section 11 hereof as to the deduction of payments, offsets, counterclaims, and demands.

SEC. 24. If any provision of this Act, or the application thereof, is held invalid, the remainder of the Act, or other applications of such provisions, shall not be affected.

Approved August 13, 1946.

Chapter XVII

Poof: Termination Policies of 1953

HOUSE RECONCURRENT Resolution 108 of 1953 and two related congressional actions—P.L. 280 and P.L. 281—ended the federally-recognized status of more than one hundred American Indian nations.[1] The effect upon tribes singled out for the termination of their official status as tribes (i.e., sovereign American Indian domestic nations) was profound. This enactment also extended state jurisdiction over tribes. The historical record shows how President Dwight Eisenhower disapproved of the fact that this legislation overlooked the obligation to consult with tribal leaders; he encouraged Congress to reconsider their wording, and then amend the legislation to assure it mandated such consultations, but "... That was never done ..."[2] In 1981, a report released by the U.S. Commission of Civil Rights summarized the impact of these and other termination acts of this era, as follows:

"I see by the papers this morning where the Department of Indian Affairs has promised that it will have its Indian Agents do better this year ... I mean, do better for the Indians, for a change."

WILL ROGERS

More than a hundred tribes were legally terminated, land and assets were lost, thousands of Indians were relocated by federal programs to the cultural shock of urban slums, states were given a broader role on many surviving reservations (a development that would exacerbate ... jurisdictional conflicts for years to come), and tribal governments were generally weakened. This was a time in American history when civil liberties generally were under substantial attack.[3]

American Indian nations "terminated" through this legislation included—with three exceptions—all tribes located within the following states: California, Minnesota, Nebraska, Oregon, and Wisconsin. Affected tribes lost all eligibility for Bureau of Indian Affairs funding of tribal health, education, and social welfare programming. The Menominee tribe of Wisconsin, terminated in 1954, had established a strong economic base through tribally-owned lumber production and sales enterprises. Their timber sales paid for Menominee health and social service programming—until this "termination" legislation opened up opportunities for their economically-advantaged competitors to acquire timbered Menominee lands.

Public Law 280

AN ACT[4] ... To confer jurisdiction on the States of California, Minnesota, Nebraska, Oregon and Wisconsin, with respect to criminal offenses and civil causes of action committed or arising on Indian reservations within such States and for other purposes. *Be it enacted by the Senate and House of Representatives of the United States of America in Congress assembled,* That chapter 53 of title 18, United States Code, is hereby amended by inserting at the end of the chapter analysis preceding section 1151 of such title the following new item: 1162 State jurisdiction over offenses committed by or against Indians in the Indian country.

SEC. 2. Title 18, United States Code is hereby amended by inserting in chapter 53 thereof immediately after section 1161 a new section to be designated as section 1162, as follows: §1162. State jurisdiction over offenses committed by or against Indians in the Indian county. (a) Each of the States listed in the following table shall have jurisdiction over offenses committed by or against Indians in the areas of Indian country listed opposite the name of the State to the same extent that such State has jurisdiction over offenses committed elsewhere within the State and the criminal laws of such State shall have the same force and effect within such Indian country as they have elsewhere within the State: *State of ... [and] ... Indian country affected ...* California – All Indian country within the State ... Minnesota –All Indian country within the State, except the Red Lake Reservation ... Nebraska – All Indian country within the State ... Oregon – All Indian country within the State, except the Warm Springs Reservation ... Wisconsin – All Indian country within the State, except the Menominee Reservation ... [later terminated in 1954] (b) Nothing in this section shall authorize the alienation, encumbrance, or taxation of any real or personal property, including water rights, belonging to any Indian or any Indian tribe, band, or community that is held in trust by the United States or is subject to a restriction against alienation imposed by the United States; or shall authorize regulation of the use of such property in a manner inconsistent with any Federal treaty, agreement, or statute or with any regulation made pursuant thereto; or shall deprive any Indian or any Indian tribe, band, or community of any right, privilege, or immunity afforded under Federal treaty, agreement, or statute with respect to hunting, trapping, or fishing or the control, licensing, or regulation thereof. (c) The provisions of sections 1162 and 1153 of this chapter shall not be applicable within the areas of Indian country listed in subsection (a) of this section. SEC. 3. Chapter 85 of title 28, United States Code, is hereby amended by inserting at the end of the chapter analysis preceding section 1331 of such title the following new item: "1360. State civil jurisdiction in actions to which Indians are parties."

SEC. 4. Title 28, United States Code, is hereby amended by inserting in chapter 85 thereof immediately after section 1359 a new section, to be designated as section 1360, as follows: "1360. State civil jurisdiction in actions to which Indians are parties." (a) Each of the States listed in the following table shall have jurisdiction over civil causes of action between Indians or to which Indians are parties which arise in the areas of Indian country listed opposite the name of the State to the same extent that such State has jurisdiction over other civil causes of action, and those civil laws of such State that are of general application to private persons or private property shall have the same force and effect within such Indian country as they have elsewhere within the State: *State of [and] Indian country affected* ...

California – All Indian country within the State ... Minnesota – All Indian country within the State, except the Red Lake Reservation ... Nebraska – All Indian country within the State ... Oregon – All Indian country within the State, except the Warm

Springs Reservation ... Wisconsin – All Indian country within the State, except the Menominee Reservation (b) Nothing in this section shall authorize the alienation, encumbrance, or taxation of any real or personal property, including water rights, belonging to any Indian or any Indian tribe, band, or community that is held in trust by the United States or is subject to a restriction against alienation imposed by the United States; or shall authorize regulation of the use of such property in a manner inconsistent with any Federal treaty, agreement., or statute or with any regulation made pursuant thereto; or shall confer jurisdiction upon the State to adjudicate, in probate proceedings or otherwise, the ownership or right to possession of such property, or any interest therein. (c) Any tribal ordinance or custom heretofore or hereafter adopted by an Indian tribe, band, or community in the exercise of any authority which it may possess shall, if not inconsistent with any applicable civil law of the State, be given full force and effect in the determination of civil causes of action pursuant to this section.

SEC. 5. Section 1 of the Act of October 5, 1949 (68 Stat. 705, ch. 604), is hereby repealed, but such repeal shall not affect any proceedings heretofore instituted under that section.

SEC. 6. Notwithstanding the provisions of any Enabling Act for the admission of a State, the consent of the United States is hereby given to the people of any State to amend, where necessary, their State constitution or existing statutes, as the case may be, to remove any legal impediment to the assumption of civil and criminal jurisdiction in accordance with the provisions of this Act: *Provided,* That the provisions of this Act shall not become effective with respect to such assumption of jurisdiction by any such State until the people thereof have appropriately amended their State constitution or statutes as the case may be.

SEC. 7. The consent of the United States is hereby given to any other State not having jurisdiction with respect to criminal offenses or civil causes of action, or with respect to both, as provided for in this Act, to assume jurisdiction at such time and in such manner as the people of the State shall, by affirmative legislative action, obligate and bind the State to assumption thereof.

Approved August 15, 1953.

Public Law 281

AN ACT[5] ... To terminate certain Federal restrictions upon Indians. *Be it enacted by the Senate and House of Representatives of the United States of America in Congress assembled, That* sections 467 and 2136 of the Revised Statutes (25 U. S. C., SEC. 266) and section 2135 of the Revised Statutes (25 U. S. C., SEC. 265), all of the said laws being laws which forbid the sale, purchase, or possession by Indians of personal property which may be sold, purchased, or possessed by non-Indians, are hereby repealed.

SEC. 2. (a) Section 1157 of title 18 of the United States Code, as amended, is further amended by striking the period at the end thereof and adding the following: *Provided,* That this section shall apply only to livestock purchased by or for Indians with funds provided from the revolving loan fund established pursuant to the Acts of June 18, 1934 (48 Stat. 984), and June 26, 1936 (49 Stat. 1967), as amended and supplemented, or from tribal loan funds used under regulations of the Secretary of the Interior, and to livestock issued to Indians as loans repayable "in kind" and to the increase of all such livestock, and only until such time as such loans are repaid: *Provided further,* That it shall be the duty of any purchaser of Indian livestock to use reasonable diligence to ascertain that such livestock are not subject to such loans. (b) Section 1 of the Act of July 4, 1884 (2 Stat. 94, 25 U. S. C., SEC. 195), is repealed.

Approved August 15, 1953.

Figure 33. The arid landscapes of many western reservations attracted little interest from outsiders until uranium was found near or on reservations—as during the early 1950s (Photo: B. L. Wilson).

Chapter XVIII

A Working Chance: Indian Vocational Training Act of 1956

THE INDIAN VOCATIONAL Training Act provided funding for businesses located on or near reservations to provide job training experiences to tribal members. This act authorized the payment of federal wage subsidies to employers in exchange for their commitment to train and employ tribal members. The impact of this legislation was limited. Nearly fifty years after its enactment, "... [statistics] ... collected by a U.S. Civil Rights Commission in 2000 calculated the average annual income for families living on the Pine Ridge Reservation in South Dakota at $3,700."[1]

The Indian Vocational Training Act of 1956

AN ACT[2] ... Relative to the employment for certain adult Indians on or near Indian reservations. *Be it enacted by the Senate and House of Representatives of the United States of America in Congress assembled,* That in order to help adult Indians who reside on or near Indian reservations to obtain reasonable and satisfactory employment, the Secretary of the Interior is authorized to undertake a program of vocational training that provides for vocational counseling or guidance, institutional training in any recognized vocation or trade, apprenticeship and on the job training, for periods that do not exceed twenty-four months, transportation to the place of training and subsistence during the transportation to the place of training and subsistence during the course of training. The program shall be available primarily to Indians who are not less than eighteen and not more than thirty-five years of age and who reside on or near an Indian reservation and the program shall be conducted under such rules and regulations as the Secretary may prescribe. For the purposes of this program the Secretary is authorized to enter into contracts or agreements with any Federal, State, or local governmental agency, or with any private school which has a recognized reputation in the field of vocational education and has successfully obtained employment for its graduates in their respective fields of training, or with any corporation or association which has an existing apprenticeship or on-the-job training program which is recognized by industry and labor as leading to skilled employment.

SEC. 2. There is authorized to be appropriated for the purposes of this Act the sum of $3,500,000 for each fiscal year and not to exceed $500,000 of such sum shall be available for administrative purposes.

Approved August 3, 1956.

Legislative Sample, Part III
1962-1990

*"... we do have an extraordinary Constitution
... We do have extraordinary sets of laws ... but ... whenever
there's a crisis like that of a war, some ... leaders set them
aside ... But there is greatness in this because, after the war, the
United States of America was strong enough to admit wrong
... they said, yes. We did something wrong. We apologize and
we want to make redress ... few countries would do this. They
... try their best to deny, but not the United States ... and for
that, I'm very proud of my country."*

SENATOR DANIEL INOUYE OF HAWAII,
REFERENCING THE WWII INTERNMENT OF JAPANESE-AMERICANS
DURING A NATIONAL PUBLIC RADIO INTERVIEW OF DECEMBER 7, 2011

Chapter XIX

One American to Another

"They are more than pretty words. They are a legislative expression of conditions, purposes, and intent." [1]

DURING THE CULTURAL turmoil of the 1960s, America's understandings of the Constitution's Life, Liberty, and Pursuit of Happiness tenets gained momentum within congressional circles. After decades of experimentation with conflicting strategies—one designed to eliminate American Indian cultures, the other designed to protect and preserve American Indian lives and lifeways—Congress opted to embrace cultural pluralism. This new horizon in congressional priorities—vis á vis tribes— marks a sea change away from earlier congressional mindsets most apparent in the boarding school legislation of the late nineteenth and early twentieth centuries, and the "termination of tribes" policies of the 1950s. Recognizing that U.S. citizenship, as established for all American Indians in 1924, brought with it

"Beginning in the late 1960s the forces of cultural pluralism once again became dominant in government circles." [2]

LAWRENCE C. KELLY

U.S. citizenship's inherent promise of fair treatment, Congress agreed on the need for legislative changes. Its members soon initiated an adaptive approach to the revision of key elements of U.S. policies toward American Indian citizens and their communities. It also demonstrates some increased awareness of Alaskan and Hawaiian Native citizens and communities.

Legislation enacted between 1962 and 1990 demonstrated the newly awakened congressional recognition—and acceptance—of the continuity, resilience, patriotism, and dignity of American Indian nations, their members and cultures. Thus, a preponderance of the public laws of this era served to enhance tribal authority, foster economic growth within reservation communities, clarify citizenship rights, and expand—albeit minimally—access to healthcare for residents of reservation communities. Acts of these years also returned a measure of autonomy to tribes, at both community and household levels, most notably in matters concerning the care and education of tribal children. Collectively, these 1962-1990 lawmaking years weakened previously imposed barriers to the involvement of members of Indian nations in the design and administration of education, health, social service, judicial, and other reservation-based programming. Some of these barriers were legislative; others were maladaptive federal, state, and local agency traditions.

During the late 1960s, Congress learned of widespread cultural bias in state-controlled child welfare strategies that adversely affected reservation children and families. In response, it enacted a child welfare law designed to incorporate the tenets of cultural relevance.

During the 1970s, Congress enacted a multitude of laws mandating the establishment and expansion of basic opportunities—i.e., those commonplace in other American communities (e.g., local health care). One public law of the 1970s assured American Indians some protection of their basic U.S. civil rights. Another mandated opportunities for residents of reservations to pursue household and business loans. An education-focused enactment provided reservation children an opportunity to attend school without leaving their families. Before the 1970s ended, Congress had also reinstated federal recognition of several previously "terminated" tribal nations, provided funding for adult education programming and the development of tribally affiliated colleges—and had restored to American Indians the right to freely practice their religions.

The 1980s and 1990s brought additional public acts that would benefit tribal citizens. In the 1980s, one such congressional act included mandates that provided a template for the governance of tribal gaming enterprises. During the 1990s, Congress passed a law designed to protect the rights of American Indians to maintain protected burial sites and exercise related stewardship.

The breadth of legislative topics addressed through legislation of this 1962-1990 era bespeaks the array of limits that had previously restricted the basic human and citizen rights of American Indian nations, individuals, and communities. It also demonstrates the capacity of a robust, committed Congress to correct past legislative errors.

Chapter XX

Better Late Than Never: American Indian Civil Rights Act of 1968

THE AMERICAN INDIAN Civil Rights Act of 1968 articulated the constitutional rights of tribal members, while also stipulating additional limits upon the powers of tribal courts.[2] Referenced as both the Indian Civil Rights Act (ICRA) and the Indian Bill of Rights Act, this legislation clarified the U.S. citizenship rights of tribally affiliated Americans.

American Indian Civil Rights Act of 1968

AN ACT[3] ... To prescribe penalties for certain acts of violence or intimidation and for other purposes. *Be it enacted by the Senate and House of Representatives of the United States of America in Congress assembled...*

TITLE II–RIGHTS OF INDIANS ...
DEFINITIONS
SEC. 201. For purposes of this title, the term—(1) "Indian tribe" means any tribe, band, or other group of Indians subject to the jurisdiction of the United States and recognized as possessing powers of self-government; (2) "powers of self-government" means and includes all governmental powers possessed by an Indian tribe, executive, legislative, and

> *"Indian people are the only group in America with no political representation. We have quasi-sovereignty. We have no vote from our sovereignty land base. So we have quasi-apartheid in America."[1]*
>
> BILLY MILLS

185

judicial, and all offices, bodies, and tribunals by and through which they are executed, including courts of Indian offenses; and (3) "Indian court" means any Indian tribal court or court of Indian offense.

INDIAN RIGHTS

SEC. 202. No Indian tribe in exercising powers of self-government shall—make or enforce any law prohibiting the free exercise of religion, or abridging the freedom of speech, or of the press, or the right of the people peaceably to assemble and to petition for a redress of grievances; (2) violate the right of the people to be secure in their persons, houses, papers and effects against unreasonable search and seizures, nor issue warrants, but upon probable cause, supported by oath or affirmation and particularly describing the place to be searched and the person or thing to be seized; (3) subject any person for the same offense to be twice put in jeopardy; (4) compel any person in any criminal case to be a witness against himself; (5) take any private property for a public use without just compensation; (6) deny to any person in a criminal proceeding the right to a speedy and public trial, to be informed of the nature and cause of the accusation, to be confronted with the witnesses against him, to have a compulsory process for obtaining witnesses in his favor and at his own expense to have the assistance of counsel for his defense; (7) require excessive bail, impose excessive fines, inflict cruel and unusual punishments and in no event impose for conviction of any one offense any penalty or punishment greater than imprisonment for a term of six months or a fine of $500 or both; (8) deny to any person within its jurisdiction the equal protection of its laws or deprive any person of liberty or property without due process of law; (9) pass any bill of attainder or ex post factor law; or (10) deny to any person accused of an offense punishable by imprisonment the right, upon request, to a trial by jury of not less than six persons.

HABEAS CORPUS

SEC. 203. The privilege of the writ of habeas corpus shall be available to any person, in a court of the United States, to test the legality of his detention by order of an Indian tribe.

TITLE III–MODEL CODE GOVERNING
COURTS OF INDIAN OFFENSES

SEC. 301. The Secretary of the Interior is authorized and directed to recommend to the Congress, on or before July 1, 1968, a model code to govern the administration of justice by courts of Indian offenses on Indian reservations. Such code shall include provisions which will (1) assure that any individual being tried for an offense by a court of Indian offenses shall have the same rights, privileges and immunities under the United States constitution as would be guaranteed any ... [other}... citizen of the United States being tried in a Federal court for any similar offense, (2) assure that any individual being tried for an offense by a court of Indian offenses will be advised and made aware of his rights under the United States Constitution and under any tribal constitution applicable to such individual, (3) establish proper qualifications for the office of judge of the court of Indian offenses and (4) provide for the establishing of educational classes for the training of judges of courts of Indian offenses. In carrying out the provisions of this title, the Secretary of the Interior shall consult with the Indians, Indian tribes and interested agencies of the United States.

Approved April 11, 1968.

Chapter XXI

Welcome Back to Parents: Indian Elementary & Secondary School Assistance Act of 1972

THE INDIAN ELEMENTARY and Secondary School Assistance Act of 1972 is part of a larger set of amendments specific to the Education Amendments Act that passed through Congress earlier the same year. This amendment expanded tribal oversight of education programs for tribal children. More specifically, it extended tribal rights central to four critical areas of education programming oversight: (1) parental involvement and community participation, (2) development and inclusion of culturally relevant programs, (3) establishment of the Office of Indian Education within the Department of Education, and (4) establishment of a National Advisory Council to review applications for funding of Indian education programs.[2]

"... My mother was a dictionary ... My mother knew words that had been spoken for thousands of years. Sometimes, late at night, she would sing one of the old songs. She would lullaby us with ancient songs. We were lullabied by our ancestors. My mother was a dictionary ..." [1]

SHERMAN ALEXIE

The Indian Elementary and Secondary School Assistance Act of 1972

AN ACT[3] ... To amend the Higher Education Act of UM, the Vocational Education Act of 1963, the General Education Provisions Act (creating a National Foundation for Post-secondary Education and a National Institute of Education), the ... Elementary and Secondary Education Act of 1965, Public Law 874, Eighty-first Congress, and related Acts, and for other purposes. *Be it enacted by the Senate and House of Representatives of the United States of America in Congress assembled,* That this Act may be cited as the "Education Amendments of 1972" ... TITLE IV— INDIAN EDUCATION SHORT TITLE ...

SEC. 401. This title may be cited as the "Indian Education Act." PART A–REVISION OF IMPACTED AREAS PROGRAM AS IT RELATES TO INDIAN CHILDREN ... AMENDMENTS TO PUBLIC LAW 874, EIGHTY-FIRST CONGRESS ... SEC. 411. (a) The Act of September 30, 1950 (Public Law 874, Eighty-first Congress), is amended by redesignating title III as title IV, by redesignating [*sic*] sections 301 through 303 and references thereto as sections 401 through 403, respectively, and by adding after title 11 the following new title:

TITLE III—FINANCIAL ASSISTANCE TO LOCAL DUCATIONAL AGENCIES FOR ... EDUCATION OF INDIAN CHILDREN
SHORT TITLE ...

SEC. 301. This title may be cited as the "Indian Elementary and Secondary School Assistance Act." DECLARATION OF POLICY SEC. 302. (a) In recognition of the special educational needs of Indian students in the United States, Congress hereby declares it to be the policy of the United States to provide financial assistance to local educational agencies to develop and carry out elementary and secondary school programs specially designed to meet these special educational needs. (b) The Commissioner shall, in order to effectuate the policy set forth in subsection (a), carry out a program of making grants to local educational agencies which are entitled to payments under this title and which have submitted, and had approved applications therefore, in accordance with the provisions of this title.

GRANTS TO LOCAL EDUCATIONAL AGENCIES

SEC. 303. (a)(1) For the purpose of computing the amount to which a local educational agency is entitled under this title for any fiscal year ending prior to July 1, 1975, the Commissioner shall determine the number of Indian children who were enrolled in the schools of a local educational agency, and for whom such agency provided free public education, during such fiscal year. (2)(A) The amount of the grant to which a local educational agency is entitled under this title for any fiscal year shall be an amount equal to (i) the average per pupil expenditure for such agency (as determined under subparagraph (e) multiplied by (ii) the sum of the number of children determined under paragraph (1). (B) A local educational agency shall not be entitled to receive a grant under this title for any fiscal year unless the number of children under this subsection, with respect to such agency, is at least ten or constitutes at least 50 per centum of its total enrollment. The requirements of this subparagraph shall not apply to any such agencies serving Indian children in Alaska, California, and Oklahoma or located on, or in proximity to, an Indian reservation. (C) For the purposes of this subsection, the average per pupil expenditure for a local educational agency shall be the aggregate current expenditures, during the second fiscal year preceding the fiscal year for which the computation is made, of all of the local educational agencies in the State in which such agency is located, plus any direct current expenditures by such State for the operation of such agencies (without regard to the sources of funds from which either of such expenditures are made), divided by the aggregate number of children who were in average daily enrollment for whom such agencies provided free Public education during such preceding fiscal year. (b) In addition to the sums appropriated for any fiscal year for grants to local educational agencies under this title, there is hereby authorized to be appropriated for any fiscal year an amount not in excess of per centum of the amount appropriated for payments on the basis of entitlements computed under subsection (a) for that fiscal year, for the purpose of enabling the Commissioner to provide financial assistance to schools on or near reservations which are not local educational agencies or have not been local educational agencies for more than three years, in accordance with the appropriate provisions of this title.

USES OF FEDERAL FUNDS

SEC. 304. Grants under this title may be used, in accordance with applications approved under section 305, for – (1) planning for and taking other steps leading to the development of programs specifically designed to meet the special educational needs of Indian children, including pilot projects designed to test the effectiveness of plans so developed; and (2) the establishment, maintenance, and operation of programs, including in accordance with special regulations of the

Commissioner, minor remodeling of classroom or other space used for such programs and acquisition of necessary equipment, specially designed to meet the special educational needs of Indian children.

SEC. 305. (a) A grant under this title, except as provided in section 303 (b), may be made only to a local educational agency or agencies, and only upon application to the Commissioner at such time or times, in such manner, and containing or accompanied by such information as the Commissioner deems necessary. Such application shall: (1) provide that the activities and services for which assistance under this title is sought will he administered by or under the supervision of the applicant; (2) set forth a program for carrying out the purposes of section 304, and provide for such methods of administration as are necessary for the proper and efficient operation of the program; (3) in the case of an application for payments for planning, provide that (A) the planning was or will be directly related to programs or projects to be carried out under this title and has resulted, or is reasonably likely to result, in a program or project which will be carried out under this title, and if the planning funds are needed because of the innovative nature of the program or project or because the local educational agency lacks the resources necessary to plan adequately for programs and projects to be carried out under this title; (4) provide that effective procedures, including provisions for appropriate objective measurement of educational achievement will be adopted for evaluating. At least annually the effectiveness of the programs and projects in meeting the special educational needs of Indian students; (5) set forth policies and procedures which assure that Federal funds made available under this title for any fiscal year will be so used as to supplement and, to the extent practical, increase the level of funds that would, in the absence of such Federal funds, be made available by the applicant for the education of Indian children and in no ease supplant such funds; (6) provide for such local control and fund accounting procedures as may be necessary to assure proper disbursement of, and accounting for, Federal funds paid to the applicant under this title; and (7) provide for making an annual report and such other reports. In such form and containing such information, as the commissioner may reasonably require to carry out his functions under this title and to determine the extent to which funds provided under this title have been effective in improving the educational opportunities of Indian students in the area served, and for keeping such record and for affording such access thereto as the Commissioner may find necessary to assure the correctness and verification of such reports. (b) An application by a local educational agency or agencies for a grant under this title may be approved only if it is consistent with the applicable provisions of this title and—(1) meets the requirements set forth in subsection (a); (2) provides that the program or project for which application is made—(A) will utilize the best available talents and resources (including persons from the Indian community) and will substantially increase the educational opportunities of Indian children in the area to be served by the applicant; and (B) has been developed - (i) in open consultation with parents of Indian children, teachers, and, where applicable, secondary school students, including public hearings at which such persons have had a full opportunity to understand the program for which assistance is being sought and to offer accommodations thereon, and (ii) with the participation and approval of a committee composed of, and selected by, parents of children participating in the program for which assistance is sought, teachers, and where applicable, secondary school students of which at least half the members shall be such parents; (C) sets forth such policies and procedures as will insure that the program for which assistance is sought will be operated and evaluated in consultation with, and the involvement of parents of the children and representatives of the area to be served, including the committee established for the purposes of clause (2) (B) (ii). (c) Amendments of applications shall, except as the Commissioner may otherwise provide by or pursuant to regulations, be subject to approval in the same manner as original applications . . .

PART B–SPECIAL PROGRAMS AND PROJECTS
TO IMPROVE EDUCATIONAL OPPORTUNITIES
FOR INDIAN CHILDREN . . .

SEC. 810. (a) The commissioner shall carry out a program of making grants for the improvement of educational opportunities for Indian children ... to support planning, pilot and demonstration projects, in accordance with subsection (b), which are designed to test and demonstrate the effectiveness of programs for improving educational opportunities for Indian children; (2) to assist in the establishment and operation of programs, in accordance with subsection (c), which are designed to stimulate (A) the provision of educational services not available to Indian children in sufficient quantity or quality and (B) the development and establishment of exemplary educational programs to serve as models for regular school programs in which Indian children are educated; (3) to assist in the establishment and operation of pre-service and in-service training programs ... for persons serving Indian children as educational personnel; and (4) to encourage the dissemination of information and materials relating to and the evaluation of the effectiveness of, education programs which may offer educational opportunities to Indian children. In the case of activities of the type described in clause (3) preference shall be given to the training of Indians. (b) The Commissioner is authorized to make grants to State and local educational agencies, federally supported elementary and secondary schools for Indian children and to Indian tribes, organizations and institutions to support planning, pilot and demonstration projects which are designated to plan for and test and demonstrate the effectiveness of, programs for improving educational opportunities for Indian children, including–(1) innovative programs related to the educational needs of educationally deprived children; (2) bilingual and bicultural education programs and projects; (3) special health and nutrition services and other related activities, which meet the special health, social and psychological problems of Indian children; and (4) coordinating the operation of other federally assisted programs which may be used to assist in meeting the needs of such children. (c) The Commissioner is also authorized to make grants to State and local educational agencies and to tribal and other Indian community organizations to assist and stimulate them in developing and establishing educational services and programs specifically designed to improve educational opportunities for Indian children. Grants may be used–to provide educational services not available to such children in sufficient quantity or quality ... remedial and compensatory instruction, school health, physical education, psychology and other services designed to assist and encourage Indian children to enter, remain in, or reenter elementary or secondary school ... comprehensive academic and vocational instruction ... instructional materials (such as library books, textbooks and other printed or published or audiovisual materials and equipment); (D) comprehensive guidance, counseling and testing services; (E) special education programs for [children with disabilities] ... bilingual and bicultural education programs; and ... other services which meet the purposes of this subsection ... (2) for the establishment and operation of exemplary and innovative educational programs and centers, involving new educational approaches, methods and techniques designed to enrich programs of elementary and secondary education for Indian children. (d) The Commissioner is also authorized to make grants to institutions of higher education and to State and local educational agencies in combination with institutions of higher education, for carrying out programs and projects–(1) to prepare persons to serve Indian children as teachers, teachers [*sic*] aides, social workers and ancillary educational personnel; and (2) to improve the qualifications of such persons who are serving Indian children in such capacities. Grants for the purposes of this subsection may be used for the establishment of fellowship programs leading to an advanced degree, for institutes and, as part of a continuing program, for seminars, symposia, workshops and conferences. In carrying out the programs authorized by this subsection, preference shall be given to the training of Indians...

SEC. 441. (a) There is hereby established, in the office of Education, a bureau to be known as the "Office of Indian Education" which under the direction of the commissioner, shall have the responsibility for administering the provisions of title III of the Act of September 30, 1950, (Public Law 874, Eighty-first Congress), as added by this Act, section 810 of title VIII of the Elementary and Secondary Education Act of 1964, as added by this Act and section 314 of title III of the Elementary and Secondary Education Amendments of 1966, as added by this Act. The Office shall be headed by a Deputy Commissioner of Indian Education, who shall be appointed by the Commissioner of Education from a list of nominees submitted to him by the national Advisory Council on Indian Education . . .

SEC. 442. (a) There is hereby established the national Advisory council on Indian Education (referred to in this title as the "National Council") which shall consist of fifteen members who are Indians and Alaska Natives appointed by the President of the

United States. Such appointments shall be made by the President from lists of nominees furnished, from time to time, by Indian tribes and organizations and shall represent diverse geographic areas of the country.

Approved June 23, 1972.

Chapter XXII

Loans at Last: Indian Financing Act of 1974

THE INDIAN FINANCING Act of 1974 increased economic opportunities for tribes and individual tribal members by making credit available at relatively affordable interest rates, i.e., rates more in alignment with banking practices common in other American communities. This public law authorized additional funding and provided loan guarantees, insurance, and interest payments to encourage tribal use of private lenders. More specifically, it encouraged the extension of credit to tribal members—for both personal and collective enterprises—through its extension of loan guarantees, insurance, and interest payments to banks.

Indian Financing Act of 1974

AN ACT[2] ... To provide for financing the economic development of Indians and Indian organizations, and for other purposes, *Be it enacted by the Senate and House of Representatives of the United States of America in Congress assembled,* That this Act may be cited as the "Indian Financing Act of 1974" ... SEC. 2. It is hereby declared to be the policy of Congress to provide capital on a reimbursable basis to help develop and utilize Indian resources, both physical and human, to a point

"... It continues to be my hope that ... we can create a new era in which the future of Indian people is determined primarily by Indian acts and Indian decisions ..."[1]

RICHARD NIXON
SPEAKING ON APRIL 13, 1974,
UPON HIS SIGNING OF THE
INDIAN FINANCING ACT

197

where the Indians will fully exercise responsibility for the utilization and management of their own resources and where they will enjoy a standard of living from their own productive efforts comparable to that enjoyed by non-Indians in neighboring communities ...

SEC. 3. For the purpose of this Act, the term—(a) "Secretary" means the Secretary of the Interior. (b) "Indian" means any person who is a member of any Indian tribe, band, group, pueblo, or community which is recognized by the Federal Government as eligible for services from the Bureau of Indian Affairs and any "Native" as defined in the Alaska Native Claims Settlement Act (85 Stat. 688). (c) "Tribe" means any Indian tribe, band, group, pueblo, or community, including Native villages and Native groups (including corporations organized by Kenai, Juneau, Sitka, and Kodiak) as defined in the Alaska Native Claims Settlement Act which is recognized by the Federal Government as eligible for services from the Bureau of Indian Affairs. (d) "Reservation" includes Indian reservations, public domain Indian allotments, former Indian reservations in Oklahoma, and land held by incorporated Native groups, regional corporations, and village corporations under the provisions of the Alaska Native Claims Settlement Act. (e) "Economic enterprise" means any Indian-owned (as defined by the Secretary of the Interior) commercial, industrial, or business activity established or organized for the purpose of profit: *Provided*, That such Indian ownership shall constitute not less than 51 per centum of the enterprise. (f) "Organization," unless otherwise specified, shall be the governing body of any Indian tribe, as defined in subsection I hereof, or entity established or recognized by such governing body for the purpose of this Act. (g) "Other organizations" means any non-Indian individual, firm, corporation, partnership, or association.

SEC. 4. No provision of this or any other Act shall be construed to terminate or otherwise curtail the assistance or activities of the Small Business Administration or any other Federal agency with respect to any Indian tribe, organization, or individual because of their eligibility for assistance under this Act.

SEC. 101. In order to provide credit that is not available from private money markets, all funds that are now or hereafter a part of the revolving fund authorized by the Act of June 18, 1934 (48 Stat. 986), the Act of June 26, 1936 (49 Stat. 1968), and the Act of April 19, 1950 (64 Stat. 44), as amended and supplemented, including sums received in settlement of debts of livestock pursuant to the Act of May 24, 1950 (64 Stat. 190), and sums collected in repayment of loans heretofore or hereafter made, and as interest or other charges on loans, shall hereafter be administered as a single Indian Revolving Loan Fund. The fund shall be available for loans to Indians having a form of organization that is satisfactory to the Secretary and for loans to individual Indians who are not members of or eligible for membership in an organization which is making loans to its members: *Provided,* That, where the Secretary determines a rejection of a loan application from a member of an organization making loans to its membership from moneys borrowed from the fund is unwarranted, he may, in his discretion, make a direct-loan to such individual from the fund. The fund shall also be available for administrative expenses incurred in connection therewith.

"... SEC. 101 ... [if] ... the Secretary determines a rejection of a loan application ... is unwarranted, he may, in his discretion, make a direct-loan to such individual from the fund ..."

SEC. 102. Loans may be made for any purpose which will promote the economic development of (a) the individual Indian borrower, including loans for educational purposes, and (b) the Indian organization and its members including loans by such organizations to other organizations and investments in other organizations regardless of whether they are organizations of Indians: *Provided,* That not more than 50 per centum of loan made to an organization shall be used by such organization for the purpose of making loans to or investments in non-Indian organizations.

SEC. 103. Loans may be made only when, in the judgment of the Secretary, there is a reasonable prospect of repayment, and only to applicants who in the opinion of the Secretary are unable to obtain financing from other sources on reasonable terms and conditions.

SEC. 104. Loans shall be for terms that do not exceed thirty years and shall bear interest at (a) a rate determined by the Secretary of the Treasury taking into consideration the market yield on municipal bonds: *Provided*, That in no event shall the rate be greater than the rate determined by the Secretary of the Treasury taking into consideration the current average yield on outstanding marketable obligations of the United States of comparable maturity, plus (b) such additional charge, if any, toward covering other costs of the program as the Secretary may determine to be consistent with its purpose: *Provided*, That educational loans may provide for interest to be deferred while the borrower is in school or in the military service.

SEC. 105. The Secretary may cancel, adjust, compromise, or reduce the amount of any loan or any portion thereof heretofore or hereafter made from the revolving loan fund established by this title and its predecessor constituent funds which he determines to be uncollectable in whole or in part, or which is collectable only at an unreasonable cost, or when such action would, in his judgment be in the best interests of the United States: *Provided*, That proceedings pursuant to this sentence shall be effective only after following the procedure prescribed by the Act of July 1, 1932 (47 Stat. 564.25 U.S.C. 386a). He may also adjust, compromise, subordinate, or modify the terms of any mortgage, lease, assignment, contract, agreement, or other document taken to secure such loans.

SEC. 106. Title to any land purchased by a tribe or by an individual Indian with loans made from the revolving loan fund may be taken in trust unless the land is located outside the boundaries of a reservation or a tribal consolidation area approved by the Secretary. Title to any land purchased by a tribe or an individual Indian which is outside the boundaries of the reservation or approved consolidation area may be taken in trust if the purchaser was the owner of trust or restricted interests in the land before the purchase, otherwise title shall be taken in the name of the purchasers without any restriction on alienation, control, or use. Title to any personal property purchased with a loan from the revolving loan fund shall be taken in the name of the purchaser ...

SEC. 108. There is authorized to be appropriated, to provide capital and to restore any impairment of capital for the revolving loan fund $50,000,000 exclusive of prior authorizations and appropriations.

TITLE II—LOAN GUARANTY AND INSURANCE

SEC. 201. In order to provide access to private money sources which otherwise would not be available, the Secretary is authorized (a) to guarantee not to exceed 90 per centum of the unpaid principal and interest due on any loan made to any organization of Indians having a form or organization satisfactory to the Secretary, and to individual Indians who are not members of or eligible for membership in an organization which is making loans to its members; and (b) in lieu of such guaranty, to insure loans under an agreement approved by the Secretary whereby the lender will be reimbursed for losses in an amount not to exceed 15 per centum of the aggregate of such loans made by it, but not to exceed 90 per centum of the loss on any one loan ...

SEC. 203. Loans guaranteed or insured pursuant to this title shall bear interest (exclusive of premium charges for insurance, and service charge, if any) at rates not to exceed such per centum per annum on the principal obligation outstanding as the Secretary determines to be reasonable taking into consideration the range of interest rates prevailing in the private market for similar loans and the risks assumed by the United States.

SEC. 204. The application for a loan to be guaranteed hereunder shall be submitted to the Secretary for prior approval. Upon approval, the Secretary shall issue a certificate as evidence of the guaranty. Such certificate shall be issued only when, in the judgment of the Secretary, there is a reasonable prospect of repayment. No loan to an individual Indian may be guaranteed or insured which would cause the total unpaid principal indebtedness to exceed $100.000. No loan to an economic enterprise (as defined in section 3) in excess of $100,000, or such lower amount as the Secretary may determine to be appropriate, shall be insured unless prior approval of the loan is obtained from the Secretary ...

SEC. 210. The maturity of any loan guaranteed or insured hereunder shall not exceed thirty years ...

SEC. 213. Whenever the Secretary finds that any lender or holder of conditions, a guaranty certificate fails to maintain adequate accounting records, or to demonstrate proper ability to service adequately loans guaranteed or insured, or to exercise proper credit judgment, or has willfully or negligently engaged in practices otherwise detrimental to the interests of a borrower or of the United States, he may refuse, either temporarily or permanently, to guarantee or insure any further loans made by such lender or holder, and may bar such lender or holder from acquiring additional loans guaranteed or insured hereunder: *Provided*, That the Secretary shall not refuse to pay a valid guaranty or insurance claim on loans previously made in good faith.

SEC. 214. Any evidence of guaranty or insurance issued by the Secretary shall be conclusive evidence of the eligibility of the loan for guaranty or insurance under the provisions of this Act and the amount of such guaranty or insurance: *Provided,* That nothing in this section shall preclude the Secretary from establishing, as against the original lender, defenses based on fraud or material misrepresentation or bar him from establishing, by regulations in force at the date of such issuance or disbursement, whichever is the earlier partial defenses to the amount payable on the guaranty or insurance.

SEC. 215. Title to any land purchased by a tribe or by an individual Indian with loans guaranteed or insured pursuant to this title may be taken in trust, unless the land is located outside the boundaries of a reservation or a tribal consolidation area approved by the Secretary. Title to any land purchased by a tribe or an individual Indian which is outside the boundaries of the reservation or approved consolidation area may be taken in trust if the purchaser was the owner of trust or restricted interests in the land before the purchase, otherwise title shall be taken in the name of the purchaser without any restriction on alienation, control, or use. Title to any personal property purchased with loans guaranteed or insured hereunder shall be taken in the name of the purchaser.

SEC. 216. The financial transactions of the Secretary incident to arising out of the guarantee or insurance of loans, and the acquisition management, and disposition of property, real, personal, or mixed, incident to such activities, shall be final and conclusive upon all officers of the Government. With respect to matters arising out of the guaranty or insurance program authorized by this title, and notwithstanding the provisions of any other laws, the Secretary may - (a) sue and be sued in his official capacity in any court of competent jurisdiction; (b) subject to the specific limitations in this title, consent to the modification, with respect to the rate of interest, time of payment on principal or interest or any portion thereof, security, or any other provisions of any note, contract, mortgage, or other instrument securing a loan which has been guaranteed or insured hereunder; (c) subject to the specific limitations in this title, pay, or compromise, any claim on, or arising because of any loan guaranty or insurance; (d) subject to the specific limitations in this title, pay, compromise, waive, or release any right, title, claim, lien, or demand, however acquired, including, but not limited to, any equity or right of redemption; (e) purchase at any sale, public or private, upon such terms and for such prices as he determines to be reasonable, and take title to property, real, personal, or mixed; and similarly sell, at public or private sale, exchange, assign, convey, or otherwise dispose of such property; and (f) complete, administer, operate, obtain, and pay for insurance on, and maintain, renovate, repair, modernize, lease, or otherwise deal with any property acquired or held pursuant to the guaranty or insurance program authorized by this title.

SEC. 217. (a) There is hereby created an Indian Loan Guaranty and Insurance Fund (hereinafter referred to as the "fund") which shall be available to the Secretary as a revolving fund without fiscal year limitation for carrying out the provisions of this title. (b) The Secretary may use the fund for the purpose of fulfilling the obligations with respect to loans guaranteed or insured under this title, but the aggregate of such loans which are insured or guaranteed by the Secretary shall be limited to $200,000,000. (c) All funds, claims, notes, mortgages, contracts, and property acquired by the Secretary under this section, and all collections and proceeds therefrom, shall constitute assets of the fund; and all liabilities and obligations of such assets shall be liabilities and obligations of the fund ...

SEC. 218. The Secretary shall promulgate rules and regulations to carry out the provisions of this title ...

TITLE IV—INDIAN BUSINESS GRANTS

SEC. 401. There is established within the Department of the Interior the Indian Business Development Program whose purpose is to stimulate and increase Indian entrepreneurship and employment by providing equity capital through non-reimbursable grants made by the Secretary of the Interior to Indians and Indian tribes to establish and expand profit-making Indian-owned economic enterprises on or near reservations.

SEC. 402. (a) No grant in excess of $50,000, or such lower amount as the Secretary may determine to be appropriate, may be made to an Indian or Indian tribe. (b) A grant may be made only to an applicant who, in the opinion of the Secretary, is unable to obtain adequate financing for its economic enterprise

"... SEC. 401 ... increase Indian entrepreneurship and employment by providing equity capital through non-reimbursable grants ... to establish and expand profit-making Indian-owned economic enterprises on or near reservations ..."

from other sources: *Provided,* That, prior to making any grant under this title, the Secretary shall assure that, where practical, the applicant has reasonably made available for the economic enterprise funds from the applicant's own financial resources. No grant may be made to an applicant who is unable to obtain at least 60 per centum of the necessary funds for the economic enterprise from other sources.

SEC. 403. There are authorized to be appropriated not to exceed the sum of $10,000,000 for each of the fiscal years 1975, 1976, and 1977 for the purposes of this title.

SEC. 404. The Secretary of the Interior is authorized to prescribe such rules and regulations as may be necessary to carry out the purposes of this Act.

TITLE V

SEC. 501 ... the Secretary shall insure that the loan or grant applicant shall be provided competent management and technical assistance consistent with the nature of the enterprise being funded.

SEC. 502 ... the Secretary is authorized to cooperate with the Small Business Administration and ACTION and other Federal agencies in the use of existing programs of this character in those agencies ... [and] ... is authorized to enter into contracts with private organizations for providing such services and assistance.

SEC. 503 ... the Secretary is authorized to use not to exceed 5 per centum of any funds appropriated for any fiscal year pursuant to section 302 of this Act.

Approved April 12, 1974.

Chapter XXIII

Administrative Rights Returned: Indian Self-Determination & Education Assistance Act of 1975

TRIBAL CONTROL OVER the education of Indian children gained strength through passage of the Indian Self-Determination and Education Assistance Act of 1975. This public law mandated tribal authority over Johnson-O'Malley education programming, including educational services delivered to tribal and other children through off-reservation boarding or day schools. Notably, it shifted control away from off-reservation public school districts, and returned to tribes the legal authority to administer all Bureau of Indian Affairs education and social service programming. In a historically unique move, American Indian community leaders were consulted prior to the drafting of this legislation.[2]

"It is the sense of Congress that the absence of locally convenient day schools may contribute to the breakup of Indian families." [1]

Indian Self-Determination & Education Assistance Act of 1975

AN ACT[3] ... To provide maximum Indian participation in the government and education of the Indian people; to provide for the full participation of Indian tribes in programs and services conducted by the Federal Government for Indians and to encourage the development of human resources of the Indian people; to establish a program of assistance to upgrade Indian education; to support the right of Indian citizens to control their own educational activities; and for other purposes. *Be it enacted by the Senate and House of Representatives of the United States of America in Congress Assembled,* That this Act maybe cited as the "Indian Self-Determination and Education Assistance Act."

CONGRESSIONAL FINDINGS

SEC. 2. (a) The Congress ... finds that—(1) the prolonged Federal domination of Indian service programs has served to retard rather than enhance the progress of Indian people and their communities by depriving Indians of the full opportunity to development leadership skills crucial to the realization of self-government, and has denied to the Indian people an effective voice in the planning and implementation of programs for the benefit of Indians which are responsive to the true needs of Indian communities; and (2) the Indian people will never surrender their desire to control their relationships both among themselves and with non-Indian governments, organizations and persons. (b) The Congress further finds that—(1) true self-determination in any society of people is dependent upon an educational process which will insure the development of qualified people to fulfill meaningful leadership roles; (2) the Federal responsibility for and assistance to education of Indian children has not affected the desired level of educational achievement or created the diverse opportunities and personal satisfaction which education can and should provide; and (3) parental and community control of the educational process is of crucial importance to the Indian people.

DECLARATION OF POLICY

SEC. 3. (a) The Congress hereby recognizes the obligation of the United States to respond to the strong expression of the Indian people for self-determination by assuring maximum Indian participation in the direction of educational as well as other Federal services to Indian communities so as to render such services more responsive to the desires of those communities. (b) The Congress declares its commitment to the maintenance of the Federal Government's unique and continuing relationship with and responsibility to the Indian people through the establishment of a meaningful Indian self-determination policy which will permit an orderly transition from Federal domination of programs for and services to Indians to effective and meaningful participation by the Indian people in the planning, conduct, and administration of those programs and services. (c) The Congress declares that a major national goal of the United States is to provide the quantity and quality of educational services and opportunities which will permit Indian children to compete and excel in the life areas of their choice, and to achieve the measure of self-determination essential to their social and economic well-being ...

"... AN ACT[3] ... To provide ... Indian participation in the government and education of the Indian people ... encourage the development of human resources of the Indian people ... upgrade Indian education ... support the right of Indian citizens to control their own educational activities ..."

SEC. 4. For the purposes of this Act, the term—(a) "Indian" means a person who is a member of an Indian tribe; (b) "Indian tribe" means any Indian tribe, band, nation, or other organized group or community, including any Alaskan Native village or regional or village corporation as established or defined in the Alaskan Native Claims Settlement Act (85 Stat. 588) which is recognized as eligible for the special programs and services provided by the United States to Indians because of their status as Indians; (c) "Tribal organization" means the tribal governing body of any Indian tribe; any legally established organization of Indians which is controlled, sanctioned, or chartered by such governing body or which is democratically elected by the adult members of the Indian community to be served by such organization and which includes the maximum participation of Indians in all phases of its activities: *Provided,* That in any case where a contract is let or grant made to an organization to perform services benefitting more than one Indian tribe, the approval of each such Indian tribe shall be a prerequisite to the letting or making of such contract or grant; (d) "Secretary," unless otherwise designated, means the Secretary of the Interior; (f)[*sic*] "State education agency" means the State board of education or other agency or officer primarily responsible for supervision by the State of public elementary and secondary schools, or, if there is no such officer or agency designated by the Governor or by State law . . .

TITLE I—INDIAN SELF-DETERMINATION ACT
SEC. 1. This title may be cited as the "Indian Self-Determination Act."

CONTRACTS BY THE SECRETARY OF THE INTERIOR
SEC. 102. (a) The Secretary of the Interior is directed, upon the request of any Indian tribe, to enter into a contract or contracts with any tribal organization of any such Indian tribe to plan, conduct, and administer programs, or portions thereof, provided for in the Act of April 16, 1934 (48 Stat. 546), as amended by this Act, any other program or portion thereof which the Secretary of the Interior is authorized to administer for the benefit of Indians under the Act of November 2, 1921 (42 Stat, 208) [i.e., the Snyder Act] ... and any Act subsequent thereto: *Provided, however,* That the Secretary may initially decline to enter into any contract requested by an Indian tribe if he finds that: (1) the service to be rendered to the Indian beneficiaries of the particular program or function to be contracted will not be satisfactory; (2) adequate protection of trust resources is not assured, or (3) the proposed project or function to be contracted for cannot be properly completed or maintained by the proposed contract: *Provided further,* That in arriving at his finding, the Secretary shall consider whether the tribe or tribal organization would be deficient in performance under the contract with respect to (A) equipment, (B) bookkeeping and accounting procedures, (C) substantive knowledge of the program to be contracted for, (D) community support for the contract, (E) adequately trained personnel, or (F) other necessary components of contract performance. (b) Whenever the Secretary declines to enter into a contract or contracts pursuant to subsection (a) of this section, he shall (1) state his objections in writing to the tribe within sixty days, (2) provide to the extent practicable assistance to the tribe or tribal organization to overcome his stated objections, and (3) provide the tribe with a hearing, under such rules and regulations as he may promulgate, and the opportunity for appeal on the objections raised. The Secretary is authorized to require any tribe requesting that he enter into a contract pursuant to the

provisions of this title to obtain adequate liability insurance ...

CONTRACTS BY THE SECRETARY OF HEALTH,
EDUCATION AND WELFARE

SEC. 103. (a) The Secretary of Health, Education, and Welfare is directed, upon the request of any Indian tribe, to enter into a contract or contracts with any tribal organization of any such Indian tribe to carry out any or all of his functions, authorities, and responsibilities under the Act of August 5, 1954 (68 Stat. 674), as amended: *Provided, however,* That the Secretary may initially decline to enter into any contract requested by an Indian tribe if he finds that: (1) the service to be rendered to the Indian beneficiaries of the particular program or function to be contracted for will not be satisfactory; (2) adequate protection of trust resources is not assured; or (3) the proposed project or function to be contracted for cannot be properly completed or maintained by the proposed contract: *Provided further,* That the Secretary of Health, Education and Welfare, in arriving at his finding, shall consider whether the tribe or tribal organization would be deficient in performance under the contract with respect to (A) equipment, (B) bookkeeping and accounting procedures, (C) substantive knowledge of the program to be contracted for, (D) community support for the contract, (E) adequately trained personnel, or (F) other necessary components of contract performance. (b) Whenever the Secretary of Health, Education, and Welfare declines to enter into a contract or contracts pursuant to subsection (a) of this section, he shall (1) state his objections in writing to the tribe within sixty days; (2) provide, to the extent practicable, assistance to the tribe or tribal organization to overcome his stated objections; and (3) provide the tribe with a hearing, under such rules and regulations as he shall promulgate, and the opportunity for appeal on the objections raised. (c) The Secretary of Health, Education, and Welfare is authorized to require any tribe requesting that he enter into a contract pursuant to the provisions of this title to obtain adequate liability insurance ...

GRANTS TO INDIAN TRIBAL ORGANIZATIONS

SEC. 104. (a) The Secretary of the Interior is authorized, upon the request of any Indian tribe from funds appropriated for the benefit of Indians pursuant to the Act of November 2, 1921 (42

Stat. 208), and any Act subsequent thereto) to contract with or make a grant or grants to any tribal organization for—(1) the strengthening or improvement of tribal government (including, but not limited to, the development, improvement, and administration of planning, financial management, or merit personnel systems; the improvement of tribally funded programs or activities; or the development, construction, improvement, maintenance, preservation, or operation of tribal facilities or resources); (2) the planning, training, evaluation of other activity designed to improve the capacity of a tribal organization to enter into a contract or contracts pursuant to section 102 of this Act and the additional costs associated with the initial years operation under such a contract or contracts; (3) the acquisition of land in connection with items (1) and (2) above; *Provided*, That in the case of land within reservation boundaries or which adjoins on at least two sides lands held in trust by the United States for the tribe or for individual Indians, the Secretary of Interior may (upon request of the tribe) acquire such land in trust for the tribe; or (4) the planning, designing, monitoring, and evaluating of Federal programs serving the tribe. (b) The Secretary of Health, Education, and Welfare may, in accordance with regulations adopted pursuant to section 107 of this Act, make grants to any Indian tribe or tribal organization for—(1) the development, construction, operation, provision, or maintenance of adequate health facilities or services including the training of personnel for such work, from funds appropriated to the Indian Health Service for Indian health services or Indian or health facilities; or (2) planning, training, evaluation or other activities designed to improve the capacity of a tribal organization to enter into a contract or contracts pursuant to section 103 of this Act. (c) The provisions of any other Act notwithstanding, any funds made available to a tribal organization under grants pursuant to this section may be used as matching shares for any other Federal grant programs which contribute to the purposes for which grants under this section are made ...

EFFECT ON EXISTING RIGHTS

SEC. 110. Nothing in this Act shall be construed as—(1) affecting, modifying, diminishing, or otherwise impairing the sovereign immunity from suit enjoyed by an Indian tribe; or (2) authorizing or requiring the termination of any existing trust responsibility of the United States with respect to the Indian people.

TITLE II—THE INDIAN EDUCATION ASSISTANCE ACT
SEC. 201. This title may be cited as the "Indian Education Assistance Act."

PART A–EDUCATION OF INDIANS IN PUBLIC SCHOOLS
SEC. 202. The Act of April 16, 1934 (48 Stat, 586), as amended, is further amended by adding at the end thereof the following new sections:

SEC. 4. The Secretary of the Interior shall not enter into any contract for the education of Indians unless the prospective contractor has submitted to, and has had approved by the Secretary of the Interior, an education plan, which plan, in the determination of the Secretary, contains educational objectives which adequately address the educational needs of the Indian students who are to be beneficiaries of the contract and assures that the contract is capable of meeting such objectives: *Provided*, That where students other than Indian students participate in such programs, money expended under such contract shall be prorated to cover the participation of only the Indian students.

SEC. 5. (a.) Whenever a school district affected by a contract or contracts for the education of Indians pursuant to this Act has a local school board not composed of a majority of Indians, the parents of the Indian children enrolled in the school or schools affected by such contract or contracts shall elect a local committee from among their number. Such committee shall fully participate in the development of, and shall have the authority to approve or disapprove, programs to be conducted under such contract or contracts, and shall carry out such other duties, and be so structured, as the Secretary of the Interior shall by regulation provide ...

SEC. 6. Any school district educating Indian students who are members of recognized Indian tribes, who do not normally reside in the State in which such school district is located, and who are residing in Federal boarding facilities for the purposes of attending public schools within such district may, in the discretion of the Secretary of the Interior, be reimbursed by him for the full per capita costs of educating such Indian students.

SEC. 203. After conferring with persons competent in the field of Indian education, the Secretary in consultation with the Secretary of Health, Education, and Welfare, shall prepare and submit to the Committees on Interior and Insular Affairs of the United States Senate and House of Representatives not later than October 4, 1975, a report which shall include: (1) a comprehensive analysis of the Act of April 16, 1934 (48 Stat.596), as amended, including—(A) factors determining the allocation of funds for the special or supplemental educational programs of Indian students and current operating expenditures; (B) the relationship of the Act of April 16, 1934 (48 Stat. 596), as amended, to- (i) title I of the Act of September 30, 1950 (64 Stat. 1100), as amended; and (ii) the Act of April 11, 1965 (79 Stat. 27), as amended; and (iii) title IV of the Act of June 23 1972 (86 Stat. 235); and (iv) the Act of September 23, 1950 (72 Stat. 548), as amended. (2) a specific program to meet the special educational needs of Indian children who attend public schools. Such program shall include, but need not be limited to, the following: (A) a plan for the equitable distribution of funds to meet the special or supplemental educational needs of Indian children and, where necessary, to provide general operating expenditures to schools and school districts educating Indian children; and (B) an estimate of the cost of such program; (3) detailed legislative recommendations to implement the program prepared pursuant to clause (2); and (4) a specific program, together with detailed legislative recommendations, to assist the development and administration of Indian-controlled community colleges.

PART B—SCHOOL CONSTRUCTION

SEC. 204. (a) The Secretary is authorized to enter into a contract or contracts with any State education agency or school district for the purpose of assisting such agency or district in the acquisition of sites for, or the construction, acquisition, or renovation of facilities (including all necessary equipment) in school districts on or adjacent to or in close proximity to any Indian reservations or other lands held in trust by the United States for Indians, if such facilities are necessary for the education of Indians residing on any such reservation or lands. (b) The Secretary may expend not less than 75 per centum of such funds as are authorized and appropriated pursuant to this part B on those projects which meet the eligibility requirements under subsections (a) and (b) of section 14 of the Act of September 23, 1950 (72 Stat. 548), as amended ... (c) The Secretary may expend not more than 25 percent of such funds as may be authorized and appropriated pursuant to this part B on any school eligible to receive funds under section 208 of this Act. (d) Any contract entered into by the Secretary pursuant to this section shall contain provisions requiring the relevant State educational agency to–(1) provide Indian students attending any such facilities constructed, acquired, or renovated, in whole or in part, from funds made available pursuant to this section with standards of education not less than those provided non-Indian students in the school district in which the facilities are situated; and (2) meet, with respect to such facilities, the requirements of the State and local building codes, and other building standards set by the State educational agency or school district for other public school facilities under its jurisdiction or control or by the government in the jurisdiction within which the facilities are situated ...

PART C—GENERAL PROVISIONS

SEC. 205. No funds from any grant or contract pursuant to this title shall be made available to any school district when the Secretary is satisfied that the quality and standard of education, including facilities and auxiliary services, for Indian students enrolled in the schools of such district are at least equal to that provided all other students from resources, other than resources provided in this title, available to the local school district.

SEC. 206. No funds from any contract or grant pursuant to this title shall be made available by any Federal agency directly to other than public agencies and Indian tribes, institutions, and organizations: *Provided,* That school districts, State education agencies and Indian tribes, institutions, and organizations assisted by this title may use funds provided herein to contract for necessary services with any appropriate individual, organization, or corporation ...

SEC. 208. The Secretary is authorized and directed to provide funds, pursuant to this Act, the Act of April 16, 1934 (48 Stat. 596), as amended or any other authority granted to him or to any tribe or tribal organization which controls and manages any previously private school ...

SEC. 209. The assistance provided in this Act for the education of Indians in the public schools of any State is in addition and supplemental to assistance provided under title IV of the Act of June 23, 1972 (88 Stat. 235).

Approved January 4, 1975.

Chapter XXIV

Access to Local Health Care: The Indian Health Care Improvement Act of 1976

THE INDIAN HEALTH Care Improvement Act of 1976 increased tribal control of health programming and healthcare services. Significantly, it expanded reservation health service eligibility to include tribal affiliates living off-reservation. Designed to improve tribal health outcomes, it mandated a broad range of educational and service-based strategies. Furthermore, it initiated a focus on the recruitment of Indian Health Service personnel from within tribal communities, and mandated the support of their studies through grant programs, college scholarships, and continuing education allowances. It also mandated the development of healthcare service sites within reservations boundaries.[2]

"On average ... men in Bangladesh can expect to live longer than Native American men in South Dakota."

U.S. COMMISSION ON CIVIL RIGHTS REPORT OF 2000[1]

The Indian Health Care Improvement Act of 1976

AN ACT[3] ... To implement the federal responsibility for the care and education of the Indian people by improving the services and facilities of federal Indian Health Programs and encouraging maximum participation of Indians in such programs and for other purposes. Be it enacted by the Senate and House of Representatives of the United States of America in Congress

217

assembled, That this act may be cited as the "Indian Health Care Improvement Act" ... Findings ... SEC. 2. The Congress finds that - (a) federal health services to maintain and improve the health of the Indians are consistent with and required by the Federal Government's historical and unique legal relationship with, and resulting responsibility to, the American Indian people. (b) A major national goal of the United States is to provide the quantity and quality of health services which will permit the health status of Indians to be raised to the highest possible level and to encourage the maximum participation of Indians in the planning and management of those services. (c) Federal health services to Indians have resulted in a reduction in the prevalence and incidence of preventable illnesses among, and unnecessary and premature deaths of, Indians. (d) Despite such services the unmet health needs of the American Indian people are severe and the health status of the Indians is far below that of the general population of the United States. For example, for Indians compared to all Americans in 1971, the tuberculosis death rate was over four and one-half times greater, the influenza and pneumonia death rate over one and one-half times greater, and the infant death rate approximately 20 percent greater. (e) All other Federal services and programs in fulfillment of the Federal responsibility to Indians are jeopardized by the low health status of the American Indian people. (f) Further improvement in Indian health is imperiled by (1) inadequate, outdated, inefficient, and undermanned facilities. For example, only twenty-four of fifty-one Indian Health Service hospitals are accredited by the Joint Commission on Accreditation of Hospitals; only thirty-one meet national fire and safety codes and fifty-two locations with Indian populations have been identified as requiring either new or replacement health centers and stations, or clinics remodeled for improved or additional service; (2) shortage of personnel. For example, about one-half of the Service hospitals, four-fifths of the Service hospital outpatient clinics, and one-half of the Service health clinics meet only 80 percent of staffing standards for their respective services; (3) insufficient services in such areas as laboratory, hospital inpatient and outpatient, eye care and mental health services, and services available through contracts with private physicians, clinics and agencies. For example, about 90 per centum of the surgical operations needed for otitis media have not been performed, over 57 per centum of required dental services remain to be provided, and about 98 per centum of hearing aid requirements are unmet; (4) related support factors. For example, over seven hundred housing units are needed for staff at remote Service facilities; (5) lack of access of Indians to health services due to remote residences, undeveloped or underdeveloped communication and transportations systems, and difficult, sometimes severe, climate conditions; and (6) lack of safe water and sanitary waste disposal services. For example, over thirty-seven thousand four hundred existing and forty-eight thousand nine hundred and sixty planned replacement and renovated Indian housing Units need new or upgraded water and sanitation facilities. (g) The Indian people's growth of confidence in Federal Indian health services is revealed by their increasingly heavy use of such services. Progress toward the goal of better Indian health is dependent on this continued growth of confidence. Both such progress and such confidence are dependent on improved Federal Indian health services.

DECLARATION OF POLICY

SEC. 3. The Congress hereby declares that it is the policy of this Nation, in fulfillment of its special responsibilities and legal obligation to the American Indian people, to meet the national goal of providing the highest possible health status to Indians and to provide existing Indian health services with all resources necessary to effect [sic] that policy.

DEFINITIONS

SEC. 4. For purposes of this Act (a) "Secretary," unless otherwise designated, means the Secretary of Health, Education, and Welfare. (b) "Service" means the Indian Health Service. (c) "Indians" or "Indian," unless otherwise designated, means any person who is a member of an Indian tribe, as defined in subsection (d) hereof, except that, for the purpose of sections 102, 103, and 201(c) (5), such terms shall mean any individual who (1), irrespective of whether he or she lives on or near a reservation, is a member of a tribe, band, or other organized group of Indians, including those tribes, bands, or groups terminated since 1940 and those recognized now or in the future by the State in which they reside, or who is a descendant, in the first or second degree, of any such member, or (2) is an Eskimo or Aleut or other Alaska Native, or (3) is considered by the Secretary of the Interior to be an Indian for any purpose, or (4) is determined to be an Indian under regulations promulgated by the Secretary. (d) "Indian tribe" means any Indian tribe, band, nation, or other organized group or community, including any Alaska Native village or group or regional or village corporation as defined in or established pursuant to the Alaska Native Claims Settlement Act (85 Stat. 688), which is recognized as eligible for the special programs and services provided by the United States to Indians because of their status as Indians. (e) "Tribal organization" means the elected governing body of any Indian tribe or any legally established organization of Indians which is controlled by one or more such bodies or by a board of directors elected or selected by one or more such bodies (or elected by the Indian population to be served by such organization) and which includes the maximum participation of Indians in all phases of its activities. (f) "Urban Indian" means any individual who resides in an urban center, as defined in subsection (g) hereof, and who meets one or more of the four criteria in subsection (c) (1) through (4) of this section. (g) "Urban center" means any community which has a sufficient urban Indian population with unmet health needs to warrant assistance under title V, as determined by the Secretary. (h) "Urban Indian organization" means a nonprofit corporate body situated in an urban center, composed of urban Indians, and providing for the maximum participation of all interested Indian groups and individuals, which body is capable of legally cooperating with other public and private entities for the purpose of performing the activities described in section 503(a).

TITLE I—INDIAN HEALTH MANPOWER PURPOSE

SEC. 101. The purpose of this title is to augment the inadequate number of health professionals serving Indians and remove the multiple barriers to the entrance of health professionals into the Service and private practice among Indians.

"... SEC. 101 ... augment the inadequate number of health professionals serving Indians. . ."

HEALTH PROFESSIONS RECRUITMENT PROGRAM FOR INDIANS

SEC. 102. (a) The Secretary, acting through the Service, shall make grants to public or nonprofit private health or educational entities or Indian tribes or tribal organizations to assist such entities in meeting the costs of- (1) identifying Indians with ... potential for education or training in the health professions and encouraging and assisting them (A) to enroll in schools of medicine, osteopathy, dentistry, veterinary medicine, optometry, podiatry, pharmacy, public health, nursing or allied health professions; or (B) if they are not qualified to enroll in any such school, to undertake such post-secondary education or training as may be required to qualify them for enrollment; (2) publicizing existing sources of financial aid available to Indians enrolled in any school referred to in clause (1) (A) of this subsection or who are undertaking training necessary to qualify them to enroll in any such school; or (3) establishing other programs which the Secretary determines will enhance and facilitate the enrollment of Indians, and the subsequent pursuit and completion by them of courses of study, in any school referred to in clause (1) (A) of this subsection. (b) (1) No grant may be made under this section unless an application therefore has been submitted to, and approved by, the Secretary. Such application shall be in such form, submitted in such manner, and contain such information, as the Secretary shall by regulation prescribe: *Provided,* That the Secretary shall give a preference to applications submitted by Indian tribes or tribal organizations. (2) The amount of any grant under this section shall be determined by the Secretary. Payments pursuant to grants under this section may be made in advance or by way of reimbursement, and at such intervals and on such conditions as the Secretary finds necessary. (c) For the purpose of making payments pursuant to grants under this section, there are authorized to be appropriated $900,000 for fiscal year 1978, $1,500,000 for fiscal year 1979, and $1,800,000 for fiscal year 1980. For fiscal years 1981, 1982, 1983, and 1984 there are authorized to be appropriated for such payments such sums as may be specifically authorized by an Act enacted after this Act.

HEALTH PROFESSIONS PREPARATORY SCHOLARSHIP
PROGRAM FOR INDIANS

SEC. 103. (a) The Secretary, acting through the Service, shall make scholarship grants to Indians who- (1) have successfully completed their high school education or high school equivalency; and (2) have demonstrated the capability to successfully complete courses of study in: schools of medicine, osteopathy, dentist, veterinary medicine, optometry, podiatry, pharmacy, public health, nursing, or allied health professions. (b)

Each scholarship grant made under this section shall be for a period not to exceed two academic years, which years shall be for compensatory paraprofessional education of any grantee. (c) Scholarship grants made under this section may cover costs of tuition, books, transportation, board, and other necessary related expenses. (d) There are authorized to be appropriated for the purpose of this section: $800,000 for fiscal year 1978, $100,000 for fiscal year 1979, and $1,300,000 for fiscal year 1980. For fiscal years 1981, 1982, 1983, and 1984 there are authorized to be appropriated for the purpose of this section such sums as may be specifically authorized by an Act enacted after this Act.

HEALTH PROFESSIONS SCHOLARSHIP PROGRAM

SEC. 104. Section 225(i) of the Public Health Service Act (42 U.S.C. 234(i) is amended (1) by inserting "(1)" after "(i)," and (2) by adding at the end the following: (2) (A) in addition to the sums authorized to be appropriated under paragraph (1) to carry out the Program, there are authorized to be appropriated for the fiscal year ending September 30, 1978, $5,450,000; for the fiscal year ending September 30, 1979, $6,300,000; for the fiscal year ending September 30, 1980, $7,200,000; and for fiscal years 1981, 1982, 1983, and 1984 such sums as may be specifically authorized by an Act enacted after the Indian Health Care Improvement Act, to provide scholarships under the Program to provide physicians, osteopaths, dentists, veterinarians, nurses, optometrists, podiatrists, pharmacists, public health personnel, and allied health professionals to provide services to Indians. Such scholarships shall be designated Indian Health Scholarships and shall be made in accordance with this section except as provided in subparagraph (B). (B) (i) The Secretary, acting through the Indian Health Service, shall determine the individuals who receive the Indian Health Scholarships, shall accord priority to applicants who are Indian, and shall determine the distribution of the scholarships on the basis of the relative needs of Indians for additional service in specific health professions. (ii) The active duty service obligation prescribed by subsection (e) shall be met by the recipient of an Indian Health Scholarship by service in the Indian Health Service, in a program assisted under title V of the Indian Health Care Improvement Act, or in the private practice of his profession if, as determined by the Secretary in accordance with guidelines promulgated by him, such practice is situated in a physician or other health professional shortage area and addresses the health care needs of a substantial number of Indians. (C) For purposes of this paragraph, the term "Indians" has the same meaning given that term by subsection (c) of section 4 of the Indian Health Care Improvement Act and includes individuals described in clauses (1) through (4) of that subsection.

INDIAN HEALTH SERVICE EXTERN PROGRAMS

SEC. 105. (a) Any individual who receives a scholarship grant pursuant to section 104 shall be entitled to employment in the Service during any nonacademic period of the year ... (b) Any individual enrolled in a school of medicine, osteopathy, dentistry, veterinary medicine, optometry, podiatry, pharmacy, public health, nursing, or allied health professions may be employed by the Service during any nonacademic period of the year. Any such employment shall not exceed one hundred and twenty days during any calendar year. (c) Any employment pursuant to this section shall be made without regard to any competitive personnel system or agency personnel limitation and to a position which will enable the individual so employed to receive practical experience in the health profession in which he or she is engaged in study. Any individual so employed shall receive payment for his or her services compared to the salary he or she would receive if he or she were employed in the competitive system. Any individual so employed shall not be counted against any employment ceiling affecting the Service or the Department of Health, Education, and Welfare ...

CONTINUING EDUCATION ALLOWANCES

SEC. 106. (a) In order to encourage physicians, dentists, and other health professionals to join or continue in the Service and to provide their services in the rural and remote areas where a significant portion of the Indian people resides, the Secretary, acting through the Service, may provide allowances to health professionals employed in the Service to enable them for a period of time each year prescribed by regulation of the Secretary to take leave of their duty stations for professional consultation and refresher training courses. (b) There are authorized to be appropriated for the purpose of this section: $100,000 for fiscal year 1978, $200,000 for fiscal year 1979, and $250,000 for fiscal year 1980. For fiscal years 1981, 1982, 1983, and 1984 there are authorized to be appropriated for the purpose of this section such sums as may be specifically authorized by an Act enacted after this Act.

TITLE II—HEALTH SERVICES . . .

SEC. 201. (a) For the purpose of eliminating backlogs in health care services and to supply known, unmet medical, surgical, dental, optometric and other Indian health needs, the Secretary is authorized to expend, through the Service, over the seven-fiscal-year period beginning after the date of the enactment of this Act the amounts authorized to be appropriated by subsection (c) Funds ... shall be in addition to the level of appropriations provided to the service under this Act and such other Federal laws in the preceding fiscal year plus an amount equal to the amount required to cover pay increases and employee benefits for personnel employed under this Act and such laws and increases in the costs of serving the health needs of Indians under this Act and such laws, which increases are caused by inflation. (b) The Secretary, acting through the Service, is authorized to employ persons to implement the provisions of this section during the seven-fiscal-year period in accordance with the schedule provided in subsection (c). Such positions authorized each fiscal year pursuant to this section shall not be considered as offsetting or limiting the personnel required by the Service to serve the health needs of Indians during and subsequent to such seven-fiscal-year period but shall be in addition to the positions authorized in the previous fiscal year. (c) The following amounts and positions are authorized, in accordance with the provisions of subsections (a) and (b), for the specific purposes noted: (1) Patient care (direct and indirect): sums and positions as provided in subsection (e) for fiscal year 1978, $8,500,000 and two hundred and twenty-five positions for fiscal year 1979, and $16,200,000 and three hundred positions for fiscal year 1980. (2) Field health, excluding dental care (direct and indirect): sums and positions as provided in subsection (e) for fiscal year 1978, $3,350,000 and eighty-five positions for fiscal year 1979, and $5,550,000 and one hundred and thirteen positions for fiscal year 1980. (3) Dental Care (direct and indirect): sums and positions as provided in subsection (e) for fiscal year 1978, $1,500,000 and eighty positions for fiscal year 1970, and $1,500,000 and fifty positions for fiscal year 1980. (4) Mental health: (A) Community mental health services: sums and positions as provided in subsection (e) for fiscal year 1978,

$1,300,000 and thirty positions for fiscal year 1979, and $2,000,000 and thirty positions for fiscal year 1980. (B) Inpatient mental health services: sums and positions as provided in subsection (e) for fiscal year 1978, $400,000 and fifteen positions for fiscal year 1979, and $600,000 and fifteen positions for fiscal year 1980. (C) Model dormitory mental health services: sums and positions as provided in subsection (e) for fiscal year 1978, $1,250,000 and fifty positions for fiscal year 1979, and $1,875,000 and fifty positions for fiscal year 1980. (D) Therapeutic and residential treatment centers: sums and positions as provided in subsection (e) for fiscal year 1978, $300,000 and ten positions for fiscal year 1979, and $400,000 and five positions for fiscal year 1980. (E) Training of traditional Indian practitioners in mental health: sums as provided in subsection (e) for fiscal year 1978, $150,000 for fiscal year 1979, and $200,000 for fiscal year 1980. (5) Treatment and control of alcoholism among Indians: $4,000,000 for fiscal year 1978, $9,000,000 for fiscal year 1979, and $9,200,000 for fiscal year 1980. (6) Maintenance and repair (direct and indirect): sums and positions as provided in subsection (e) for fiscal year 1978, $3,000,000 and twenty positions for fiscal year 1979, and $4,000,000 and thirty positions for fiscal year 1980. (7) For fiscal years 1981, 1982, 1983, and 1984 there are authorized to be appropriated for the items referred to in the preceding paragraphs such sums as may be specifically authorized by an Act enacted after this Act. For such fiscal years, positions are authorized for such items (other than the items referred to in paragraphs (4) (E) and (5) as may be specified in an Act enacted after the date of the enactment of this Act. (d) The Secretary, acting through the Service, shall expend directly or by contract not less than 1 per centum of the funds appropriated under the authorizations in each of the clauses (1) through (5) of subsection (c) for research in each of the areas of Indian health care for which such funds are authorized to be appropriated. (e) For fiscal year 1978, the Secretary is authorized to apportion not to exceed a total of $10,025,000 and 425 positions for the programs enumerated in clauses (c) (1) through (4) and (c) (6) of this section.

TITLE III – HEALTH FACILITIES CONSTRUCTION
AND RENOVATION OF SERVICE FACILITIES

Sec. 301. (a) The Secretary, acting through the Service, is authorized to expend over the seven-fiscal-year period beginning after the date of the enactment of this Act the sums authorized by subsection (b) for the construction and renovation of hospitals, health centers, health stations, and other facilities of the Service. (b) The following amounts are authorized to be appropriated for purposes of subsection (a): (1) Hospitals: $67,180,000 for fiscal year 1978, $73,256,000 for fiscal year 1979, and $49,742,000 for fiscal year 1980. For fiscal years 1981, 1982, 1983, and 1984, there are authorized to be appropriated for hospitals such sums as may be specifically authorized by an Act enacted after this Act. (2) Health centers and health stations: $6,960,000 for fiscal year 1978, $6,226,000 for fiscal year 1979, and $3,720,000 for fiscal year 1980. For fiscal years 1981, 1982, 1983, and 1984, there are authorized to be appropriated for health centers and health stations such sums as may be specifically authorized by an Act enacted after this Act. (3) Staff housing: $1,242,000 for fiscal year 1978, $21,725,000 for fiscal year 1979, and $4,116,000 for fiscal year 1980. For fiscal years 1981, 1982 1983, and 1984, there are authorized to be appropriated for staff housing such sums as may be specifically authorized by an Act enacted after this Act. (c) Prior to the expenditure of, or the making of any firm commitment to expend, any funds authorized in subsection (a), the Secretary, acting through the Service shall (1) consult with any Indian tribe to be significantly affected consultation by any such expenditure for the purpose of determining and, wherever practicable, honoring tribal preferences concerning the size, location, type, and other characteristics of any facility on which such expenditure is to be made; and (2) be assured that, wherever practicable, such facility, not later than one year after its construction or renovation, shall meet the standards of the Joint Committee on Accreditation of Hospitals.

CONSTRUCTION OF SAFE WATER AND SANITARY
WASTE DISPOSAL FACILITIES

SEC. 302. (a) During the seven-fiscal-year period beginning after the date of the enactment of this Act, the Secretary is authorized to expend under section 7 of the Act of August 5, 1954 (42 U.S.C. 2004a), the sums authorized under subsection (b) to supply unmet needs for safe water and sanitary waste disposal facilities in existing and new Indian homes and communities ...

PREFERENCE TO INDIANS AND INDIAN FIRMS

SEC. 303. (a) The Secretary, acting through the Service, may utilize the negotiating authority of the Act of June 25, 1910 (25 U.S.C. 47), to give preference to any Indian or any enterprise, partnership, or corporation, or other type of business organization owned and controlled by an Indian or Indians including former or currently federally recognized Indian tribes in the State of New York (hereinafter referred to as an "Indian firm") in the construction and renovation of Service facilities pursuant to section 301 and in the construction of safe water and sanitary waste disposal facilities pursuant to section 302. Such preference may be accorded by the Secretary unless he finds, pursuant to rules and regulations promulgated by him, that the projector function to be contracted for will not be satisfactory or such projector function cannot be properly completed or maintained under the proposed contract ... the Secretary shall assure that the rates of pay for personnel engaged in the construction or renovation of facilities constructed or renovated in whole or in part by funds made available pursuant to this title are not less than the prevailing local wage rates for similar work as determined in accordance with the Act of March 3, 1931 (40 U.S.C. 276a-276a-5, known as the Davis-Bacon Act) ...

SEC. 304. The Act of December 11, 1970 (84 Stat. 1465) is hereby amended by adding the following new section 9 at the end of SEC. 9: Nothing in this Act shall preclude the Soboba Band of Mission Indians and the Soboba Indian Reservation from being provided with sanitation facilities and services under the authority of section 7 of the Act of August 5, 1954 (68 Stat. 674), as amended by the Act of July 31, 1959 (73 Stat. 267) ...

INDIAN HEALTH SERVICE FACILITIES

SEC. 1880. (a) A hospital or skilled nursing facility of the Indian Health Service, whether operated by such Service or by an Indian tribe or tribal organization (as those terms are defined in section 4 of the Indian Health Care Improvement Act), shall be eligible for payments under this title, notwithstanding sections 1814(c) and1835(d), if and for so long as it meets all of the conditions and requirements for such payments which are applicable generally to hospitals or skilled nursing facilities (as the case may be) under this title. (b) Notwithstanding subsection (a), a hospital or skilled nursing facility of the Indian Health Service which does not meet all of the conditions and requirements of this title which are applicable generally to hospitals or skilled nursing facilities (as the case may be), but which submits to the Secretary within six months after the date of the enactment of this section an acceptable plan for achieving compliance with such conditions and requirements, shall be deemed to meet such conditions and requirements (and to be eligible for payments under this title) ... (c) Notwithstanding any other provision of this title, payments to which any hospital or skilled nursing facility of the Indian Health Service is entitled by reason of this section shall be placed in a special fund to be held by the Secretary and used by him (to such extent or in such amounts as are provided in appropriation Acts) exclusively for the purpose of making any improvements in the hospitals and skilled nursing facilities of such Service which may be necessary to achieve compliance with the applicable conditions and requirements of this title ...

SERVICES PROVIDED TO MEDICAID ELIGIBLE INDIANS
SEC. 402. (a) Title XIX of the Social Security Act is amended by adding at the end thereof the following new section:

INDIAN HEALTH SERVICE FACILITIES
SEC. 1911. (a) A facility of the Indian Health Service (including a hospital, intermediate care facility, or skilled nursing facility), whether operated by such Service or by an Indian tribe or tribal organization (as those terms are defined in section 4 of the Indian Health Care Improvement Act), shall be eligible for reimbursement for medical assistance provided under a State plan if and for so long as it meets all of the conditions and requirements which are applicable generally to such facilities under this title. (b) Notwithstanding subsection (a), a facility of the Indian Health Service (including a hospital, intermediate care facility, or skilled nursing facility) which does not meet all of the conditions and requirements of this title which are applicable generally to such facility, but which submits to the Secretary within six months after the date of the enactment of this section an acceptable plan for achieving compliance with such conditions and requirements, shall be deemed to meet such conditions and requirements (and to be eligible for reimbursement under this title), without regard to the extent of its actual compliance with such conditions and requirements, during the first twelve months after the month in which such plan is submitted. (b) The Secretary is authorized to enter into agreements with the appropriate State

agency for the purpose of reimbursing such agency for health care and services provided in Service facilities to Indians who are eligible for medical assistance under title XIX of the Social Security Act, as amended. (c) Notwithstanding any other provision of law, payments to which any facility of the Indian Health Service (including a hospital, intermediate care facility, or skilled nursing facility) is entitled under a State plan approved under title XIX of the Social Security Act by reason of section 1911 of such Act shall be placed in a special fund to be held by the Secretary and used by him (to such extent or in such amounts as are provided in appropriation Acts) exclusively for the purpose of making any improvements in the facilities of such Service which may be necessary to achieve compliance with the applicable conditions and requirements of such title. The preceding sentence shall cease to apply when the Secretary determines and certifies that substantially all of the health facilities of such Service in the United States are in compliance with such conditions and requirements. (d) Any payments received, for services provided recipients hereunder shall not be considered in determining appropriations for the provision of health care and services to Indians. (e) Section 1905 (b) of the Social Security Act is amended by inserting at the end thereof the following: "Notwithstanding the first sentence of this section, the Federal medical assistance percentage shall be 100 per centum with respect to amounts expended as medical assistance for services which are received through an Indian Health Service facility whether operated by the Indian Health Service or by an Indian tribe or tribal organization (as defined in section 4 of the Indian Health Care Improvement Act)."

REPORT

SEC. 403. The Secretary shall include in his annual report required by section 701 an accounting on the amount and use of funds made available to the Service pursuant to this title as a result of reimbursements through titles XVIII and XIX of the Social Security Act, as amended.

TITLE V—HEALTH SERVICES FOR URBAN INDIANS PURPOSE
SEC. 501. The purpose of this title is to encourage the establishment of programs in urban areas to make health services more accessible to the urban Indian population ...

RURAL HEALTH PROJECTS

SEC. 508. Not to exceed 1 per centum of the amounts authorized by Section 506 shall be available for not to exceed two pilot projects providing outreach services to eligible Indians residing in rural communities near Indian reservations.

"... SEC. 601 ... conduct a study to determine the need for, and the feasibility of, establishing a school of medicine to train Indians to provide health services for Indians ..."

TITLE VI—AMERICAN INDIAN SCHOOL OF MEDICINE
FEASIBILITY STUDY

SEC. 601. The Secretary, in consultation with Indian tribes and appropriate Indian organizations, shall conduct a study to determine the need for, and the feasibility of, establishing a school of medicine to train Indians to provide health services for Indians. Within one year of the date of the enactment of this Act the Secretary shall complete such study and shall report to the Congress findings and recommendations based on such study ...

PLAN OF IMPLEMENTATION

SEC. 703. Within two hundred and forty days after enactment of this Act, a plan will be prepared by the Secretary and will be submitted to the Congress. The plan will explain the manner and schedule (including a schedule of appropriation requests), by title and section, by which the Secretary will implement the provisions of this Act ...

Approved September 30, 1975

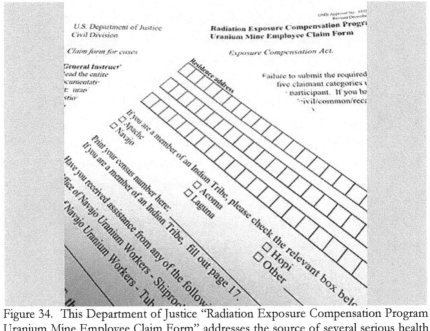

Figure 34. This Department of Justice "Radiation Exposure Compensation Program Uranium Mine Employee Claim Form" addresses the source of several serious health problems common within reservation populations living in close proximately to mining sites, e.g., residents of uranium-exposed sections of the Apache, Navajo, Acoma, Laguna, and Hopi lands. The need for efficacy in the cleanup of active and closed mines is ongoing. The limited water sources of some desert lands remain compromised by decades of radioactive pollution resulting from mining runoff.

Figure 35. The Indian Health Care Improvement Act of 1976, as amended on Oct. 29, 1992, mandated a priority in "locating ... [health service facilities] ... and projects on Indian lands if requested by the Indian tribes with jurisdiction over such lands." This contemporary nurse station is located within the borders of a southwestern reservation; many of those residents served by this site live more than a one hour drive away. Some families of this health care site's locale must travel another two hours to off-reservation appointments with the nearest physician. (Photo: C. Breeman).

Chapter XXV

Recognized in the USA: Reinstatement of the Modoc, Wyandotte, Peoria, and Ottawa Tribes Act of 1978

THE REINSTATEMENT OF the Modoc, Wyandotte, Peoria, and Ottawa Tribes Act of 1978 overturned three public acts passed by Congress in 1956. The previous legislation had ended ("terminated") all federal recognition of these four tribes and many others. Although federal recognition had been withdrawn, these tribes had continued operating as cohesive, functioning American Indian nations. This 1978 legislation returned to the Modoc, Wyandotte, Peoria, and Ottawa tribes their status as federally-recognized American Indian tribes. It also demonstrated a congressional acceptance and legal recognition of the endurance and continuity of these tribes, their tribal governance capacities, and their communities.

Reinstatement of the Modoc, Wyandotte, Peoria, and Ottawa Tribes Act of 1978

AN ACT[1] ... To reinstate the Modoc, Wyandotte, Peoria, and Ottawa tribes of Oklahoma as federally supervised and recognized Indian tribes. *Be it enacted by the Senate and House of Representatives of the United States of America in Congress assembled,* That (a) federal recognition is hereby extended where confirmed with respect to the Wyandotte Indian tribe of

"Don't run for that Senate. You would be sunk in there. They wouldn't listen to Abraham Lincoln his first ten years in there if he was to come back and be elected to it."

WILL ROGERS

233

Oklahoma, Ottawa Indian tribe of Oklahoma, and the Peoria Indian tribe of Oklahoma, the provisions of the acts repealed by subsection (b) of this section notwithstanding. (b) The following acts are hereby repealed: (1) the Act of August 1, 1956 (70 Stat. 893; 25 U. S. C. 791–807), relating to the Wyandotte tribe; (2) the Act of August 2, 1956 (70 Stat. 937; 25 U. S. C. 821–826), relating to the Peoria tribe; and (3) the Act of August 3, 1956 (70 Stat 963; 25 U. S. C. 841–853), relating to the Ottawa tribe. (c) There are hereby reinstated all rights and privileges of each of the tribes described in subsection (a) of this section and their members under federal treaty, statute, or otherwise which may have been diminished or lost pursuant to the act relating to them which is repealed by subsection (b) of this section. Nothing contained in this act shall diminish any rights or privileges enjoyed by each of such tribes or their members now or prior to enactment of such act, under federal treaty, statute, or otherwise, which are not inconsistent with the provisions of this act. (d) except as specifically provided in this act, nothing contained in this act shall alter any property rights or obligations, any contractual rights or obligations, including existing fishing rights, or any obligation for taxes already levied.

SEC. 2. (a)(1) The Modoc Indian tribe of Oklahoma is hereby recognized as a tribe of Indians residing in Oklahoma and provisions of the act of June 26, 1936, as amended (49 Stat. 1967; 25 U.S.C. 501–509), are hereby extended to such tribe and its members. The Secretary of the Interior shall promptly offer the said Modoc tribe assistance to aid them in organizing under section 3 of said Act of June 26, 1936 (25 U.S.C. 503). (2) The provisions of the Act of August 13, 1954 (68 statute. 718; 25 U.S.C. 564–564w), hereafter shall not apply to the Modoc Tribe of Oklahoma or its members except for any right to share in the proceeds of any claim against the United States as provided in sections 6 (c) and 21 of said Act, as amended (25 U.S.C 564e and 564t). (3) The Modoc Indian tribe of Oklahoma shall consist of those Modoc Indians who are direct lineal descendants of those Modoc's removed to Indian territory (now Oklahoma) in November 1873, and who did not return to Klamath, Oregon, pursuant to the act of March 9, 1909 (35 Stat. 751), as determined by the Secretary of the Interior, and the descendants of such Indians who otherwise meet the membership requirements adopted by the tribe. (b) The Secretary of the

Interior shall promptly offer the Ottawa tribe of Oklahoma and the Peoria Tribe of Oklahoma assistance to aid them in reorganizing under section 3 of the Act of June 26, 1936 (49 Stat. 967; 25 U.S.C. 503), which Act is re-extended to them and their members by this Act. (c) The validity of the organization of the Wyandotte Indian tribe of Oklahoma under section 3 of the Act of June 26, 1936 (49 stat. 1967; 25 U.S.C. 503), and the continued application of said Act to such tribe and its members is hereby confirmed.

SEC. 3 (a) It is hereby declared that enactment of this Act fulfills the requirements of the first proviso in section 2 of the Act of January 2, 1975 (88 Stat. 1920, 1921), with respect to the Wyandotte tribe of Oklahoma, the Ottawa tribe of Oklahoma, and the Peoria tribe of Oklahoma. (b) It is hereby declared that the organization of the Modoc tribe of Oklahoma as provided in section 3 (a) of this Act shall fulfill the requirements of the second proviso in section 2 of the Act of January 2, 1973 (88 stat. 1920, 1921). (c) Promptly after organization of the Modoc Tribe of Oklahoma, the Secretary of the Interior shall publish a notice of such fact in the Federal Register including a statement that such organization completes fulfillment of the requirements of the provisos in section 2 of the Act of January 2, 1975 (88 Stat. 1920, 1921), and that the land described in section 1 of said Act is held in trust by the United States for the eight tribes named in said Act.

SEC. 4. The Wyandotte, Ottawa, Peoria, and Modoc Tribes of Oklahoma and their members shall be entitled to participate in the programs and services provided by the United States to Indians because of their status as Indians, including, but not limited to, those under the Act of November 2, 1921 (42 Stat. 208; 25 U.S.C. 13), and for purposes of the Act of August 16, 1957 (71 Stat. 370; 42 U.S.C. 2005–2005F). The members of such tribes shall be deemed to be Indians for which hospital and medical care was being provided by or at the expense of the Public Health Service on August 16, 1957.

Approved May 15, 1978.

Chapter XXVI

Homegrown Degrees: The Tribally-Controlled Community College Assistance Act of 1978

THE TRIBALLY-CONTROLLED Community College Assistance Act of 1978 provided federal funding for a portion of the development and continuity of tribally owned colleges. Diné College, founded by the Navajo Nation in 1968, served as the model for this legislation.[1] At present, these reservation-based colleges award two-year and, in some cases, four-year degrees. This legislation emerged the same day Congress overturned the House Reconcurrent Resolution 108 (i.e., a "termination" policy Congress enacted in 1953).[2]

Tribally-Controlled Community College Assistance Act

AN ACT[3] ... To provide for grants to tribally controlled community colleges, and for other purposes. *Be it enacted by the Senate and House of Representatives of the United States of America in Congress assembled,* That this Act may be cited as the "Tribally-Controlled Community College Assistance Act of 1978."

TITLE I – TRIBALLY CONTROLLED COMMUNITY COLLEGES
SEC. 1. It is the purpose of this title to provide grants for the operation and improvement of tribally controlled community colleges to insure continued and expanded educational opportunities for Indian students.

TITLE II – NAVAJO COMMUNITY COLLEGE
SEC. 201. This title may be cited as the "Navajo College Assistance Act of 1978."

SEC. 202. The Congress after careful study and deliberation, finds that–(1) the Navajo Tribe constitutes the largest American Indian tribes in the United States; (2) the Navajo Tribe has, through its duly constituted tribal council and representatives, established a community college within the boundaries of the reservation; (3) the population of the Navajo Tribe and the best area of the Navajo reservation requires that the Navajo Community College expand to better serve the needs of such population; and (4) that Congress has already recognized the need for that institution by the passage of the Navajo Community College Act.

Approved October 17, 1978.

Figure 36. Oglala Lakota College (shown above) is located in Oglala Lakota County, SD. Founded in 1971, it became eligible for "operations and improvement" grants mandated by the Tribally-Controlled Community Colleges Act of 1978. The Diné Community College, also known as Navajo Community College, served as the model for this 1978 legislation. Oglala Lakota College was the first tribal college to offer four-year degree programs (Photo: B. L. Wilson).

Chapter XXVII

Family Care at Last: Indian Child Welfare Act of 1978

THE INDIAN CHILD Welfare Act (ICWA) of 1978 began as a Senate bill. It was voted into law in the House of Representatives—without further debate—on November 8, 1978. This act facilitated the placement of at-risk Indian children in local (i.e., tribally affiliated) foster or adoptive homes—and mandated tribal jurisdiction over all child custody cases involving tribal families. It required tribes—not BIA representatives, the FBI, or state officials—to oversee tribal child custody, child healthcare, and related social service programming. This act mandated that reservation-specific federal and state policies must be brought into alignment with the adaptive, reasonable, and humane practices commonly applied in all other American communities. The Indian Child Welfare Act of 1978 made it more possible for tribal children to maintain contact with their immediate and extended families, while being nurtured within the context of their own languages, cultures, and communities.

In 2015, an ICWA report found that "... no federal agency is tasked with ensuring state compliance with the protections mandated by ICWA ..." [1]

The Indian Child Welfare Act of 1978

AN ACT[2] ... To establish standards for the placement of Indian children in foster or adoptive homes, to prevent the breakup of Indian families, and for other purposes. *Be it enacted by the Senate and House of Representatives of the United States of America in Congress assembled,* That this Act may be cited as the Indian Child Welfare Act.

SEC. 2. Recognizing the special relationship between the United States and Indian tribes and their members and the Federal responsibility to Indian people, the Congress finds – (1) That cause 3, section 8, article I of the United States Constitution provides that the Congress shall have Power * * * [sic] to regulate Commerce * * * [*sic*] with Indian tribes; and, through this and

"... SEC. 2 ... an alarmingly high percentage of ... [tribal] ... children are placed in non-Indian foster and adoptive homes and institutions ..."

other constitutional authority, Congress has plenary power over Indian affairs; (2) That Congress, through statues, treaties and the general course of dealing with Indian tribes, has assumed the responsibility for the protection and preservation of Indian tribes and their resources; (3) that there is no resource that is more vital to the continued existence and integrity of Indian tribes than their children and that the United States has a direct interest, as trustee, in protecting Indian children who are members of or are eligible for membership in an Indian tribe; (4) that an alarmingly high percentage of Indian families are broken up by the removal, often unwarranted, of their children from them by nontribal public and private agencies and that an alarmingly high percentage of such children are placed in non-Indian foster and adoptive homes and institutions; and (5) that the States, exercising their recognized jurisdiction over Indian child custody proceedings through administrative and judicial bodies, have often failed to recognize the essential tribal relations of Indian people and the cultural and social standards prevailing in Indian communities and families.

SEC. 3. The Congress hereby declares that it is the policy of this nation to protect the best interest of Indian children and to promote the stability and security of Indian tribes and families by the establishment of minimum Federal standards for the removal of Indian children from their families and the placement of such children in foster or adoptive home which will reflect the unique values of Indian culture and by providing for assistance to Indian tribes in the operation of children and family service programs.

SEC. 4. For the purposes of this Act, except as may be specifically provided otherwise, the term "child custody proceeding" shall mean and include ... (i) "foster care placement" which shall mean an action removing an Indian child from ... [his/her] parent or Indian custodian for temporary placement in a foster home or institution or the home of a guardian or conservator where the parent or Indian custodian cannot have the child returned upon demand, but where parental rights have not been terminated

TITLE I–CHILD CUSTODY PROCEEDINGS
SEC. 101. (a) An Indian tribe shall have jurisdiction exclusive as to any State over any child custody proceedings involving an Indian child who resides or is domiciled within the reservation of such tribe, except where such jurisdiction is otherwise vested in the State by existing Federal law. Where an Indian child is a ward of a tribal court, the Indian tribes shall retain exclusive jurisdiction, notwithstanding the residence or domicile of the child.

SEC. 104. Any Indian child who is the subject of any action for foster care placement or termination of parental rights under state law, any parent or Indian custodian from whose custody such child was removed and the Indian child's tribe may petition any court of competent jurisdiction to invalidate such action upon a showing that such action violated any provision of sections 101, 102 and 103 of this Act.

SEC. 105. (a) In any adoptive placement of an Indian child under State law, a preference shall be given in the absence of good cause to the contrary to a placement with (1) a member of the child's extended family; (2) other members of the Indian child's tribe; or (3) other Indian families. (b) Any child accepted for foster care or pre-adoptive placement shall be placed in the least restrictive setting which most approximates a family and in which his special needs, if any, may be met. The child shall also be placed within reasonable proximately to his or her home, taking into account any special needs of the child. In any foster care or pre-adoptive placement, a preference shall be given, in the absence of a good cause to the contrary, to a placement with – (i) a member of the Indian child's extended family; (ii) a foster home licensed, Approved or specified by the Indian child's tribes; (iii) an Indian foster home licensed or approved by an authorized non-Indian licensing authority; or, (iv) an institution for children approved by an Indian tribe or operated by an Indian organization which has a program suitable to meet the Indian child's needs ...

TITLE II–INDIAN CHILD AND FAMILY PROGRAMS
SEC. 201. (a) The Secretary is authorized to make grants to Indian tribes and organizations in the establishment and operation of Indian child and family service programs on or near reservations and in the preparation and implementation of child welfare codes. The objective of every Indian child and family service program shall be to prevent the breakup of Indian families and, in particular, to insure that the permanent removal of an Indian child from the custody of his parent or Indian custodian shall be a last resort.

TITLE IV—MISCELLANEOUS
SEC. 401. (a) It is the sense of Congress that the absence of locally convenient day schools may contribute to the breakup of Indian families. (b) The Secretary is authorized and directed to prepare, in consultation with appropriate agencies in the Department of Health, Education and Welfare, a report on the feasibility of providing Indian children with schools located near their homes and to submit such report to the Select Committee on Indian Affaires of the United States Senate and the Committee on Interior and Insular Affairs of the United States House of Representatives within two years from the date of this Act. In developing this report the Secretary shall give particular consideration to the provision of educational facilities for children in the elementary grades.

Approved November 8, 1978.

Chapter XXVIII

Worship as You Will: American Indian Religious Freedom Act of 1978

THE AMERICAN INDIAN Religious Freedom Act of 1978 clarified freedom of religion tenets of the U.S. Constitution—as applied to the practice of traditional Native American, Native Hawaiian, and Alaskan Native religions. This act clarified the federal responsibility to protect all religious rights. It also required federal action be taken to adjust existing federal systems in order to assure the establishment and maintenance of federal agency capacities to fulfil all requirements of this act.

"America does not need to violate the religions of her native peoples. There is room for ... and great value in cultural and religious diversity. We would all be poorer if these American Indian religions disappeared from the face of the Earth." [1]

During Senate proceedings held one week prior to its passage, the following summary of congressional findings—a report on the history and status quo, vis à vis restrictions on indigenous religious practices—was read into the Congressional Record, as follows:[2]

Mr. ROBERT C. BYRD. "Mr. President, I ask unanimous consent that the amendments be considered and agreed to en bloc."

The ACTING PRESIDENT pro tempore. "Without objection, it is so ordered."

245

The joint resolution was ordered to be ... read the third time ...
and passed. The preamble was agreed to.

Mr. ROBERT C. BYRD. "Mr. President, I ask unanimous consent to have printed in the Record an excerpt from the report (No. 25-709), explaining the purposes of the measure."

There being no objection, the excerpt was ordered to be printed
in the Record, as follows:

PURPOSE OF THE MEASURE

The intent of the Senate Joint Resolution 102 is to insure that the policies and procedures of a variety of Federal agencies are brought into compliance with the constitutional injunction that Congress shall make no laws abridging the free exercise of religion.

BACKGROUND

Native Americans have an inherent right to the free exercise of their religion. That right is reaffirmed in the U.S. Constitution in the Bill of Rights, as well as by many State and tribal constitutions. The practice of traditional Native Indian religions, outside the Judeo-Christian mainstream or in combination with it, is further upheld in the 1968 Indian Civil Rights Act.

Despite these laws, a lack of U.S. governmental policy has allowed infringement in the practice of native traditional religions. These infringements came about through the enforcement of policies and regulation based on laws which are basically sound and which the large majority of Indians strongly support. These laws often embody principles such as the preservation of wilderness areas and the preservation of endangered species for which Indians have actively fought, literally generations before the non-Indian became convinced of their importance.

But, because such laws were not intended to relate to religion and because there was a lack of awareness of their effect on religion, Congress neglected to fully consider the impact of such laws on the Indians' religious practices. It is only within the last decade that it has become apparent that such laws, when combined with more restrictive regulations, insensitive enforcement procedures and administrative policy directives, in fact, have interfered severely with the culture and religion of American Indians. Interference with the free exercise of native religions has taken place in three general areas. The first restrictions are denials of access to Indians to certain physical locations. Often, these locations include certain sites–a hill, a lake, or a forest glade–which are sacred to Indian religions. Ceremonies are often required to be performed in these spots. To deny access to them is analogous to preventing a non-Indian from entering his church or temple. Many of these sites not in Indian possession are owned by the Federal Government and a few are on State lands. Federal agencies such as the Forest Service, Park Service, Bureau of Land Management and others have prevented Indians in certain cases from entering onto these lands. The issue is not ownership or protection of the lands involved. Rather, it is a straightforward question of access in order to worship and perform the necessary rites.

"... In some instances, these lands were put under Federal supervision because they were Indian cemeteries. Yet today, the same tribes cannot bury their religious and political leaders there ... There is no overriding reason to deny Indians the right to inter their dead in sanctified ground ..."

Further, there is the question of cemeteries which were in use at the time of Federal subjugation. In some instances, these lands were put under Federal supervision because they were Indian cemeteries. Yet today, the same tribes cannot bury their religious and political leaders there. There is no overriding reason to deny Indians the right to inter their dead in sanctified ground. Revised regulations and enforcement procedures, could allow access for religious purposes and still follow the intent of these laws. The second major area of Federal violations is the restrictions on use of substances. To the Indians, these natural objects have religious significance because they are sacred, they have power, they heal, they are necessary to the exercise of the rites of the religion, they are necessary to the culture integrity of the tribe and, therefore, religious survival or a combination of these reasons. To the Federal Government, these substances are restricted because the non-Indian has made them scarce, as in endangered species, or because they pose a health threat to those who misuse them, as in peyote.

The Federal court system has shown that this apparent conflict can be overcome with the institution of well thought-out exceptions.

Although acts of Congress prohibit the use of peyote as a hallucinogen, it is established Federal law that peyote is constitutionally protected when used by a bona fide religion as a sacrament. Yet, a lack of awareness or understanding of the law has led some Federal officials to confiscate sacramental substances. Things which have never been prescribed by law, such as pine leaves or sweet grass, have been confiscated by Federal officials who were suspicious that they were some form of drugs. Even worse, medicine bundles once sealed by religious leaders are never to be opened or handled by others. They are worn or carried by Indians for health, protection and purity. Although containing only legal substances, these medicine bags or bundles have been opened by custom officials searching for drugs, thus making them unclean and valueless. Another example of overzealous officials is the confiscation of turkey feathers and the feathers of other common birds which are legal for all Americans to possess, but which are taken with the fear that they might be from some endangered bird. Even the most ardent conservationist cannot match the need of traditional Indians for preserving eagles and hawks. For some plains tribes, much of their religion depends on the existence of these species. It does prevent the exercise of American Indian religions. Although the enforcement problems create more difficult administrative issue and requires more careful consideration of regulation changes in this area, it is possible to both uphold the intent of the laws and allow for religious freedom. Where necessary, tribal representatives will be able to institute self-enforcement procedures designed to insure that any exception to general regulatory laws surrounding access to sites, use of sacred objects, et cetera, will be confined to tribal members actually participating in the religious exercise or event ... The third area of concern is actual interference in religious events. In some instances, those who interfere have good motives or are merely curious. Those instances include being present at ceremonies which require strict isolation, even to the extent of circling the ceremony in small aircraft. Unlike the other areas, some of these incidents happen because of Federal omissions, rather than actions. In areas where the Federal Government has a duty to act or is the only law enforcement at the site, Federal officials have failed to protect Indian religions from interruptions. In other instances, it is the Government official who directly interferes. This direct Federal interference in the religious ceremonies imposes upon one religion, by Government action, the values of another. Such action is a direct threat to the foundation of religious freedom in America. It comes far too close to an informal state religion. America does not need to violate the religions of her native peoples. There is room for and great value in cultural and religious diversity. We would all be poorer if these American Indian religions disappeared from the face of the Earth. Much can be done to prevent the destruction of Indian religions. For instance, several States have already taken supportive action. During the eagle feather crisis of 1974, many Oklahoma State officials issued statements of support. Montana went beyond rhetoric to pass a State resolution setting forth the policy of free exercise and protection for Indian religions. The State of California has enacted the Native American Historical, Cultural and Sacred Sites Act of 1976 which takes giant strides in overcoming the problems of access. Unfortunately, to date, with the exception of sporadic efforts by a few individuals, the Federal Government's lack of policy has allowed infringements of religious rights to continue.

The American Indian Religious Freedom Act of 1978

JOINT RESOLUTION
AMERICAN INDIAN RELIGIOUS FREEDOM[3]

Whereas the freedom of religion for all people is an inherent right, fundamental to the democratic structure of the United States and is guaranteed by the First Amendment of the United States Constitution:

Whereas the United States has traditionally rejected the concept of a government denying individuals the right to practice their religion and, as a result, has benefited from a rich variety of religious heritages is in this country;

Whereas the religious practices of the American Indian (as well as Native Alaskan and Hawaiian) are an integral part of their culture, tradition and heritage, such practices forming the basis of Indian identity and value systems;

Whereas the traditional American Indian religions, as an integral part of Indian life, are indispensable and irreplaceable;

Whereas the lack of a clear, comprehensive, and consistent Federal policy has often resulted in the abridgment of religious freedom for traditional American Indians;

Whereas such religious infringements result from the lack of knowledge or the insensitive and inflexible enforcement of Federal policies and regulations premised on a variety of laws;

Whereas such laws and policies often deny American Indians access to sacred sites required in their religions, including cemeteries;

Whereas such laws at times prohibit the use and possession of sacred objects necessary to the exercise of religious rites and ceremonies;

Whereas traditional American Indian ceremonies have been intruded upon, interfered with, and in a few instances banned: Now, therefore, be it *Resolved by the Senate and House of Representatives of the United States of America in Congress assembled,* That henceforth it shall be the policy of the United States to protect and preserve for American Indians their inherent right of freedom to believe, express, and exercise the traditional religions of the American Indian, Eskimo, Aleut, and Native Hawaiians, including but not limited to access to sites, use and possession of sacred objects, and the freedom to worship through ceremonials and traditional rites.

SEC. 2. The President shall direct the various Federal departments, agencies, and other instrumentalities responsible for administering relevant laws to evaluate their policies and procedures in consultation with native traditional religious leaders in order to determine appropriate changes necessary to protect and preserve Native American religious cultural rights and practices 12 [*sic*] months after approval of this resolution, the President shall report back to the Congress the results of this evaluation, including any changes which were made in administrative policies and procedures, and any recommendations he may have for legislative action.

Approved August 11, 1978.

Figure 37. The American Indian Freedom of Religion Act of 1978 legalized the religious aspects of tribal community activities which had been criminalized during the late nineteenth century. This intentionally pixelated photograph was taken with permission of powwow organizers during a public powwow held in 1989 at the convention center in Rapid City, SD (Photo: B. L. Wilson).

Chapter XXIX

No New Jobs:
Indian Employment Act of 1979

THE MISLEADING TITLE notwithstanding, the Indian Employment Act of 1979 made no provisions for enhancing—or in any other way addressing—employment issues relative to American Indians. The initial proposal was vetoed by President Gerald Ford in 1975 for being "discriminatory and costly":

"This bill is designed to increase employment opportunities 'for Indians' by providing special compensation to *non-Indian employees* ... [italics added] ... in BIA [Bureau of Indian Affairs] and IHS [Indian Health Services] ... who retire early. It seeks to accomplish this purpose by authorizing payment of extraordinary retirement benefits under certain conditions to non-Indian employees of those agencies who retire before 1986 ..."[1]

> *"I could study all my life and not think up half the amount of funny things they can think of in one session of Congress."*
>
> WILL ROGERS

A second version of the initial proposal made it through Congress in 1979.[2] At the time of its initial enactment, the Bureau of Indian Affairs (BIA) retirement benefits it mandated for distribution benefited only those staff members who were not tribally affiliated.

The Indian Employment Act of 1979

AN ACT[3] -- To amend Civil Service retirement provisions as they apply to certain employees of the Bureau of Indian Affairs and of the Indian Health Service who are not entitled to Indian employment preference and to modify the application of the Indian employment preference laws as it applies to those agencies. Be it enacted by the Senate and House of Representatives of the United States of America in Congress assembled, That (a) section 8336 of title 5, United States Code, is amended by re-designating subsection (j) as subsection (k) and inserting after subsection (i) the following new subsection: (j)(1) Except as provided in paragraph (3), an employee is entitled to an annuity if he-(A)(i) is separated from the service after completing 25 years of service or after becoming 50 years of age and completing 20 years of service, or (ii) is involuntarily separated, except by removal for cause on charges of misconduct or delinquency, during the 2-year period before the date on which he would meet the years of service and age requirements under clause (i), (B) was employed in the Bureau of Indian Affairs, the Indian Health Service, a tribal organization (to the extent provided in paragraph (2)), or any combination thereof, continuously from December 21, 1972, to the date of his separation, and (C) is not entitled to preference under the Indian preference laws. (2) Employment in a tribal organization may be considered for purposes of paragraph (1)(B) of this subsection only if—(A) the employee was employed by the tribal organization after January 4, 1975, and immediately before such employment he was an employee of the Bureau of Indian Affairs or the Indian Health Service, and (B) at the time of such employment such employee and the tribal organization were eligible to elect, and elected, to have the employee retain the coverage, rights, and benefits of this chapter under section 105 (e)(2) of the Indian Self-Determination Act (25 U.S.C. 450i(a)(2); 88 Stat. 2209). (3)(A) The provisions of paragraph (1) of this subsection shall not apply with respect to any separation of any employee which occurs after the date 5 years after-(i) the date the employee first meets the years of service and age requirements of paragraph (1)(A)(i), or (ii) the date of the enactment of this paragraph, if the employee met those requirements before that date. (B) For purposes of applying this paragraph with respect to any employee of the Bureau of Indian Affairs in the Department of the Interior or of the Indian Health Service in the Department of Health, Education, and Welfare, the Secretary of the department involved may postpone the date otherwise applicable under subparagraph (A) if-(i) such employee consents to such postponement, and (ii) the Secretary finds that such postponement is necessary for the continued effective operation of the agency. The period of any postponement under this subparagraph shall not exceed 12 months and the total period of all postponements with respect to any employee shall not exceed 5 years. (4) For the purpose of this subsection—(A) "Bureau of Indian Affairs" means (i) the Bureau of Indian Affairs and (ii) all other organizational units in the Department of the Interior directly and primarily related to providing services to Indians and in which positions are filled in accordance with the Indian preference laws. (B) "Indian preference laws" means section 12 of the Act of June 18, 1934 (25 U.S.C. 472; 48 Stat. 986), or any other provision of law granting a preference to Indians in promotions or other Federal personnel actions. (b) Section 8339(d) of title 5, United States Code, is amended by adding at the end thereof the following new paragraph: (5) The annuity of an employee retiring under section 8336(j) of this title is computed under subsection (a) of this section, except that with respect to service on or after December 21, 1972, the employee's annuity is—(A) 2 ½ percent of the employee's average pay multiplied by so much of the employee's service on or after that date as does not exceed 20 years; plus (B) 2 percent of the employee's average pay multiplied by so much of the employee's service on or after that date as exceeds 20 years. (c) The first sentence of section 8339(h) of title 5, United States Code, is amended—(1) by inserting: "(d)(5)" after (b); and (2) by striking out "or (h)" and inserting "in lieu thereof," (h), or (d) The amendments made by this section shall take effect on the date of the enactment of this Act. SEC. 2. (a) For purposes of applying reduction-in-force procedures under subsection (a) of section 3502 of title 5, United States Code, with respect to positions within the Bureau of Indian Affairs and the Indian Health Service, the competitive and excepted service retention registers shall be combined, and any employee entitled to Indian preference who is within a retention category established under regulations prescribed under such subsection to provide due effect to military preference shall be entitled to be retained in preference to other employees not entitled to Indian preference who are within such retention category. (b) The Indian preference laws shall not apply in the case of any reassignment within the Bureau of Indian Affairs or within the Indian Health Service (other than to a position in a higher grade) of an employee not entitled to Indian preference if it is determined that under the circumstances such reassignment is necessary— (A) to assure the health or safety of the employee or of any member of the employee's household; (B) in the course of a reduction in force; or (C) because the employee's working relationship with a tribe has so deteriorated that the employee cannot provide effective service for such tribe or the Federal Government. (2) The authority to make any determination under subparagraph (A), (B), or (C) of paragraph (1) is vested in the Secretary of the Interior with respect to the Bureau of Indian Affairs and the Secretary of Health, Education, and Welfare with respect to the Indian Health Service, and, notwithstanding any other provision of law, the Secretary involved may not delegate such authority to any individual other than an Under Secretary or Assistant Secretary of the respective department ...

"... such laws shall not apply in the case of any personnel action respecting an employee not entitled to Indian preference if each tribal organization concerned grants, in writing, a waiver ..."

Notwithstanding any provision of the Indian preference laws, such laws shall not apply in the case of any personnel action respecting an employee not entitled to Indian preference if each tribal organization concerned grants, in writing, a waiver of the application of such laws with respect to such personnel action. (2) The provisions of section 8336(j) of title 5, United States Code (as added by the preceding section of this Act), shall not apply to any individual who has accepted a waiver with respect to a personnel action pursuant to paragraph (1) of this subsection or to section 1131(0 of the Education Amendments of 1978 (25 U.S.C. 2011(f); 92 Stat. 2324). (d) The Secretaries of the Interior and Health, Education, and Welfare shall each submit to the

Congress a report following the close of each fiscal year with respect to the actions which they took in such fiscal year to recruit and train Indians to qualify such Indians for positions which are subject to preference under the Indian preference laws. Such report shall also include information as to the grade levels and occupational classifications of Indian and non-Indian employees in the Bureau of Indian Affairs and the Indian Health Service. (e) The Office of Personnel Management shall provide all appropriate assistance to the Bureau of Indian Affairs and the Indian Health Service in placing non-Indian employees of such agencies in other Federal positions. All other Federal agencies shall cooperate to the fullest extent possible in such placement efforts. (2) The Secretaries of the Interior and Health, Education, and Welfare, and the Director of the Office of Personnel Management shall each submit a report to Congress following the close of each fiscal year with respect to the actions which they took in such fiscal year to place non-Indian employees of the Bureau of Indian Affairs and the Indian Health Service in other Federal positions. (f) For purposes of this section—(1) The term "tribal organization" means—(A) the recognized governing body of any Indian tribe, band, nation, pueblo, or other organized community, including a Native village (as defined in section 3(c) of the Alaska Native Claims Settlement Act (43 U.S.C. 1602(c); 85 Stat. 688); or (B) in connection with any personnel action referred to in subsection (c)(1) of this section, any legally established organization of Indians which is controlled, sanctioned, or chartered by a governing body referred to in subparagraph (A) of this paragraph and which has been delegated by such governing body the authority to grant a waiver under such subsection with respect to such personnel action. (2) The term "Indian preference laws" means section 12 of the Act of June 18, 1934 (25 U.S.C. 472; 48 Stat. 986) or any other provision of law granting a preference to Indians in promotions and other personnel actions. (3) The term "Bureau of Indian Affairs" means (A) the Bureau of Indian Affairs and (B) all other organizational units in the Department of the Interior directly and primarily related to providing services to Indians and in which positions are filled in accordance with the Indian preference laws.

Approved December 5, 1979.

Chapter XXX

Cash Infusion: The Indian Gaming Regulatory Act of 1988

THE INDIAN GAMING Regulatory Act of 1988 provided a regulatory framework for all reservation-based gaming operations. The legislation was considered and passed by the U.S. Senate on September 15, 1988, and by the House of Representatives on September 26, 1988. The final version of this enactment mandated federal jurisdiction over tribal gaming, while returning to tribes a measure of tribal authority and economic opportunity.

The Indian Gaming Regulatory Act of 1988

AN ACT[1] ... To regulate gaming on Indian lands. *Be it enacted by the Senate and House of Representatives in Congress assembled,* That this Act may be cited as the "Indian Gaming Regulatory Act."

FINDINGS

SEC. 2. The Congress finds that – (1) numerous Indian tribes have become engaged in or have licensed gaming activities on Indian lands as a means of generating tribal governmental revenue; (2) Federal courts have held that section 2103 of the Revised Statutes (25 U.S.C. 81) requires Secretarial review of management contracts dealing with Indian gaming, but does not provide standards for approval of such contracts; (3) existing Federal law does not provide clear standards or regulations for the conduct of gaming on Indian lands; (4) a principal goals of Federal Indian policy is to promote tribal economic development, tribal self-sufficiency and strong tribal government; and (5) Indian tribes have the exclusive right to regulate gaming

259

activity on Indian lands if the gaming activity is not specifically prohibited by Federal law and is conducted within a Statute which does not, as a matter of criminal law and public policy, prohibit such gaming activity.

DECLARATION OF POLICY

SEC. 3. The purpose of this Act is – (1) to provide a statutory basis for the operation of gaming by Indian tribes as a means of promoting tribal economic development, self-sufficiency and strong tribal governments; (2) to provide a statutory basis for the regulation of gaming by an Indian tribe adequate to shield it from organized crime and other corrupting influences, to ensure that the Indian tribes is the primary beneficiary of the gaming operation and to assure that gaming is conducted fairly and honestly by both the operator and players; and (3) to declare that the establishment of independent Federal regulatory authority for gaming on Indian lands, the establishment of Federal standards for gaming on Indian lands and the establishment of a national Indian Gaming Commission are necessary to meet congressional concerns regarding gaming and to protect such gaming as a means of generating tribal revenue ...

> *"... Under the Indian Gaming Regulatory Act there are special rules governing the use of tribal gaming revenues. Tribes must ... use gaming resources: to pay for tribal government operations ... provide for the general welfare of the tribe and its members ... support economic development ... [and] ... fund and local government agencies ..."*
>
> ADA E. DEER[2]

NATIONAL INDIAN GAMING COMMISSION

SEC. 5. (a) There is established within the Department of the Interior a Commission to be known as the National Indian Gaming Commission. (b)(1) The Commission shall be composed of three full-time members who shall be appointed as follows: (A) A chairman, who shall be appointed by the President with the advice and consent of the Senate; and (B) two associate members who shall be appointed by the Secretary of the Interior.

(2)(A) The Attorney General shall conduct a background investigation on any person considered for appointment to the Commission. (B) The Secretary shall publish the name and other information the Secretary deems pertinent regarding a nominee for the Commission and shall allow a period of not less than thirty days for receipt of public comment. (3) Not more than two members of the Commission shall be of the same political party. At least two members of the Commission shall be enrolled members of any Indian tribe ...

Approved October 17, 1988.

Figure 38. Revenues from tribally-owned casinos continue to fund upgrades in tribal health, education, and social service programming. Most tribal nations, however, do not operate casinos (Photo: B. Lee Wilson).

Chapter XXXI

Common Decency: The Native American Graves & Repatriation Act of 1990

THE NATIVE AMERICAN Graves and Repatriation Act of 1990 returned to tribes control over the physical remains of their ancestors. Congress created this legislation to address human rights offenses and myriad related ethical dilemmas posed by the ongoing collection and maintenance of Native American, Alaskan Native, and Hawaiian Native human remains, e.g., those gathered primarily during the nineteenth and twentieth centuries. These remains—kept on-site at public museums, universities, and in private collections—often included associated personal objects.

> *"... When human remains are displayed in museums or historical societies, it is never the bones of white soldiers or the first European settlers that came to this continent that are lying in glass cases. It is Indian remains ... "*
>
> SENATOR INOUYE
> OF HAWAII

The Native American Graves and Repatriation Act required the near immediate removal of Native American and Native Hawaiian human remains from private and public collections, and their return to direct descendants for burial or other culturally relevant disposition. The act also included provisions for the protection of civil rights in matters specific to religious funerary practices. In the case of tribally-linked human remains of great antiquity, such as those unearthed in the course of reconstruction archeological surveys of building sites, the act established a process to follow in determining which American Indian nation could claim the remains upon conclusion of a scientific review.

While this act does address the disposition of Native American human remains of thousands of years in antiquity, most of the remains and associated personal belongings affected by this legislation were collected during recent generations—sometimes legally, sometimes illegally. One example of a legal collection followed the March 25, 1916, death of a quiet celebrity named Ishi, the last remaining member of the Yahi people. Well-known cultural anthropologist Alfred Kroeber was in Europe when his informant-turned-friend, Ishi, died in California. Kroeber tried to block an autopsy, yet before he could return, one was performed; Kroeber soon learned that a portion of his friend's remains had been commoditized and sent to the Smithsonian Institution for display.[1]

Prior to the November 16, 1990 passage of the Native American Graves and Repatriation Act, U.S. senators discussed the merits of its precursor, House of Representatives Bill 5237.[2] A congressional subcommittee had been created after the completion of a three-year consultation with tribal representatives, national museum staff members, archeologists, cultural anthropologists, and many others. The report of the subcommittee's findings and recommendations provided the foundation for the House proposal, as it informed members of Congress of tribal interests in the return of skeletal remains, funeral clothing, and other personal items displayed in public and private museums or in storage. The subcommittee investigation included a review of records of federally/state tolerated, yet specious, military actions—i.e., the massacres of captive family groups during the 1860s and 1890s.

The following excerpt of the Senate's discussion of this proposed legislation, as recorded in the Congressional Record of October 26, 1990, provides an overview of the depth and range of the congressional considerations framed within this act.[3]

Excerpt from the Congressional Record of October 26, 1990

Mr. INOUYE: "Mr. President, I am pleased to rise in support of H. R. 5237, the Native American Grave Protection and Repatriation Act. Native Americans have waited a long time for this restoration of their rights and I urge the Senate to not delay any longer in undoing this injustice that began so long ago ... When the Army Surgeon General ordered the collection of Indian osteological remains during the second half of the nineteenth century, his demands were enthusiastically met not only by Army medical personnel, but by collectors who made money from selling Indians skulls to the Army Medical Museum. The desires of

Indians to bury their dead were ignored. In fact, correspondence from individuals engaged in robbing graves often speaks of the dangers these collectors faced when Indians caught them digging up burial grounds."

> *"... When the Army Surgeon General ordered the collection of Indian osteological remains during the second half of the Nineteenth Century, his demands were enthusiastically met not only by Army medical personnel, but by collectors who made money from selling Indians skulls to the Army Medical Museum. The desires of Indians to bury their dead were ignored ..."*

When human remains are displayed in museums or historical societies, it is never the bones of white soldiers or the first European settlers that came to this continent that are lying in glass cases. It is Indian remains. The message that this sends to the rest of the world is that Indians are culturally and physically different from and inferior to non-Indians. This is racism. In light of the important role that death and burial rites play in Native American cultures, it is all the more offensive that the civil rights of America's first citizens have been so flagrantly violated for the past century. Even today, when supposedly great strides have been made to recognize the rights of Indians to recover the skeletal remains of their ancestors and to reprocess items of sacred value or cultural patrimony, the wishes of Native Americans are often ignored by the scientific community. In cases where Native Americans have attempted to regain items that were inappropriately alienated from the tribe, they have often met with resistance from museums and have not had the legal ability or financial resources to pursue the return of the goods. It is virtually only in instances where a Museum has agreed for moral or political reasons to return the goods that tribes have had success in retrieving property. Tribes have had similar difficulties in preventing the excavation and sale of goods that unscrupulous collectors have acquired. The legislation before us today is the product of a great deal of dialogue and compromise and I believe it is a good bill and is fair to all sides. In 1987, the Select Committee on Indian Affairs held a hearing on legislation to provide a process for the repatriation of Native American human remains and cultural patrimony. At that time, the representative of the American Association of Museums asked the committee if it would consider delaying action on the measure for one year, while the museum community attempted to fashion a dialogue with representatives of the Indian community to see whether they could develop a policy together to guide the repatriation of Native American remains and cultural patrimony. The committee agreed, and that dialogue proceeded. Their final report was submitted to the committee in February of this year. I believe we all recognize the value of the work carried out by museums. When we visit museums and look at remnants of past civilizations, we are really learning about ourselves, and how our societies and civilizations have evolved. Museums enhance our quality of life. As enlightened people we welcome scientific inquiry and the opportunity to know more about ourselves. Accordingly, we welcome the preservation and scientific purposes that museums fulfill. Mr. President, the bill before us today is not about the validity of museums or the value of scientific inquiry. Rather, it is about human rights. I did not anticipate that this legislation will result in a wholesale raid on Museum collections, as I have heard previous versions of this bill characterized. I do not believe the rights of antique collectors will be taken away. It is ironic to note that the greatest opposition to this proposal has come from those who have most strongly ignored Native Americans in their efforts to retrieve items that were improperly alienated from their tribes or who are trying to prevent inappropriate and insensitive display of their ancestral goods and remains. This legislation is designed to facilitate a more open and cooperative relationship between Native Americans and museums. For museums that have dealt honestly and in good faith with Native Americans, this legislation will have little effect. For museums and institutions which have consistently ignored the requests of Native Americans, this legislation will give Native Americans greater ability to negotiate. Mr. President, I believe this bill represents a major step in correcting an injustice that started over 100 years ago. It is appropriate that the Congress take an active role in helping to restore these rights to Native Americans and I urge the adoption of the measure by the Senate."

Mr. AKAKA: "Mr. President, I rise in support of H. R. 5237, the Native American Grave Protection and Repatriation Act. I testified in July before the House Committee on Interior and Insular Affairs in support of this measure for several reasons. Native Hawaiians have always considered the burial of their kapuna, or ancestors, the epitome of cultural respect. It is understood that once the kapuna leaves this world to journey on to the spiritual world, their remains should never be disturbed. Their bones are the only connection between the spirit world and the physical world. However, over the decades Native Hawaiian remains and objects uncovered accidentally or during scientific excavations, have been placed in museums such as the Smithsonian Institution. Mr. President, the National Museum of the American Indian Act of 1989 has set a precedent for the return of Native Hawaiian and Native American remains and funerary objects from the Smithsonian Institution to their rightful resting places. I am proud to say that a Native Hawaiian organization, Hui Malama I Na Kupuna o Hawai'i, received the first repatriated Hawaiian remains under the act this July. Native Hawaiian remains still at the Smithsonian will be repatriated next year when land set aside to receive the remains is properly prepared. H.R. 5237 is the next step in returning remains and objects still in the possession of other federally funded museums and government agencies to the native homeland. The bill is a comprehensive effort to repatriate Native American, Native Alaskan, and Native Hawaiian remains, prohibit the trafficking and profiting from the sale of Native American human remains without the right of possession, and eliminate the long-standing policy of scientific research on future remains found. I also strongly support a provision that would name the Office of Hawaiian Affairs and Hui Malama I Na Kupuna o Hawai'i as the Native Hawaiian organizations responsible for receiving the repatriated remains and objects. Mr. President, I am pleased that the Hawaii State Legislature, and other State legislatures, have also taken strides in providing for the protection of native remains and burial grounds. With this gesture, they have reaffirmed their recognition of cultural sensitivity and respect toward their Native American and Native Hawaiian populations. It is long overdue that the remains of Native Hawaiians and Native Americans can be accorded proper dignity and respect, and not allowed to be treated as objects of curiosity."

Mr. MOYNIHAN: "Mr. President, first let me say that this is a hugely important legislation. The treatment of Native Americans has been one of our Nation's greatest failures. It is due to the distinguished chairman of the Select Committee of Indian Affairs that we shall now rightfully move to restore tens of thousands of remains to the families and tribes to whom these remains are most appropriately to be entrusted. It is also my understanding that many museums, including the American Museums of Natural History, the Field Museum of Natural History, Harvard University, and others, have now, because of the efforts of the chairman, changed their policy relating to Native American remains by agreeing to return these remains to the tribes that request them. Many museums have recognized the rights and concerns of Native Americans. As well, the museums want to deal fairly with the funerary objects. Is it not the view of the chairman of the Select Committee on Indian Affairs that the useums have changed their position on the return of Native American remains and funerary objects?"

Mr. INOUYE: "Yes; the senior Senator of New York is correct."

Mr. MOYNIHAN: "Would it not be possible to encourage the museums and Native Americans to resolve in a similar manner the return of artifacts, such as sacred objects and objects of cultural patrimony? The distinguished chairman of the select committee, of course, has been much more involved than I. And I would accept his view."

Mr. INOUYE: "This legislation does nothing to prevent voluntary agreements from being negotiated between museums and Native Americans with respect to the return of remains or any other items."

Mr. MOYNIHAN: "I thank the distinguished senior Senator from Hawaii."

The Native American Graves and Repatriation Act

AN ACT[4] to provide for the protection of Native American Graves, and for other purposes. *Be it enacted by the Senate and House of Representatives of the United States of America in Congress assembled,*

SECTION 1, SHORT TITLE

.This act may be cited as the "Native American Graves Protection and Repatriation Act."

SEC. 2. DEFINITIONS

For purposes of this act, the term-(1) "burial site" means any natural or prepared physical location, whether originally below, on, or above the surface of the earth, into which is part of the death right or ceremony of a culture, individual human remains are deposited. (2) "cultural affiliation" means that there is a relationship of shared group identity which can be reasonably traced historically or prehistorically between a present-day Indian tribe or Native Hawaiian organization and an identifiable earlier group. (3) "cultural items" means human remains and (A) "associated funerary objects" which shall mean objects that, as part of the death rite or ceremony of a culture, are reasonably believed to have been placed with individual human remains either at the time of death or later, and both the human remains

268

and associated funerary objects are presently in the possession or control of a federal agency or museum, except that other items exclusively made for burial purposes or to contain human remains shall be considered as associated funerary objects. (B) "unassociated funerary objects" which shall mean objects that, as a part of the death rite or ceremony of a culture, are reasonably believed to have been placed with individual human remains either at the time of death or later, where the remains are not in the possession or control of the federal agency or museum and the objects can be identified by a preponderance of the evidence is related to specific individuals or families or to known human remains or, by a preponderance of the evidence, as having been removed from a specific burial site of an individual culturally affiliated with a particular Indian tribe, (C) "sacred objects" which shall mean specific ceremonial objects which are needed by traditional Native American religious leaders for the purpose of traditional Native American religions by their present-day adherents, and (D) "cultural patrimony" which shall mean an object having ongoing historical, traditional, or cultural importance central to the Native American group or culture itself, rather than property owned by an individual Native American, and which, therefore, cannot be alienated, appropriated, or conveyed by any individual regarding us of whether or not the individual is a member of the Indian tribe or Native Hawaiian organization and such objects shall have been considered inalienable by such Native American group at any time the object was separated from such group. (4) "Federal agency" means any department, agency, or instrumentality of the United States. Such term does not include the Smithsonian Institution. (5) "federal lands" means any land other than tribal lands which are controlled or owned by the United States, including land selected by but not yet conveyed to Alaska Native corporations and groups organized pursuant to the Alaska Native Claims Settlement Act of 1971. (6) "Hui Malama I Na Kupuna O Hawai'i Nei" means the nonprofit, Native Hawaiian organization incorporated under the laws of the state of Hawaii by that name on April 17, 1989, for the purpose of providing guidance and expertise in decisions dealing with Native Hawaiian cultural issues, particularly burial issues. (7) "Indian tribe" means any tribe, band, nation, or other organized group or community of Indians, including any Alaska native village (as defined in, or established pursuant to, the Alaska Native Claims Settlement Act in per annum, which is recognized as eligible for the special programs and services provided by the United States to Indians because of their status as Indians. (8) "museum" means any institution or state or local government agency (including any institution of higher learning) that receives federal funds and has possession of, or control over, Native American cultural items. Such term does not include the Smithsonian Institution or any other federal agency. (9) "Native American" means of, or relating to, a tribe, people, or culture that is indigenous to the United States. (10) "Native Hawaiian" means any individual who is a descendent of the aboriginal people who, prior to 1778, occupied and exercised sovereignty in the area that now constitutes the State of Hawaii. (11) "Native Hawaiian organization" means any organization which - (A) serves and represents the interests of Native Hawaiians, (B) has as a primary and stated purpose the provision of services to Native Hawaiians, and (C) has expertise in Native Hawaiian Affairs, and shall include the Office of Hawaiian Affairs and Hui Malama I Na Kupuna O Hawai'i Nei. (12) "Office of Hawaiian Affairs" means the Office of Hawaiian Affairs established by the Constitution of the State of Hawaii. (13) "right of possession" means possession obtained with the voluntary consent of an individual or group that had authority of alienation. The original acquisition of a Native American unassociated funerary object, sacred object or object of cultural patrimony from an Indian tribe or Native Hawaiian organization with the voluntary consent of an individual or group with authority to alienate such object is deemed to give right of possession of that object, unless the phrase so defined would, as applied in section 7 (c), result in a Fifth Amendment taking by the United States as determined by the United States Claims Court pursuant to 28 U.S.C. 1491 by which event the "right of possession" shall be as provided under otherwise applicable property law. The original acquisition of Native American human remains and associated funerary objects which were excavated, exhumed, or otherwise obtained with full knowledge and consent of the next of kin or the official governing body of the appropriate culturally affiliated Indian tribe or Native Hawaiian organization is deemed to give right of possession to those remains. (14) "Secretary" means the Secretary of the Interior. (15) "tribal land" means (A) all lands within the exterior boundaries of any Indian reservation; (B) all dependent Indian communities; (C) any lands administered for the benefit of

Native Hawaiians pursuant to the Hawaiian Homes Commission Act, 1920, and section 4 of Public Law 86-3 ["... An Act To provide for the admission of the State of Hawaii into the Union ..."] ...

SEC. 3. OWNERSHIP.

Native American Human Remains and Objects. The ownership or control of Native American cultural items which are excavated or discovered on Federal or tribal lands after the date of enactment of this Act shall be (with priority given in the order listed) - (1) in the case of Native American human remains and associated funerary objects, in the lineal descendants of the Native American; or (2) in any case in which such lineal descendants cannot be ascertained, and in the case of unassociated funerary objects, sacred objects, objects of cultural patrimony - (A) in the Indian tribe or Native Hawaiian organization on whose tribal land such objects or remains were discovered; (B) in the Indian tribe or Native Hawaiian organization which has the closest cultural affiliation with such remains or objects and which, upon notice, states a claim for

"... SEC. 3 ... If the discovery occurred in connection with an activity ... [e.g.,] ... construction, mining, logging, and agriculture, the person shall cease the activity ... [and] ... make a reasonable effort to protect the items discovered before resuming such activity ..."

such remains or objects; or (C) if the cultural affiliation of the objects cannot be reasonably ascertained and if the objects were discovered on Federal land that is recognized by a final judgment of the Indian Claims Commission or the United States Court of Claims as the aboriginal land of some Indian tribe - (1) in the Indian tribe that is recognized as aboriginal occupying the area in which the objects were discovered, if upon notice, such tribe states a claim for such remains are objects, or (2) if it can be shown by a preponderance of the evidence that a different tribe has a stronger cultural relationship with remains or objects than the tribe or organization specified in paragraph (1), in the Indian tribe that has the strongest demonstrated relationship, if upon notice, such tribe states claim for such remains or objects. (b)

Unclaimed Native American Human Remains and Objects. Native American cultural items not claimed under subsection (a) shall be disposed of in accordance with regulations promulgated by the Secretary in consultation with the review committee established under section 8, Native American groups, representatives of museums and the scientific community. (c) Intentional Excavation and Removal of Native American Human Remains and Objects. The intentional removal from excavation of Native American cultural items from Federal or tribal lands for purposes of discovery, study, or removal of such items is permitted only if - (1) such remains are excavated or removed pursuant to a permit issued under section 4 of the Archaeological Resources Protection Act of 1979 (93 Stat. 721; 16 U.S.C. 470aa et seq.) which shall be consistent with this Act; (2) such items are excavated or removed after consultation with the or, in the case of tribal lands, consent of the appropriate (if any) Indian tribe or Native Hawaiian organization; (3) the ownership and right of control of the disposition of such items shall be as provided in subsections (a) and (b); and (4) proof of consultation or consent under paragraph (2) is shown.

INADVERTENT DISCOVERY OF NATIVE AMERICAN REMAINS AND OBJECTS.

any person who knows, or has reason to know, that such person has discovered Native American cultural items on Federal or tribal lands after the date of enactment of this Act shall notify, in writing, the Secretary of the Department, or head of any other agency or instrumentality of the United States, having primary management authority with respect to Federal lands and the appropriate Indian tribe or Native Hawaiian organization with respect to tribal lands, if known or readily ascertainable, and, in the case of lands that have been selected by and Alaska Native Corporation or group organized pursuant to the Alaska Native Claims Settlement Act of 1971, the appropriate Corporation or group. If the discovery occurred in connection with an activity, including (but not limited to) construction, mining, logging, and agriculture, the person shall cease the activity in the area of the discovery, make a reasonable effort to protect the items discovered before resuming such activity, and provide notice under this subsection. Following the notification under this subsection, and upon certification by the Secretary of the Department or the head of any agency or instrumentality of the

United States or the appropriate Indian tribe or Native Hawaiian organization that notification has been received, the activity may resume after 30 days of such certification. (2) The disposition of and control over any cultural items excavated and or removed under this subsection shall be determined as provided for in this section. (3) If the Secretary of the Interior consents, the responsibilities (in whole or in part) under paragraphs (1) and (2) of the Secretary of any department (other than the Department of the Interior) or they had any other agency or instrumentality may be delegated to the Secretary with respect to any land managed by such other Secretary or agency head. (e) Relinquishment. Nothing in this section shall prevent the governing body of the Indian tribe or Native Hawaiian organization from expressly relinquishing control over any Native American human remains, or title to or control over any funerary objects, or sacred object . . .

SEC. 4. ILLEGAL TRAFFICKING, ILLEGAL TRAFFICKING
Chapter 53 of title 18, United States code, is amended by adding at the end thereof the following new section: "1170. Illegal Trafficking in Native American Human Remains and Cultural Items." (b) Whosoever knowingly sells, purchases, uses for-profit, or transports for sale or profit, the human remains of a Native American without the right of possession to those remains as provided in the Native American Graves Protection and Repatriation Act shall be fined in accordance with this title, or imprisoned not more than 12 months, or both, and in the case of a second or subsequent violation, defined in accordance with this title, or imprisoned not more than 5 years, or both ... (b) Table of Contents. The table of contents for chapter 53 of title 18, United States Code, is amended by adding at the end thereof the following new item: "1170. Illegal Trafficking in Native American Human Remains and Cultural Items."

SEC. 5. INVENTORY FOR HUMAN REMAINS
AND ASSOCIATED FUNERARY OBJECTS
In General. Each Federal agency and each museum which has possession or control over holdings or collections of Native American human remains and associated funerary objects shall compile an inventory of such items and, to the extent possible based on information possessed by such museum or Federal agency, identify the geographical and cultural affiliation of such item. (b) Requirements. (1) the inventories and identifications

required under subsection (a) shall be – (A) completed in consultation with tribal government and Native Hawaiian organization officials and traditional religious leaders; (B) completed by not later than the date that is five years after the date of enactment of this Act, and (C) made available both during the time they are being conducted and afterward to a review committee established under section 8. (2) Upon request by an Indian tribe or Native Hawaiian organization which receives or should have received notice, a museum or Federal agencies shall supply additional available documentation to supplement the information required by subsection (a) of this section. The term "documentation" means a summary of existing museum or Federal agency records, including inventories or catalogs, relevant studies, or other pertinent data for the limited purpose of determining the geographical origin, cultural affiliation, and basic facts surrounding acquisition and access of Native American human remains and associated funerary objects subject to this section. Such term does not mean, and this Act shall not be construed to be an authorization for, the initiation of new scientific studies of such remains and associated funerary objects or other means of acquiring or preserving additional scientific information from such remains and objects. (c) Extension of Time for Inventory. Any museum which has made a good-faith effort to carry out an inventory and identification under this section, but which has been unable to complete the process, may appeal to The Secretary for an extension of the time requirements set forth in subsection (b) (1) (B). The Secretary may extend such time requirements for any such museum upon a finding of good faith effort. An indication of good faith shall include the development of a plan to carry out the inventory and identification process. (d) Notification. (1) If the cultural affiliation of any particular Native American human remains or associated funerary objects is determined pursuant to this section, the Federal agency or museum concerned shall, not later than 6 months after the completion of the inventory, notify the affected Indian tribes or Native Hawaiian organizations. (2) The notice required by paragraph (1) shall include information- (A) which identifies each Native American human remains or associated funerary objects and the circumstances surrounding its acquisition; (B) which lists the human remains or associated funerary objects that are clearly identifiable as to tribal origin; and (C) which lists the Native American human remains and associated peer itinerary objects that are not clearly identifiable as being culturally affiliated with that Indian tribe or Native Hawaiian organization, but which, given the totality of circumstances surrounding acquisition of the remains or objects, are determined by a reasonable belief to be remains or objects culturally affiliated with the Indian tribe or Native Hawaiian organization. (3) A copy of each notice provided under paragraph (1) shall be sent to the Secretary who shall publish such notice in the Federal Register. (e) Inventory. For the purposes of this section, the term "inventory" means a simple itemized list that summarizes the information called for by this section.

"... SEC.7 ... Native American human remains ... shall be expeditiously returned where the requesting Indian tribe or Native Hawaiian organization can show cultural affiliation ..."

SEC. 6. SUMMARY FOR UNASSOCIATED FUNERARY
OBJECTS, SACRED OBJECTS, AND CULTURAL PATRIMONY
In General. Each Federal agency or museum which has possession or control over holdings or collections of Native American associated funerary objects, sacred objects, or objects of cultural patrimony shall provide a written summary of such objects based upon available information held by such agency or museum. The summary shall describe the scope of the collection, kinds of objects included, reference to the geographical location, means and period of acquisition and cultural affiliation, where readily ascertainable. (b) Requirements. (1) The summary required under subsection (a) shall be-(A) in lieu of an object-by-object inventory; (B) followed by consultation with tribal government and Native Hawaiian organization officials and traditional religious leaders; and (C) completed by not later than the date that is 3 years after the date of enactment of this Act. (2) Upon request, Indian Tribes and Native Hawaiian organizations shall have access to records, catalogs, relevant studies or other pertinent data for the limited purposes of determining the geographic origin, cultural affiliation, and basic facts surrounding acquisition and accession of Native American objects subject to this section. Such information shall be provided in a reasonable manner to be agreed upon by all parties.

SEC. 7. REPATRIATION

Repatriation of Native American Human Remains and Objects Possessed or Controlled by Federal Agencies and Museums. (1) if, pursuant to section 5, the cultural affiliation of Native American human remains and associated funerary objects with particular Indian tribe or Native Hawaiian organization is established, then the Federal agency or museum, upon the request of the known lineal descendent of the Native American or of the tribal organization and pursuant to subsections (b) and (e) of this section, shall expeditiously return such remains and associated funerary objects. (2) If, pursuant to section 6, the cultural affiliation with particular Indian tribe or Native Hawaiian organization is shown with respect to unassociated funerary objects, sacred objects or objects of cultural patrimony, then the federal agency or museum, upon the request of the Indian tribe or Native Hawaiian organization and pursuant to subsections (b), (c) and (e) of this section, shall expeditiously return such objects. (3) The return of cultural items covered by this Act shall be in consultation with requesting lineal descendent or tribe or organization to determine the place and manner of delivery of such items. (4) Where cultural affiliation of Native American human remains and funerary objects has not been established in an inventory prepared pursuant to sections 5, or the summary pursuant to section 6, or where Native American human remains and funerary objects are not included upon any such inventory, then, upon request and pursuant to subsections (b) and (e) and, in the case of unassociated funerary objects, subsection (c), such Native American human remains in funerary objects shall be expeditiously returned where the requesting Indian tribe or Native Hawaiian organization can show cultural affiliation by a preponderance of the evidence based upon geographical, kinship, biological, archaeological, anthropological, linguistic, folkloric, oral traditional, historical, or other relevant information or expert opinion. (5) Upon request and pursuant to subsections (b), (c) and (e), sacred objects and objects of cultural patrimony shall be expeditiously returned to where - (A) the requesting party is the direct lineal descendent of an individual who owned the sacredobject; (B) the requesting Indian tribe or Native Hawaiian organization can show that the object was owned or controlled by the tribe or organization; or (C) the requesting Indian tribe or Native Hawaiian organization can show that the sacred object was owned or controlled by a member thereof, provided that in the case where a sacred object was owned by a member thereof, there are no identifiable lineal descendants of said member or the lineal descendants, upon notice, has failed to make a claim for the object under this Act. (b) Scientific Study. If the lineal descendent, Indian tribe or Native Hawaiian organization requests the return of culturally affiliated Native American cultural items, the Federal agency or museum shall expeditiously return such items unless such items are indispensable for completion of a specific scientific study, the outcome of which would be of major benefit to the United States. Such items shall be returned by no later than 90 days after the date on which the scientific study is completed. (c) Standard of Repatriation. If unknown lineal descendent or an Indian tribe or Native Hawaiian organization request the return of Native American unassociated funerary objects, sacred objects or objects of cultural patrimony pursuant to this Act and presents evidence which, if standing alone before the introduction of evidence to the contrary, would support a finding that the Federal agency or museum did not have the right of possession, and such agency or museum shall return such objects unless they can overcome such inference and prove that it has a right of possession to the objects. (d) Sharing of Information by Federal Agencies and Museums.-Any Federal agency or museum shall share what information it does possess regarding the object in question with the known lineal descendent, Indian tribe, or Native Hawaiian organization to assist in making a claim under this section. (e) Competing Claims. Where there are multiple requests for repatriation of any cultural item and, after complying with the requirements of this Act, the Federal agency or museum cannot clearly determine which requesting party is the most appropriate claimant, the agency or museum may retain such item until the requesting parties agree upon its disposition or the dispute is otherwise resolved pursuant to the provisions of this Act or by a court of competent jurisdiction. (f) Museum Obligation. Any museum which repatriates any item in good faith pursuant to this Act shall not be liable for claims by an aggrieved party or for claims of breach of fiduciary duty, public trust, or violations of state law that are inconsistent with the provisions of this Act.

SEC. 8. REVIEW COMMITTEE

Establishment. Within 120 days after the date of enactment of this Act, the Secretary shall establish a committee to monitor and review the implementation of the inventory and identification process and repatriation activities required under sections 5, 6 and 7. (b) Membership. (1) The committee established under subsection (a) shall be composed of 7 members, (A) 3 of whom shall be appointed by the Secretary from nominations submitted by Indian tribes, Native Hawaiian organizations, and traditional Native American religious leaders with at least two of such persons being traditional Indian religious leaders; (B) 3 of whom shall be appointed by the Secretary from nominations submitted by national Museum organizations and scientific organizations; and (C) 1 who shall be appointed by the Secretary from a list of persons developed and consented to by all of the members appointed pursuant to sub paragraphs (A) and (B). (2) The Secretary may not appoint Federal officers or employees to the committee. (3) In the event vacancies shall occur, such vacancies shall be filled by the Secretary in the same manner as the original appointment within 90 days of the occurrence of such vacancy (4) Members of the committee established under subsection (a) shall serve without pay, but shall be reimbursed at a rate equal to the daily rate for GS-18 of the General Schedule for each day (including travel time) for which the member is actually engaged in committee business. Each member shall receive travel expenses, including per diem in lieu of subsistence, in accordance with the sections 5702 and 5703 of title 5, United States Code. (c) Responsibilities. The committee established under subsection (a) shall be responsible for - (1) designating one of the members of the committee as chairman; (2) monitoring the inventory and identification process conducted under sections 5 and 6 to ensure a fair, objective consideration and assessment of all available relevant information and evidence; (3) upon the request of any affected party, reviewing and making findings related to- (A) the identity or cultural affiliation of cultural items, or (B) the return of such items; (4) facilitating the resolution of any disputes among Indian tribes, Native Hawaiian organizations, or lineal descendants and Federal agencies or museums relating to the return of such items including convening the parties to the dispute if deemed desirable; (5) compiling an inventory of culturally unidentifiable human remains that are in the possession or control of each Federal agency and museum and ... recommending specific actions for developing a process for disposition of such remains; (6) consulting with Indian tribes in Native Hawaiian organizations and museums on matters within the scope of the work of the committee affecting such tribes or organization; (7) consulting with the Secretary in the development of regulations to carry out this Act; (8) performing such other related functions as the Secretary may assign to the committee; and (9) making recommendations, if appropriate, regarding future care of cultural items which are to be repatriated. (d) Any records and findings made by the review committee pursuant to this Act relating to the identity or cultural affiliation of any cultural items in the return of such items may be admissible in any action brought under section 15 of this Act. (e) Recommendations and Report. The committee shall make the recommendations under paragraph (c) (5) in consultation with Indian tribes and Native Hawaiian organizations and appropriate scientific and museum groups. (f) Access. The Secretary shall ensure that the committee established under subsection (a) and the members of the committee have reasonable access to Native American cultural items under review and to associated scientific and historic documents. (g) Duties of Secretary. The Secretary shall - (1) establish such rules and regulations for the committee as may be necessary, and (2) provide reasonable administrative and staff support necessary for the deliberations of the committee. (h) Annual Report. The committee established under subsection (a) shall submit an annual report to the Congress on the progress made, and any barriers encountered, in implementing this section during the previous year. (i) Termination. The committee established under subsection (a) shall terminate at the end of the 120-day period beginning on the day the Secretary certifies, a report submitted to Congress, that the work of the committee has been completed.

SEC. 9. PENALTY

Penalty. Any museum that fails to comply with the requirements of this Act may be assessed a civil penalty by the Secretary of the Interior pursuant to procedures established by the Secretary through regulation. A penalty assessed under the subsection shall be determined on the record after opportunity for an agency hearing. Each violation under this subsection shall be a separate offense. (b) Amount of Penalty. - The amount of the penalty assessed under this subsection (a) shall be determined under regulations promulgated pursuant to this Act, taking into account, in addition to other factors-(1) the archaeological, historical, or commercial value of the item involved; (2) the damages suffered, both economic and noneconomic, by an aggrieved party, and (3) the number of violations that have occurred. (c) Actions To Recover Penalties. - If any museum fails to pay an assessment of a civil penalty pursuant to a final order of the Secretary that has been issued under subsection (a) and not appealed or after a final judgment has been rendered on appeal of such order, the Attorney General may institute a civil action in an appropriate district court of the United States to collect the penalty. In such action, the validity and amount of such penalty shall not be subject to review. (d) Subpoenas. In hearings held pursuant to subsection (a), subpoenas may be issued for the attendance and testimony of witnesses and the production of relevant papers, books, and documents. Witnesses so summoned shall be paid the same fees and mileage that are paid to witnesses of the courts of the United States.

SEC. 10. GRANTS

(a) Indian Tribes and Native Hawaiians Organizations. - The Secretary is authorized to make grants to Indian tribes and Native Hawaiian organizations for the purpose of assisting such tribes and organizations in the repatriation of Native American cultural items. (b) Museums. The Secretary is authorized to make grants to museums for the purpose of assisting the museums in conducting the inventories and identification required under sections 5 and 6.

"... SEC. 15 ... The United States district court shall have jurisdiction over any action brought by any person alleging a violation of this Act and shall have the authority to issue such orders as may be necessary to enforce the provisions of this Act ..."

SEC. 11. SAVING PROVISIONS.

Nothing in this Act shall be construed to - (1) limit the authority of any Federal agency or museum to (A) return or repatriate Native American cultural items to Indian tribes, Native Hawaiian organizations, or individuals, and (B) enter into any other agreement with the consent of the culturally affiliated tribe or organization as to the disposition of, or control over, items covered by this Act; (2) delay actions on repatriation requests that are pending on the date of enactment of this Act; (3) deny or otherwise affect access to any court; (4) limit any procedure rule or substantive right which may otherwise be secured to individuals or Indian tribes or Native Hawaiian organizations; or

(5) limit the application of any State or Federal law pertaining to theft or stolen property.

SEC. 12. SPECIAL RELATIONSHIP BETWEEN FEDERAL GOVERNMENT AND INDIAN TRIBES.

This Act reflects the unique relationship between the Federal Government and Indian tribes and Native Hawaiian organizations and should not be construed to establish a precedent with respect to any other individual, organization or foreign government.

SEC. 13. REGULATIONS.

The Secretary shall promulgate regulations to carry out this Act within 12 months of enactment.

SEC. 14. AUTHORIZATION OF APPROPRIATIONS.

There is authorized to be appropriated such sums as may be necessary to carry out this Act.

SEC. 15. ENFORCEMENT.

The United States district court shall have jurisdiction over any action brought by any person alleging a violation of this Act and shall have the authority to issue such orders as may be necessary to enforce the provisions of this Act.

Approved November 16, 1990.

Chapter XXXII

Toward A More Perfect Union

"We desperately wish that we could change this history...but of course we cannot."

THE EMANCIPATION Proclamation signed by President Lincoln during the Civil War grew out of an enduring national commitment to the concepts of *Life, Liberty, and the Pursuit of Happiness.* Yet even the power and eloquence of this proclamation could not overcome the uneasy social norms that continued the ranking of America's racial and ethnic groups. For decades, this ranking affected all cross-cultural American relationships. The fact that such ideologies precipitated disastrous compromises of the most fundamental human rights of African Americans, well into the twentieth and twenty-first centuries, is well known. Lesser known, however, is the intensity and frequency of hate crimes committed against Native Americans throughout the nineteenth and twentieth centuries, and continuing into the twenty-first. Indeed, throughout the years of this democracy's adolescence, the murders, starvation, rapes, and displacement of members of American Indian nations were accepted on some amorphous national level as unseemly rites of an enduring American belief in the dogma of Manifest Destiny.

Reservation histories testify to the disastrous outcomes of a series of hastily constructed policies of the past—from the 1800s into the 1960s—public laws grounded in rumors, bravado, and erroneous reporting. The resulting ill-informed legislating cost tribes innumerable lives and generated decades of despair. Conversely, later Congresses crafted a measure of corrective legislation—beginning in the mid-1930s and continuing into contemporary times—layers of public laws based more on inquiry and review than on innuendo. These latter efforts seem worthy of a collective and retrospective nod of respect.

Congress represents just one piece of America's governance puzzle. The public laws its legislators place on the books may or may not be apparent in day-to-day interpretations and applications of those very laws. Vine Deloria, Jr, co-author of an exhaustive study of treaties, agreements, and other documents pertinent to the topic of American Indian Diplomacy, concluded that the Congressional Record demonstrates that Congress had, more often than not, acted responsibly toward tribes: "The historical record ... [of congressional legislation] ... is far more positive than most people would believe." Although his analysis addressed this nation's legacy of disparate treatment of tribally affiliated Americans, he found the root cause of that disparity not within the actions of Congress, but rather in the ways courts historically, and within contemporary timelines, had interpreted these laws:

> Some treaties and agreements were not ratified by Congress because its members believed they would be harmful to Indians ... Federal and State courts, however, in an effort to reconcile the interpretations of treaties and agreements with prevailing public sentiments of the time, often twisted language beyond its natural meaning to fit predetermined results. The Supreme Court has been notoriously guilty of violating Indian rights in that respect. Many treaties and agreements, clearly articulating Indian rights in their language, have been interpreted narrowly by the courts, resulting in a loss of rights for Indians.[2]

Whether or not individual legislative mandates are ever implemented in the manner intended by Congress is a reality further mediated at state government, local government, and individual citizenry levels. Consequently, many mandates of this legislative set have been implemented in ways inconsistent with the expressed original intentions and expectations of Congress. This phenomenon is most apparent in limited state and local responses to legislative mandates specific to citizenship, emergency appropriations, land allotment, health and water safety, boarding schools, child welfare, law enforcement, and those mandates requiring consultations with tribal nations.

Certainly Congress intended its granting of citizenship in 1924 to carry with it the basic rights of citizenship, yet decades passed before some states allowed American Indians, even veterans of WWI and WWII, to register to vote.[3] During the late nineteenth century, Congress tried to send cattle to western reservations to stave off starvation epidemics, but unscrupulous contractors countered that intent through corrupt deals involving the purchase of thin, sick cattle, most of which never reached reservation lands. And it was local reservation agents, not members of Congress, who used land allotment legislation as a rationale for prohibiting tribal relatives from walking from one land allotment (e.g., a 160-acre plot) onto another on the basis of their own free will. Since its early boarding school legislation required parental consent, it is unlikely that members of Congress expected any reservation agents to withhold emergency food from families who did not give permission for their child's removal. Furthermore, Congress never authorized agents to forcibly remove children from their communities, nor did Congress authorized any agent to send children away to work in "Wild West Shows" in New York and Europe.[4]

Local, state, or federal actions that fall outside of the limits of regulatory compliance standards (i.e., congressional mandates) undercut even the most adaptive legislative actions. For example, in 2016, congressional lawmaking specific to the disposition of tribal remains and burial sites—and related treaty agreements previously ratified by Congress—did nothing to prevent the denigration of tribal cemeteries during the course of a corporate pipeline project.

And although Congress did block tribal jurisdiction in matters of serious crimes in 1885, it simultaneously transferred jurisdictional responsibilities to U.S. governmental law enforcement agencies (e.g., today's Federal Bureau of Investigation)—with an expectation that serious crimes would still be investigated and prosecuted. However, Congress eventually learned about related patterns of neglect, i.e., law enforcement agents of some locations failing to investigate rapes or murders of tribal members. These and other illegal, locally defined actions—all contrary to the intent expressed within the public laws of this set—compromised in some regions the safety of generations of reservation families.

"... I feel that the ... [U.S. Judicial] ... system has failed ... and continued incarceration of Leonard Peltier* is a sad commentary on the U.S ... and the humanitarian values America professes to have ... "

ARCHBISHOP
DESMOND TUTU [6]

*Citizen of Anishinabe and Dakota/Lakota Nations

Federal Findings

Field work of congressional subcommittees, intermittently—over the course of this collection's 1885-1990 time line—informed members of Congress of ways earlier legislative actions had adversely affected tribal nations. Over time, such fact-finding contributed to the development of legislation which generated more positive outcomes, a reality most apparent in public laws enacted since 1961. This congressional fact-finding continues into contemporary times. In 1981, the U.S. Commission on Civil Rights recommended changes in federal law enforcement on reservations—the long-standing federal responsibility first established in the 1885 Seven Major Crimes Act. The commission's findings resulted in the following recommendation for changes in federal policies toward American Indian nations:

> The FBI should be relieved of its primary role for investigating major crimes occurring in Indian country, and this responsibility should be assumed by the Bureau of Indian Affairs and tribal investigators, with the FBI providing backup support as requested. The FBI should also be utilized on reservations similarly to the ways it is utilized in other governmental jurisdictions [e.g., U.S. states].[5]

This recommendation to transfer reservation law enforcement responsibilities from the Federal Bureau of Investigations (FBI) to the Bureau of Indian Affairs (BIA) did not lead to any actual jurisdictional changes. Twenty-seven years later, in 2008, yet another federal report further documented the lack of consistent federal law enforcement in and around reservation communities:

> Indian Country continues to face a crisis of violent crime. A Bureau of Justice Statistics Report covering the period 1992–2002 found that American Indians are victims of violent crime at a rate more than twice that of the national population ... American Indians experienced an estimated 1 violent crime for every 10 residents over age 12. The figures are even worse for Native American women, who are the victims of rape or sexual assault at a rate more than 2.5 times that of American women in general ... 34.1 percent of American Indian and Alaska Native women—more than one in three—will be raped in their lifetime. This level of violence against native women is tragic and unacceptable. The majority of perpetrators of violent crime against Indians were non-Indian. [7]

Bureau of Indian Affairs Y2000 Apology

Laws of this legislative set are outgrowths of the 1819 Civilization Act's call for the repression of all American Indian cultures. Nearly two hundred years later, 338 federally recognized American Indian nations and 229 Alaskan Native tribes continue to demonstrate their endurance and cultural resilience—by their very existence.[8]

On September 8, 2000, the Bureau of Indian Affairs announced its 175th year of operation as an "Occasion for Reflection." In a related news release, portions of the BIA public apology delivered earlier that day by Kevin Gover, then Assistant Secretary of Indian Affairs, to all American Indian and Alaska Native peoples, were made public. In his delivery of the apology, Gover pointed out the bureau's lengthy history of cultural assaults upon American Indian and Alaska Native cultures, giving emphasis to the enrollment of tribal children into distant BIA boarding schools. Here is one portion of that release:

> We desperately wish that we could change this history ... but of course we cannot. On behalf of the Bureau of Indian Affairs, I extend this formal apology to Indian people for the historical conduct of this agency ... These wrongs ... must be acknowledged if the healing is to begin ... The Bureau of Indian Affairs was born in 1824 in a time of war on Indian people ... May it live in the year 2000 and beyond as an instrument of their prosperity.[9]

"This country is a thousand times bigger than any two men in it, or any two parties in it."

WILL ROGERS

Chapter Notes

PREFACE

[1]The Library of Congress in Washington, D.C., is the result of a public law enacted in 1800; another public law, enacted in 1891, provided funding for "...continuing the construction of the building for the Library of Congress, and for each and every purpose connected with the same, six hundred thousand dollars."

[2]Here's one example: "... An Act to expand the powers of the Indian Arts and Crafts Board, and for other purposes ..." became a public law on November 29, 1990 (104 U.S. Stat. 4662). It amended the 1935 Indian Arts and Crafts Act relative to what the Department of the Interior website described as a "... truth in advertising ..." amendment. This same public law amended several other existent public laws, e.g., the Indian Self-Determination and Education Assistance Act of 1978, and the Indian Financing Act of 1974,

[3]The Public Library of Cincinnati and Hamilton County, Ohio, is one of twelve repositories of U.S. National Archives collections; therefore, its collections include copies of the official Congressional Record; most of the Congressional Record excerpts featured within this publication were collected at this southern Ohio site.

[4]The creek called Wounded Knee is situated within the Pine Ridge Reservation of the Oglala Lakota. High atop a hill near the creek is a mass gravesite—one sacred reminder of the U.S. Calvary's December 29, 1890 massacre of hundreds of captives—children, men, and women.

EPIGRAPH

[1]"In 1830, at the urging of southern and western Congressmen and Senators, the Indian Removal Act was passed, and this act marks the emergence of the legislative branch as the dominant factor in the formation

of Indian policy." Deloria. "The Application of the Constitution to American Indians," in Lyons et al., *Exiled in the Land of the Free: Democracy, Indian Nations, and the U.S. Constitution, 287.*

INTRODUCTION

[1]Source: Whaples, Robert. "Child Labor in the United States." EH.Net Encyclopedia, edited by Robert Whaples. October 7, 2005. URL: http://eh.net/encyclopedia/article/whaples.childlabor.

[2]Indian Employment Act (93 Stat. 1056); for insightful commentary as to the purpose of this public law, as well as a euphemism inspired by this act, see Feraca, *Why Don't They Give Them Guns? The Great American Indian Myth, 178.*

[3]The *Congressional Record* is the fourth of a series of publications of congressional actions, its records spanning the times from the 43rd Congress to present; further information can be found online a t http://memory.loc.gov.

[4]H.R. 684 - https://www.gpo.gov/fdsys/pkg/BILLS-113hr684ih/pdf/BILLS-113hr684ih.pdf.

[5]Indian Removal Act (21 Stat. 411).

[6]The term *sui generis* is here used to denote a body of law that is limited in its applicability to a singular, prescribed set of circumstances, as is the case of laws applicable only to American Indian tribes and tribal members.

[7]Lyons et al., "Application of the Constitution," in *Exiled in the Land of the Free: Democracy, Indian Nations, and the U.S. Constitution, 287.*

[8]More than a century later, on April 27, 1991, the New York Times published an article, written by Gustav Neubuhrl, that addressed the 1864 massacre and featured a public apology offered by the United Methodist Church to all descendants of the Sand Creek survivors. The "Sand Creek Apology" acknowledged this post-surrender massacre of more than 200 unsuspecting men, women, and children. A subsequent New York Times article, *"132 Years Later, Methodists Repent Forebear's Sins,"* appeared on April 27, 1996.

[8]Library of Congress, Prints & Photographs Division, National Child Labor Committee Collection, [reproduction number, e.g., LC-USZ62-108765].

LEGISLATED GEOGRAPHIES

[1]http://www.bia.gov.
[2]Prucha, *Andrew Jackson's Indian Policy: A Reassessment, 528.* The Journal of American History. Vol. 56, No. 3 (Dec., 1969), pp. 527-539.

[3]Sheehan, *Seeds of Extinction: Jeffersonian Philanthropy and the American Indian*, 542-544.

[4]Many left behind well-established gardens, plowed fields, workhorses, riding horses, chickens, dairy cattle, hogs, frame houses, barns, root cellars, quilts, fences, gardening tools, and shelves of hom

[5](4 U.S. Stat. 411); for more information on the removal act, see Gibson's article in the *Handbook of North American Indians, Volume 4*, 221-223.

[6]Source: https://www.nps.gov/scbl/planyourvisit/upload/Horse-Creek-Treaty.pdf: "... This treaty, as signed, was ratified by the Senate on May 24, 1852, with an amendment changing the annuity in Article 7 from 50 to 10 years, subject to acceptance by the tribes."

[7]Richard White's book, *Railroaded*, provides an in-depth history of the concept and development of the transcontinental railroad. His work catalogues the federal grants distributed to railroad companies, including grants of tribal lands: "Railroads received the land equivalent of small countries or, in North American terms, the equivalent of an American state or a Canadian province. The federal grant to the Union Pacific roughly equaled the square mileage of New Hampshire and New Jersey combined. The main line of the Central Pacific got slightly more than the landmass of Maryland. The Trans Pacific, one of the branches connecting with the Union Pacific trunk, had to settle for Vermont and Rhode Island. A later transcontinental, the Northern Pacific ... received a total land grant that was the equivalent of converting all of New England into a strip twenty miles wide in the states and forty miles wide in the territories stretching from Lake Superior to Puget Sound. In all, the land grant railroads east and west of the Mississippi received [in excess of 130 million acres] from the United States. If all these federal land grants had been concentrated into a single state ... it would now rank third, behind Alaska and Texas, in size."

[8]Lyons et al., *Exiled in the Land of the Free: Democracy, Indian Nations, and the U.S. Constitution*, 287.

[9]"The surrender of Crazy Horse and more than 13,000 followers at Camp Robinson, Nebraska, on May 6, 1877, signified the end of the Sioux War." It also signified the last day any tribe roamed free. See Utley, *Handbook of North American Indians, Volume 4*, 176.

[10]The twenty-eight-year imprisonment of an Apache tribe is described on the following website: www.fortsillapache-nsn.gov. It tells of the imprisonment of the entire Chiricahua Apache tribe from 1886 through 1914: "Peaceful and hostile alike were taken to Florida, including the scouts who took the oath to serve the United States under the flag at Fort Apache, Arizona Territory. They were lined up under the same flag and were

disarmed and sent to the Florida prisons. Approximately 512 women, children, and men were imprisoned. While at Florida 112 children were sent to the Indian school at Carlisle, Pennsylvania. Nearly one-third of them died at Carlisle. Due to the unhealthy condition of the prisons in Florida, many died. The prisoners were transferred to Mount Vernon Barracks, Alabama in 1888. This was not a significant improvement for the death rate."

ACTS OF AN INSECURE VICTOR
[1]The futility of the treaty-making process stemmed from the extreme imbalance of military power, in tandem with the American mainstream ambivalence regarding the legal and human rights of indigenous populations (Nabokov, *Native American Testimony: An Anthology of Indian and White Relations: First Encounter to Dispossession*, 225-226).

[2]On page 21 of Peter Matthiessen's book, *In the Spirit of Crazy Horse*, he writes, "Custer's Regiment was harshly chastised by old 'Bearcoat' Miles, an Indian fighter since the Civil War, who had sent out that Seventh Cavalry detachment in response to the unwarranted panic of an Indian agent, caused by the ghost dances. As an old man in 1916, General Miles was still bitterly repudiating the massacre [Wounded Knee, 1890] as 'most reprehensible, most unjustifiable, and worthy of the severest condemnation.'"

[3]Gagnon and White Eyes, *Pine Ridge Reservation: Yesterday and Today*, 19.

[4] "The surrender of Crazy Horse [and more than 13,000 followers] at Camp Robinson, Nebraska, on May 6, 1877, signified the end of the Sioux War." It also signified the last day any tribe roamed free. Utley, *Handbook of North American Indians, Volume 4*, 176.

[5]Hagan, "Indian and White Relations," in *Handbook of North American Indians*, 62-63. Here quoted: "[I]n 1892 Congress (27 U.S. Stat. 120) directed that the president should fill vacancies as they occurred with army officers unless he believed a civilian were preferable. Under President Cleveland almost half of the nearly 60 agents were army officers. The number declined under President William McKinley and of the 15 serving as agents when the Spanish-American War began, 11 were recalled to active duty."

FEDERAL AGENTS ONLY: THE SEVEN MAJOR CRIMES ACT OF 1885
[1]U.S. Department of Justice report: *Indian Tribes: A Continuing Quest for Survival, A Report of the United States Commission on Civil Rights, 1981*, p. 163.

[2]23 Stat. 362, 385; U.S. Department of Justice, *Native Americans in South Dakota: An Erosion of Confidence in the Justice System*, Chapter 1: "In Indian country, tribal governments hold exclusive jurisdiction over all crimes committed by one Indian against another that are not subject to federal prosecution…"

[3]15 Stat. 635-647.

[4]Lyons et al., *Exiled in the Land of the Free: Democracy, Indian Nations, and the U.S. Constitution, 319:* "[T]he act for the first time extended federal jurisdiction '... over strictly internal crimes of Indians against Indians, a major blow at the integrity of the Indian tribes and a fundamental readjustment in relations between the Indians and the United States government.'"

[5]The Meriam (congressional subcommittee) Report of 1928 identified a general state of confusion, still apparent more than forty years after enactment of the Major Crimes Act, as to what entity (tribe, state, or federal government) held responsibility for the "legal jurisdiction over the restricted Indians in such important matters as crimes and misdemeanors and domestic relations..."

[6]U. S. Department of Justice, *Indian Tribes: A Continuing Quest for Survival,* 5.

[7]U.S. Department of Justice, *Native Americans in South Dakota: An Erosion of Confidence in the Justice System,* Introduction, 5.

[8]U.S. Department of Justice, *Native Americans in South Dakota: An Erosion of Confidence in the Justice System,* 8. The Department of Justice found most sexual assaults of tribal women were committed by white men ("82 percent of all cases").

[9]Archbishop Desmond Tutu, in a letter dated July 8, 2009, and addressed to a Parole Commission prior to a parole hearing for Leonard Peltier.

CHECKERBOARD SHELL GAME OF GIGANTIC PROPORTIONS: THE GENERAL ALLOTMENT ACT OF 1887

[1]Deloria, ed., *American Indian Policy in the Twentieth Century,* 4.

[2] Lawrence C. Kelly is here quoted from page 66 of his 1988 article: *United States Indian Policies, 1900-1980.* In Handbook of North American Indians. William C. Sturtevant, ed., 66-80. Washington, DC: Smithsonian Institution.

[3]24 Stat. 388-391.

[4]Meriam, *The Problem of Indian Administration. Report of a Survey made at the Request of Honorable Hubert Work.*

[5]Beckman, Stephan Dow, *History Since 1846,* Handbook of North American Indians, from 1985 publication: Exercise of Congressional Plenary Power, Presidential Authority, and Bureau of Indian Affairs Procedures, Colvile Indian Reservation, 1872-1944. (Report to U.S. Department of Justice, Docket 181-D, Colville Tribe v. U.S.; U.S. Claims Court, Washington, D.C.).

ERASING TRIBAL SPACES: 1888 DAWES AMENDMENT TO REDUCE LAKOTA LANDS

[1]15 Stat. 635.

[2]Penalties varied, but for this and other behavior that in any other context would be seen as law-abiding, included thirty to sixty days of incarceration.

[3]25 Stat. 94-104; the act did not address those tribal members living within the Great Sioux Reservation who *did not* collect rations at designated agencies.

THE SPOILS OF SOIL: THE LEASING OF INDIAN LANDS ACT OF 1891

[1]Hagan, "United States Indian Policies, 1860-1900," in *Handbook of North American Indians*, 61-62.

[2]Farming success was unlikely for many tribal landowners, due to their often limited access to water and livestock—and, in some cases, barriers to cooperative farming (e.g., certain reservation agents incarcerated landowners who traveled off their own land allotments without prior permission).

[3]26 Stat. 794.

TAKE THE CHILDREN AWAY: THE INDIAN EDUCATION ACT OF 1891

[1]24 Stat. 45; Hagan, "United States Indian Policies, 1860-1900," in *Handbook of North American Indians*, 61.

[2]26 Stat. 989, 1012-1014.

FAIR PLAY IN THE BALANCE: THE BURKE ACT OF 1906

[1]24 Stat. 388-391 ("The General Allotment Act," also referenced in various sources as the Dawes Allotment Act, the Dawes Act, and the Dawes Severalty Act); Kelly, "United States Indian Policies," in *Handbook of North American Indians*, 67-68.

[2]Deloria and Wilkins, *Tribes, Treaties, and Constitutional Tribulations*, 170.

[3]35 Stat. 182 ("The Burke Act").

THIRTY YEARS IN COMING: THE SIOUX PONY ACT OF 1906

[1]35 Stat. 325, 374-375.

WITNESS TO ECONOMIC BARRIERS: BUY INDIAN ACT OF 1910

[1]36 Stat. 861; Castile, *To Show Heart: North American Self-Determination and Federal Indian Policy*, 56; 96.

[2]36 Stat. 855-863

KEEPING THE WHEELS TURNING: ADMINISTRATION ACT OF 1921

[1]On pages 362-363 of Dee Brown's book, *Bury My Heart at Wounded Knee*, the author describes circumstances surrounding a court decision in a civil rights action that began 4/18/1879, and called for the release of Chief Standing Bear and his Ponca band, having found no "arbitrary authority" in American law to support the removal of peaceable people away from their homes (in this case, removal to a destination hundreds of miles distant and within "Indian Territory").

[2]42 Stat. 208-209, P. L. 84.

PUBLIC ACTS OF MIXED INTENT

[1]Warren Petoskey, author of *Dancing My Dream*, Elder at Dawnland Native Ministries.

[2] Lawrence C. Kelly is here quoted from page 66 of his 1988 article: *United States Indian Policies, 1900-1980*. In Handbook of North American Indians. William C. Sturtevant, ed., 66-80. Washington, DC: Smithsonian Institution.

[3]Philleo Nash, speaking in reference to Felix S. Cohen's 1942 completion of *The Handbook of Federal Indian Law*, as noted in Nash's "Twentieth Century United States Government Agencies" article in the *Handbook of North American Indians, 268.*

[4]Matthiessen, *In the Spirit of Crazy Horse*, 31; also 67 Stat. 588-590, P. L. 280; 67 Stat. 590-591, P. L. 281.

[5]Several tribal elders interviewed (2001-2009) with a social worker who documented their experiences as students of Indian boarding schools (Brunner, *Remnants of a Shattered Past*). They recalled long hours of baboring in the fields of local farmers or on school grounds, and doing laundry, kitchen, and garden duties. Some recalled sexual abuse. Their testimonies attested to the long-term impact of the harsh treatment. They recounted how they were forced to exchange their home cultures for the rigid, distorted cultures of the schools. They spoke of loneliness, fear, isolation, punishments, meager meals—and anguish over the loss of family, privacy, safety, and their own languages. They lamented their loss of home, religion, and ethnic identity, and reflected upon a shared *ethno-stress*—the residue of an endemic, multigenerational historical trauma.

[6]Meriam, *The Problem of Indian Administration. Report of a Survey made at the Request of Honorable Hubert Work*, February 21, 1928; quoted in Wilson, *The Impact of 110 Years of U.S. Indian Policy Legislation (1880-1990) on Ten Aspects of Reservation-Based Childrearing, 44:* "These outcomes were systemic in effect. For example, laws enacted in 1888, 1892, and 1904 stipulated the incarceration of adults found speaking Indian languages; consequently

virtually all adults (if speakers of Lakota, Cheyenne, or any other Indian language) were subject to arrest. Similarly, laws that forced the removal of children from their families affected all households that cared for children. The land transfer laws (enacted in 1887, 1889, 1891, 1894, 1897, 1946, 1953, 1961) generated systemic political, social, and geographic barriers to traditional cultural patterns of extended family contact."

[6]This quotation appeared in a 1983 Oklahoma State University Press publication, as recorded during Rogers' radio broadcast of March 30, 1931. See Gragert, ed., *Radio Broadcasts of Will Rogers*, 145-46.

CLOSING THE LOOPHOLES: THE INDIAN CITIZENSHIP ACT OF 1924
[1]Tyler, *A History of Indian Policy*, 315.

[2]Deloria, ed., *American Indian Policy in the Twentieth Century*, 29.
[3]Quoted from page 150 of *Tribes, Treaties, and Constitutional Tribulations*, by Vine Deloria Jr. and David E. Wilkins

[4]43 Stat. 253.

GOOD NEWS AT LAST: THE JOHNSON-O'MALLEY ACT OF 1934
[1]U.S. Department of Justice, *Indian Tribes: a Continuing Quest for Survival*, U.S. Commission on Civil Rights report.

[2]49 Stat. 891.

MIXED INTENTIONS: THE INDIAN REORGANIZATION ACT OF 1934
[1]Deloria, ed., *American Indian Policy in the Twentieth Century*, 43.

[2]Gibson, "Indian Land Transfers," in *Handbook of North American Indians*, 265.

[3]Washburn, *Red Man's Land, White Man's Law*, 80.

[4]Meyn, *More Than Curiosities: A Grassroots History of the Indian Arts and Crafts Board and its Precursors, 1920-1942.*

[5]48 Stat. 984, P. L. 383.

AN ECONOMIC BOOST: THE ARTS & CRAFTS BOARD ACT OF 1935
[1]"In supplementing the Indian incomes and in home decoration, encouragement should be given to native Indian arts and industries ... they ... afford an opportunity for self-expression and, properly managed, will yield considerable revenue, much more than can be secured by encouraging them to duplicate the handiwork of the whites. Their designs can be readily adapted to articles for which the commercial demand is reasonably good ...

the demand for Indian art [*sic*] work of high quality materially exceeds the supply ... A little intelligent cooperation and aid in marketing would doubtless tend rapidly to correct this difficulty."

[2]Congressional Record transcripts show the bill found unanimous support: "There being no objection, the Senate proceeded to consider the bill (S.2203) to promote the development of Indian arts and crafts and to create a board to assist therein, and for other purposes, which have been from the Committee on Indian Affairs, with amendments."

[3]49 Stat. 891; *Meyn, More Than Curiosities: A Grassroots History of the Indian Arts and Crafts Board, 1920–1942;* present-day vendor applications for tribal members interested in being included in a national source directory can be accessed through the Indian Arts and Crafts webpage on the Department of the Interior website.

AN HONORABLE MOVE: U.S. INDIAN CLAIMS COMMISSION ACT OF 1946

[1]Nash, "Twentieth Century United States Government Agencies," in *Handbook of North American Indians, 270*

[2]60 Stat. 1049.

POOF: TERMINATION POLICIES OF 1953

[1]Lawrence Baca, on pages 235-236 of his article, "The Legal Status of American Indians," in *Handbook of North American Indians,* discusses

House Concurrent Resolution 108, Public Law 83-280 (67 U.S. Sat. 588), and a 1968 amendment (67 U.S. Stat. 590).

[2]Lawrence C. Kelly, on page 76 of his article, "United States Indian Policies, 1900-1980," in *Handbook of North American Indians,* summarized the termination acts as follows: "Two bills and one resolution, all designed to remove federal controls from Indians, passed through Congress and were signed into law;" House Reconcurrent Resolution 108, known euphemistically as "The Temptation Resolution," for lifting restrictions on the sale of liquor to Indians, was overturned in 1978 with the passage of *tribal college* legislation (P. L. 100-297).

[3]U.S. Department of Justice, *Indian Tribes: a Continuing Quest for Survival,* U.S. Commission on Civil Rights report—June 1981, iii.

[4]67 Stat. 588-590.

[5]67 Stat. 590-591.

A WORKING CHANCE: INDIAN VOCATIONAL TRAINING ACT OF 1956

[1]U.S. Commission of Civil Rights, U.S. Department of Justice, *Native Americans in Dakota: An Erosion of Confidence in the Justice System (March 2000)*, Chapter 1, Introduction, 6.

[2]70 Stat. 986.

ONE AMERICAN TO ANOTHER

[1]This quotation was collected from Congressional Record archives. It's part of a speech given by Senator Fred M. Vinson of Kentucky to other members of the Senate. Born on January 20, 1890, within weeks of the 1890 Wounded Knee Massacre, this politician's career included his service within all three branches of the U.S. government. He died in 1953.

[2] Lawrence C. Kelly is here quoted from his 1988 article: *United States Indian Policies, 1900-1980*. In Handbook of North American Indians. William C. Sturtevant, ed., 66-80. Washington, DC: Smithsonian Institution.

BETTER LATE THAN NEVER: AMERICAN INDIAN CIVIL RIGHTS ACT OF 1968

[1]Billy Mills, Olympic Gold Medalist, as quoted in the 1994 publication, *Vision Quest: Men, Women, and Sacred Sites of the Sioux Nation.*

[2]"Tribal government seemed weakened by interposing federal courts [via the American Indian Civil Rights Act] between itself and Indian citizens. It was not until 1978 that the bill's impact was much narrowed with the Supreme Court decision Santa Clara Pueblo v. Martinez, establishing that tribal governments retained a large degree of sovereign immunity from such suits in federal courts" (Pevar, *The Rights of Indian and Tribes: The Basic ACLU Guide to Indian and Tribal Rights, 245, as quoted by Castile, To Show Heart: North American Self-Determination and Federal Indian Policy, 66).*

[3]82 Stat. 77, P. L. 90-284.

WELCOME BACK TO PARENTS: INDIAN ELEMENTARY AND SECONDARY SCHOOL ACT OF 1972

[1]Quoted from page 118 of Sherman Alexie's most recent book, *You Don't Have to Say You Love Me*. Publisher: Little, Brown, and Company, 2017.

[2]Szasz and Ryan, "American Indian Education," *in Handbook of North American Indians*, 298.

[3]86 Stat. 235, 334-345.

LOANS AT LAST: INDIAN FINANCING ACT OF 1974

[1]Quoted from the collaborative "American Presidency Project" website maintained through a collaboration between UC Santa Barbara and Citrus

collaboration. See item "109 ... Statement About Signing the Indian Financing Act of 1974 ..."

[2]88 Stat. 27.

ADMINISTRATIVE RIGHTS RETURNED: INDIAN SELF-DETERMINATION AND EDUCATION ASSISTANCE ACT OF 1975
[1]Gagnon and White Eyes, *Pine Ridge Reservation: Yesterday and Today,* 25; Deloria, ed., *American Indian Policy in the Twentieth Century,* 28-29.

[2]Szasz and Ryan, "American Indian Education," in *Handbook of North American Indians,* 298.

[3]88 Stat. 2203, P. L. 93-638.

ACCESS TO LOCAL HEALTH CARE: THE INDIAN HEALTH CARE IMPROVEMENT ACT OF 1976
[1]U.S. Commission of Civil Rights, U.S. Department of Justice, *Native Americans in Dakota: An Erosion of Confidence in the Justice System [2000],* Chapter 1, 7.

[2]For example, "[it] lifted the prohibition against Medicare and Medicaid reimbursement for services performed by the Indian Health Service" and "paid off backlogs of health care bills, while providing means for some development of health care facilities within reservation communities..." (Prucha, *The Indian in American Society: From the Revolutionary War to the Present,* 378).

[3]25 Stat. 1901, P. L. 94-437.

RECOGNIZED IN THE USA: REINSTATEMENT OF THE WYANDOTTE, PEORIA, AND OTTAWA TRIBES ACT OF 1978
[1]92 Stat. 246-247, P. L. 95-281.

HOMEGROWN DEGREES: THE TRIBALLY-CONTROLLED COMMUNITY COLLEGE ASSISTANCE ACT OF 1978
[1]The first college founded by Native Americans was established in 1887, as addressed in the anthropology textbook, *This Land Was Theirs* (Oswalt and Neely 1996): "In 1887 the Lumbee became the first native American group to found an Indian college. It became Pembroke State College for Indians and in 1971 Pembroke State University."

[2]This legislation overturned the termination provisions of House Reconcurrent Resolution 108 (P. L. 100-297) of 1953; *Prucha, Atlas of American Indian Affairs,* 315.

[3]92 Stat. 1325.

FAMILY CARE AT LAST: INDIAN CHILD WELFARE ACT OF 1978
[1]The March 2015 report, *Indian Child Welfare Act Measuring Compliance*, was authored by representatives of the Casey Family Programs (casey.org), the Center for Regional Tribal Child Welfare Studies, National Council of Juvenile and Family Court Judges, and the Minneapolis American Indian Center.

[2]92 Stat. 3069-3078, P. L. 95-608; in most other American communities, any child considered to be "at risk" (e.g., neglected or abused) would typically be removed from the home by state authorities and placed temporarily in the home of a reliable local relative or other approved local foster care provider (i.e., safe homes within child's local community).

WORSHIP AS YOU WILL: AMERICAN INDIAN RELIGIOUS FREEDOM ACT OF 1978
[1]Congress, speaking through excerpted text of this act, 92 Stat. 469, P. L. 95-341.

[2]April 4, 1978, transcript of Senate proceedings, quoted from Volume 124, Part 7, pages 8365-8366 of the Congressional Record.

[3]102 Stat. 2467.

NO NEW JOBS: INDIAN EMPLOYMENT ACT OF 1979
[1]Gerald R. Ford, "Veto of the Indian Employment Bill," September 24, 1976. Online by Gerhard Peters and John T. Woolley, *The American Presidency Project*. http://www.presidency.ucsb.edu.

[2]Castile, *To Show Heart: North American Self-Determination and Federal Indian Policy*, 166.

[3]93 Stat. 1056, P. L. 96-135; Feraca, *Why Don't They Give Them Guns? The Great American Indian Myth*, 178.

CASH INFUSION: INDIAN GAMING REGULATORY ACT OF 1988
[1]102 Stat. 2467.

[2]Ada E. Deer served as the Assistant Secretary-Indian Affairs of the U.S. Department of the Interior, 1993-1997

COMMON DECENCY: THE NATIVE AMERICAN GRAVES AND REPATRIATION ACT OF 1990

[1]Kroeber, *Ishi in Two Worlds: A Biography of the Last Wild Indian in North America*, 234.

[2]H.R. 5237 (a proposal read into the Congressional Record during a session of the House of Representatives on October 26, 1990, titled "The Native American Graves and Repatriation Act").

[3]Congressional Record of October 26, 1990.

[4]104 Stat. 3048-3058.

TOWARD A MORE PERFECT NATION

[1]Kevin Gover, speaking on September 8, 2000, in his role as Bureau of Indian Affairs Assistant Secretary, in acknowledgement of the bureau's 175th anniversary, its "Occasion for Reflection."

[2]Deloria and DeMaille, *Documents of American Indian Diplomacy: Treaties, Agreements, and Conventions (Legal History of America Vol. 4)*, 5.

[3]"Returning Indian war veterans [WWII] ... found themselves barred from registering to vote ... They began to pressure the Bureau of Indian Affairs to help them secure the vote in Arizona and New Mexico, two of the last states to bar Indians" as quoted from p. 150, *Tribes, Treaties, and Constitutional Tribulations* by Vine Deloria Jr. and David E. Wilkins.

[4]Starita, *The Dull Knives of Pine Ridge*, 146-146.

[5]This quoted passage is taken from page 176 of a U.S. Department of Justice report published in 1981, *Indian Tribes: A Continuing Quest for Survival. A Report of the United States Commission on Civil Rights*. Related points can be found on the following pages, i.e., "... the report concludes that the present system for protecting Indian rights has significant limitations, that coherent mechanisms for determining and implementing Indian policy are lacking, and that conflicts over Indian rights exacerbate pre-existing problems Indians face concerning denials of equal protection of the laws ..." [p. ii]; "There is little or no monitoring on a national level of the FBI investigative work in Indian country ..." [p. 163]; "Despite the FBI's key role in Federal law enforcement in Indian country, there is no systematic communication with other divisions of the Department of Justice or other Federal agencies on issues of policy ... 'Statistics are not collected or monitored that would permit an evaluation of the problems on a reservation-by-reservation basis . . .[p. 164]; "... statistics kept by the Federal Government regarding law enforcement on Indian reservations do not permit accurate analysis or systematic monitoring of the quality of law enforcement ..." [p. 175].

[6]In a letter dated July 8, 2009, Archbishop Desmond Tutu addressed the U.S. Parole Commission prior to Anishinabek-Lakota Leonard Peltier's parole hearing. Tutu advocated for the release of Peltier, due to the lack of any credible evidence being presented prior to his 1976 guilty conviction for the alleged murder of two FBI agents. Amnesty International, the Southern Christian Leadership Conference, the National Congress of American Indians, and other justice advocates, have identified Peltier as a political prisoner and have asked for his release from prison. The year 2017 marked Leonard Peltier's fortieth year of imprisonment.

[7]*Tribal Courts and the Administration of Justice in Indian Country Hearing Before the Committee on Indian Affairs United States Senate One Hundred Tenth Congress Second Session,* July 24, 2008, 32: "Because tribes have been stripped of jurisdiction over non-Indian offenders, tribes need the assistance of federal law enforcement. The Department of Justice must work cooperatively with Tribal law enforcement and dramatically step up its efforts to combat this crisis. Tulalip has shared in this experience of unacceptable levels of violent crime, and has worked hard to forge a relationship with federal law enforcement. In recent years, Tulalip has built a good relationship with the U.S. Attorney's Office on major crimes enforcement on the Tulalip Reservation. However, as President of the Northwest Tribal Court Judges Association, I know many Indian tribes do not share the same positive relationship with federal law enforcement. Tribes in more remote locations have experienced problems getting federal support and assistance in investigating and prosecuting crimes. These problems have worsened in recent years with the reallocation of federal law enforcement resources to foreign terrorism matters." An earlier U.S. Department of Justice report, *Native Americans in Dakota: An Erosion of Confidence in the Justice System* "Executive Summary," is the source of this quotation: "In 2000, a governmental inquiry into the state of law enforcement in South Dakota found preferential treatment of non-Indians and corresponding patterns of discrepancies in the patterns of longer sentences given to Indians, as compared to those sentences given to non-Indians."

[8]According to the Bureau of Indian Affairs website, fewer than half of the total number of Native Americans identified through the U.S. Census are enrolled members of federally recognized American Indian tribes: "According to the U.S. Bureau of the Census, the estimated population of American Indians and Alaska Natives, including those of more than one race, as of July 1, 2007, was 4.5 million, or 1.5 per cent of the total U.S. population. In the BIA's 2005 American Indian Population and Labor Force Report, the latest available, the total number of enrolled members of the [then] 561 federally recognized tribes was shown to be less than half the Census number, or 1,978,099." As of 2018, the BIA website notes a heightened count of federally recognized tribes/nations, i.e., 567. [9]The source of this quotation is a press release posted on the Bureau of Indian

Affairs website, www.bia.gov. For statistics about the lack of economic opportunities available within many reservation communities, see U.S. Department of Justice report, *Native Americans in Dakota: An Erosion of Confidence in the Justice System*, 6; e.g., "Despite a booming economy [Y2000], nationwide, half of the potential workforce in Indian Country is unemployed ... For American Indians in South Dakota the statistics are even worse. Unemployment rates for Indians living on or near South Dakota's reservations... [i.e., range from 40% to 85%]."

Bibliography

Alexie, Sherman
2017 You Don't Have to Say You Love Me. Boston: Little, Brown, and Company.

Bachman, Ronet
1992 Death and Violence on the Reservation. Westport, Connecticut: Auburn House.

Biolsi, Thomas
1992 Organizing the Lakota: The Political Economy of the New Deal on the Pine Ridge and Rosebud Reservations. Tucson: University of Arizona Press.

Bordewich, Fergus M.
1996 Killing the White Man's Indian. New York: Doubleday.

Brown, Dee
1970 Bury My Heart at Wounded Knee. New York: Holt, Rinehart, and Winston.

Brunner, Sharon.
2011 Remnants of a Shattered Past: A Journey of Discovery and Hope. Sault Ste. Marie: Freedom Eagles Publishing and Research, LLC.

Bucholz, Roger, William Fields, and Ursala P. Roach
1996 20th-Century Warriors: Native American Participation in the United States Military. http:// www.denix.osd/Public/Native/ Outreach/warriors.html.

Cahn, Edgar S.
1969 Our Brother's Keeper: The Indian in White America. Washington, DC: New Community Press.

Castile, George P.
1998 To Show Heart: North American Self-Determination and Federal Indian Policy, 1960-1975. Tucson: University of Arizona Press.

Collier, John
1947 Indians of the Americas. Chicago: Mentor Books.

Cronon, William
1983 Changes in the Land: Indians, Colonists, and the Ecology of New England. New York: Hill and Wang.

Cronon, William and Richard White
1998 Ecological Change and Indian-White Relations. In Handbook of North American Indians, William C. Sturtevant, ed., 417-429. Washington, DC: Smithsonian Institution.

Deloria, Vine, Jr., ed.
1985 American Indian Policy in the Twentieth Century. Norman: University of Oklahoma Press.

Deloria, Vine, Jr. and Sandra L. Cadwalader, eds.
1984 The Aggressions of Civilization: Federal Indian Policy Since the 1880s. Philadelphia: Temple University Press.

Deloria, Vine, Jr. and Raymond J. DeMaille
1999 Legal History of America, Vol. 4: Documents of American Indian Diplomacy: Treaties, Agreements, and Conventions. Norman: University of Oklahoma Press.

Deloria, Vine, Jr. and David E. Wilkins
1999 Tribes, Treaties, and Constitutional Tribulations. Austin: University of Texas Press.

Dorris, Michael
1989 The Broken Cord. New York: Harper Perennial.

Feraca, Stephen E.
1990 Why Don't They Give Them Guns? The Great American Indian Myth. Maryland: University Press of America.

Forstall, Richard L., ed.
1996 Population of the States and Counties of the United States, 1790-1900. Department of Commerce, Bureau of Census (C3.2:P81/26). Washington, DC: Government Printing Office.

Gagnon, Gregory and Karen White Eyes
1992 Pine Ridge Reservation: Yesterday and Today. Interior: Badlands Natural History Association.

Gibson, Arrell M.
1988 Indian Land Transfers. In Handbook of North American Indians. William C. Sturtevant, ed., 211-229. Washington, DC: Smithsonian Institution.

Gragert, Steven K., ed.
1983 Radio Broadcasts of Will Rogers. Stillwater: Oklahoma State University Press.

Grobsmith, Elizabeth S.
1981 Lakota of the Rosebud: A Contemporary Ethnography. Lincoln: University of Nebraska Press.

Hagan, William T.
1988 United States Indian Policies, 1860-1900. In Handbook of North American Indians. William C. Sturtevant, ed., 51-65. Washington, DC: Smithsonian Institution.

1988 Indian and White Relations. In Handbook of North American Indians. William C. Sturtevant, ed., 62-63. Washington, DC: Smithsonian Institution.

Herman, Robin and Gary Neidenthal
1996 Hanbleceya: A Quest for Vision: A Mental Health Curriculum Based Upon the Circle of Courage, A Native American Approach to Child Development. Beavercreek, OH: Hanbleceya House.

Herman, Robin, PhD., Khalil Osiris, and Tony Villa, Sr.
2004 The Psychology of Incarceration: A Distortion of the State of Belonging. Beavercreek, OH: Hanbleceya House.

Holm, Tom
1996 Strong Hearts, Wounded Souls: Native American Veterans of the Vietnam War. Austin: University of Texas Press.

Kelly, Lawrence C.
1988 United States Indian Policies, 1900-1980. In Handbook of North American Indians. William C. Sturtevant, ed., 66-80. Washington, DC: Smithsonian Institution.

Kroeber, Theodora
1971 Ishi in Two Worlds: A Biography of the Last Wild Indian in North America. Berkeley: University of California Press.

Lester, David
1997 Suicide in American Indians. Commack, NY: New Nova Science Publishers.

Lurie, Nancy O.
1988 Relations Between Indians and Anthropologists. In Handbook of North American Indians. William C. Sturtevant, ed., 548-556. Washington, DC: Smithsonian Institution.

Lyons, Oren, with John Mohawk, Vine Deloria, Jr, Laurence Hauptman, Howard Berman, Donald Grinde, Jr., Curtis Berkey, and Robert Venables.
1992 Exiled in the Land of the Free: Democracy, Indian Nations, and the U.S. Constitution. Santa Fe: Clear Light Publishers.

Matthiessen, Peter
1983 In the Spirit of Crazy Horse. New York: Viking Penguin.

Meriam, Lewis
1928 The Problem of Indian Administration. Baltimore: Johns Hopkins Press.

Meyn, Susan L.
1998 More Than Curiosities: A Grassroots History of the Indian Arts and Crafts Board and Its Precursors, 1920 to 1942. Ph.D. dissertation. University of Cincinnati.

Mooney, James
1973 The Ghost Dance Religion and Wounded Knee (The Dover Edition). New York: Dover Publications.

Nabokov, Peter
1978 Native American Testimony: An Anthology of Indian and White Relations: First Encounter to Dispossession. New York: Harper and Row Publishers.

Nash, Philleo
1988 Twentieth Century United States Government Agencies. In Handbook of North American Indians. William C. Sturtevant, ed., 264-275. Washington, DC: Smithsonian Institution.

Oglala Lakota College
1997 Oglala Lakota College Annual Report 1997. Kyle: Mintom.

Oswalt, Wendell H. and Sharlotte Neely
1996 This Land Was Theirs. California: Mayfield Publishing Company.

Petoskey, Warren
2009 Dancing My Dream. Michigan: Read the Spirit Books.

Pevar, Stephen L.
1992 The Rights of Indians and Tribes: The Basic ACLU Guide to Indian and Tribal Rights. Carbondale: Southern Illinois University Press.

Price, Katherine
1996 The Oglala People, 1841-1879. Lincoln: University of Nebraska Press.

Prucha, Francis P.
1969 Andrew Jackson's Indian Policy: A Reassessment. Journal of American History, Vol. 56, No.3:527-539.

1971 The Indian in American History: American Problem Studies. Hinsdale: The Dryden Press.
1986 The Great Father: The United States Government and the American Indians. Abridged edition. Lincoln: University of Nebraska Press.
1988 The Indian in American Society: from the Revolutionary War to the Present. Berkeley: University of California Press.
1990 Atlas of American Indian Affairs. Lincoln: University of Nebraska Press.

Rothstein, Richard
2017 The Color of Law: A Forgotten History of How Our Government Segregated America. New York: Liveright Publishing Corporation.

Roleff, Tamara L., ed.
1998 Native American Rights. San Diego: Greenhaven Press.

Sheehan, Bernard W.
1974 Seeds of Extinction: Jeffersonian Philanthropy and the American Indian. New York: Norton.

Sneve, Virginia Driving Hawk
1995 Completing the Circle. University of Nebraska Press.

Starita, Joseph
1995 The Dull Knives of Pine Ridge: A Lakota Odyssey. New York: Putnam.

Szasz, Margaret C., and C. S. Ryan
1988 American Indian Education. In Handbook of North American Indians. William C. Sturtevant, ed., 284-300. Washington, DC: Smithsonian Institution.

Tyler, S. Lyman
1973 A History of Indian Policy. Bureau of Indian Affairs. Washington, DC: U.S. Department of the Interior.

U.S. Department of Commerce, Bureau of the Census
1920 Fourteenth Census of the United States Taken in the Year 1920. Population 1920 – Number and Distribution of Inhabitants.
1930 Fifteenth Census of the United States. Population, Vol. III, Part 2.
1960 Census of Population. Vol. I. Characteristics of the Population, Chapter B, General Population Characteristics. Nebraska only, 29-142.
1970 We, The First Americans. Report.
1980 Census of Population. Vol. I. Characteristics of the Population, Chapter B, General Population Characteristics. Part 43, South Dakota.
1980 We, The First Americans. Report.
1981 1980 Census of Population. Vol. I. Characteristics of the Population, Chapter C, General Population Characteristics, Part 29. Nebraska.
1990 Census of Population. Subject Report: Federal and State Indian Reservations.

1992 1990 Census of Population. General Population Characteristics, American Indian and Alaska Native Areas.

U.S. Department of Education
1998 Office of Educational Research and Improvement. National Center for Education Statistics. State Comparisons of Education Statistics: 1969-70, NCES, 98-018, by Charlene M. Hoffman, Tomas D. Snyder, Project Officer. Washington, DC.

U.S. Department of Health and Human Services
1991 Trends in Indian Health. Indian Health Service. Washington, DC: Government Printing Office.
2000 Indian Health Service History and Tribal Movement and Facilities Today. Indian Health Service. Website: http:/www.IHS. gov/FacilitiesServices/AreaOffices/Aberdeen/today2.asp

U.S. Department of Justice
1983 Indian Tribes: A Continuing Quest for Survival. U.S. Commission of Civil Rights.
2000 Native Americans in South Dakota: An Erosion of Confidence in the Justice System. South Dakota Advisory Committee on the United States Commission on Civil Rights. U.S. Commission on Civil Rights.

Utley, Robert M.
1988 Indian-United States Military Situation, 1848-1891. In Handbook of North American Indians. William C. Sturtevant, ed., 163-184. Washington, DC: Smithsonian Institution.

Washburn, Wilcomb
1971 Red Man's Land, White Man's Law: A Study of the Past and Present Status of the American Indian. New York: Charles Scribner's Sons.

White, Richard
2012 Railroaded: The Transcontinentals and the Making of America. New York: W.W. Norton & Co.

Wilson, B. Lee
2000 The Impact of 110 Years of U.S. Indian Policy Legislation (1880-1990) on Ten Aspects of Reservation-Based Childrearing. Master's thesis, Department of Anthropology, University of Cincinnati.

Young Bear, Severt and R. D. Theisz
1994 Standing in the Light: A Lakota Way of Seeing. Lincoln, Nebraska: University of Nebraska Press.

Acknowledgements

Many talented and generous individuals contributed to the evolution of this publication. Dr. Susan Meyn introduced me to the most salient anthropological reviews of federal policies toward tribal nations—and shared her research into a public law enacted in 1935. Archeologist Dr. Frank L. Cowan (Ohio Hopewell Culture expert) introduced me to a Native American Graves and Repatriation Act (NAGPRA) field expert; he also provided invaluable critiques of early chapters. The cover photo and two interior photos appear thanks to Cherie Breeman. Expert editorial advice was provided by Dorothy Binder during multiple iterations of this book's varied and complicated texts. Jeannette Ramirez encouraged my pursuit of this project, and introduced me to the attorney who enlightened my understanding of relevant legal concepts. Charles Finney's sound advice assured this book's inclusion of historically concurrent national events—those which could have influenced the mindsets of nineteenth, twentieth, and twenty-first century legislators. Further support for this project came by way of Richard J. C. Hoskin and Sharon Brunner; both offered steady encouragement, critique, and inspiration. Geraldine Wilson's review of key passages, and Karen Sims' proofreading of this manuscript's first edition, streamlined the completion of the final phases of this second edition.

Photographs & Maps

Images appearing on the cover and within the interior of this publication were provided through the courtesy of multiple public and private sources.

The Sand Creek Massacre National Historic Site photograph (Figure 1) appears courtesy of the staff of the Sand Creek National Historic Site located in Kiowa County, Eads, Colorado.

The image of George Bent and his wife, Magpie, were provided courtesy of the staff of the Denver Public Library's Western History Collections (Figure 2).

The photograph of Will Rogers (Figure 25) was provided courtesy of the Will Rogers Museum located in Claremore, Oklahoma.

Five images were gleaned from the historic photograph collections of the Library of Congress (Figures 4, 5, 17, 30, 31).

The public domain map of contemporary American Indian reservations (Figure 9) was accessed through the U.S. Department of the Interior/U.S. Geological Survey.

The Cumberland County Historical Society of Carlisle, PA, provided the historic image of the student body of the Carlisle Indian School (Figure 22); their website—www. historicalsociety.com.—features a variety of other unique photographs and historic documents.

The Carlisle Indian School Digital Resource Center provided six historic photographs (Figures 23, 24, 26, 27, 29, and 30); additional images and related documents can be viewed on the Carlisle Indian School Digital Resource Center's website (http://carlisleindian.dickinson.edu).

The cover photo and three interior photos (Figures 10, 13, 35) were contributed by Cherie Breeman.

Three maps (Figures 7, 16, 21) and photographs taken during travels throughout the USA (Figures 3, 6, 8, 11-12, 14-15, 18-20, 28, 32-34, 36-38) are part of the author's personal collections.

Appendix A

The Horse Creek Treaty

The Horse Creek Treaty—also known as the Fort Laramie Treaty of 1851—emerged upon conclusion of a gathering of thousands of American Indians and representatives of the United States. What follows is a transcript of that treaty agreement, formalized approximately thirty miles from Ft. Laramie, a site located in present-day Wyoming:

ARTICLES OF A TREATY MADE AND CONCLUDED at Fort Laramie, in the Indian Territory, between D. D. Mitchell, superintendent of Indian Affairs, and Thomas Fitzpatrick, Indian agent, commissioners specially appointed and authorized by the President of the United States, of the first part, and the chiefs, headmen, and braves of the following Indian nations, residing south of the Missouri River, east of the Rocky Mountains, and north of the lines of Texas and New Mexico, viz [*sic*], the Sioux or Dahcotahs [*sic*], Cheyennes, Arrapahoes [*sic*], Crows, Assinaboines [*sic*], Gros-Ventre, Mandans, and Arrickaras [*sic*], parties of the second part, on the seventeenth day September, A. D. one thousand eight hundred and fifty-one.

Article 1: The aforesaid nations, parties to this treaty, having assembled for the purpose of establishing and confirming peaceful relations amongst themselves, do hereby covenant and agree to abstain in future from all hostilities whatever against each other, to maintain good faith and friendship in all their mutual intercourse, and to make an effective and lasting peace.

Article 2: The aforesaid nations do hereby recognize the right of the United States Government to establish roads, military and other posts, within their respective territories. ...

Article 3: In consideration of the rights and privileges acknowledged in the preceding article, the United States bind themselves to protect the aforesaid Indian nations against the commission of all depredations by the people of the said United States, after the ratification of this treaty ...

Article 4: The aforesaid Indian nations do hereby agree and bind themselves to make restitution or satisfaction for any wrongs committed, after the ratification of this treaty, by any band or individual of their people, on the people of the United States, whilst lawfully residing in or passing through their respective territories …

Article 5: The aforesaid Indian nations do hereby recognize and acknowledge the following tracts of country, included within the metes and boundaries hereinafter designated, as their respective territories … [The remaining elements of Article 5 describe the respective territories for the Sioux or Dahcotah [*sic*] Nation; the Gros Ventre, Mandans and Arrickara [*sic*] Nations; the Assinaboine [*sic*] Nation; the Blackfoot Nation; the Crow Nation and the Cheyenne and Arrapahoe [*sic*] Nations.] …

Article 6: The parties to the second part of this treaty have selected principals or head-chiefs for their respective nations, through whom all national business will hereafter be conducted, do hereby bind themselves to sustain said chiefs and their successors during good behavior …

Article 7: In consideration of the treaty stipulations, and for the damages which have or may occur by reason thereof to the Indian nations, parties hereto, and for their maintenance and the improvement of their moral and social customs, the United States bind themselves to deliver to the said Indian nations the sum of fifty thousand dollars per annum for the term of ten years, with the right to continue the same at the discretion of the President of the United States for a period not exceeding five years thereafter, in provisions, merchandise, domestic animals, and agricultural implements, in such proportions as may be deemed best adapted to their condition by the President of the United States, to the distributed in proportion to the population of the aforesaid Indian nations …

Article 8: It is understood and agreed that should any of the Indian nations, parties to this treaty, violate any of the provisions thereof, the United States may withhold the whole or a portion of the annuities mentioned in the preceding article from the nation so offending, until in the opinion of the President of the United States, proper satisfaction shall have been made. In testimony whereof the said D. D. Mitchell and Thomas Fitzpatrick commissioners as aforesaid, and the chiefs, headmen, and braves, parties hereto, have set their hands and affixed their marks, on the day and at the place first above written.

Appendix B

Signatories of the Fort Laramie Treaty of 1868

In 1868, the second Fort Laramie treaty was signed in follow-up to its 1851 predecessor. Both defined the boundaries of the Great Sioux Reservation. These next few pages provide a listing of all official signatories of the Fort Laramie Treaty of 1868.

N. G. TAYLOR, [SEAL].
W. T. SHERMAN, [SEAL].
Lt. Genl.[*sic*] WM. S. HARNEY,
Bvt. Maj. Gener [*sic*] *U.S.A.,*
JOHN B. SANBORN, [SEAL]
S. F. TAPPAN, [SEAL].
C. C. AUGUR, [SEAL]
Bvt. Gen.
ALFRED H. TERRY, [SEAL]
Bvt. M. Gen. U.S.A.
Attest: A. S. H. WHITE, *Secretary* . . .

Executed on the part of the Brulé band of Sioux by the chief and headmen whose names are hereto annexed, they being thereunto duly authorized, at Fort Laramie, D. T. ... [Dakota Territory] ... the twenty-ninth day of April, in the year A.D. 1868.

MA-ZA-PON-KASKA, his x mark, Iron Shell.
WAH-PAT-SHAH, his x mark, Red Leaf.
HAH-SAH-PAH, his x mark, Black Horn.
ZIN-TAH-GAH-LAT-SKAH, his x mark, Spotted Tail.
ZIN-TAH-SKAH, his x mark, White Tail.
ME-WAH-TAH-NE-HO-SKAH, his x mark, Tall Mandas.
SHE-CHA-CHAT-KAH, his x mark, Bad Left Hand.

NO-MAH-NO-PAH, his x mark, Two and Two.
TAH-TONKA-SKAH, his x mark, White Bull.
CON-RA-WASHTA, his x mark, Pretty Coon.
HA-CAH-CAH-SHE-CHAH, his x mark, Bad Elk.
WA-HA-KA-ZAH-ISH-TAH, his x mark, Eye Lance.
MA-TO-HA-KE-TAH, his mark, Bear That Looks Behind.
BELLA-TONKA-TONKA, his x mark, Big Partisan.
MAH-TO-HO-HONKA, his x mark, Swift Bear.
TO-WIS-NE, his x mark, Cold Place.
ISH-TAH-SKAH, his x mark, White Eyes.
MA-TA-LOO-ZAH, his x mark, Fast Bear.
AS-HAH-KAH-NAH-ZHE, his x mark, Standing Elk.
CAN-TE-TE-KI-YE, his x mark, The Brave Heart.
SHUNKA-SHATON, his x mark, Day Hawk.
TATANKA-WAKON, his x mark, Sacred Bull.
MAPIA SHATON, his x mark, Hawk Cloud.
MA-SHA-A-OW, his x mark, Stands And Comes.
SHON-KA-TON-KA, his x mark, Big Dog.
Attest:
Ashton S. H. White, *Secretary of Commission.*
George B. Withs, *Phonographer to Commission.*
Geo. H. Holtzman.
John D. Howland.
James C. O'Connor.
CHARLES E. GUREN, *Interpreter.*
Leon F. Pallardy, *Interpreter.*
Nicholas Janis, Interpreter.
NICHOLAS JANIS, *Interpreter.*

Executed on the part of the Ogallalah [*sic*] band of Sioux by the chiefs and headmen whose names are hereto subscribed, they being thereunto duly authorized, at Fort Laramie, the twenty-fifth day of May, in the year A. D. 1868.

TAH-SHUN-KA-CO-QUI-PAH, his x mark, Man-Afraid-of-His-Horses.
SHA-TON-SKAH, his x mark, White Hawk.
SHA-TON-SAPAH, his x mark, Black Hawk.
E-GA-MON-TON-KA-SAPAH, his x mark, Black Tiger.
OH-WAH-SHE-CHA, his x mark, Bad Wound.
PAH-GEE, his x mark, Grass.
WAH-NON-REH-CHE-GEH, his x mark, Ghost Heart.
CON-REEH, his x mark, Crow.
OH-HE-TE-KAH his x mark, The Brave.
TAH-TON-KAH-HE-YO-TA-KAH, his x mark, Sitting Bull.
SHON-KA-OH-WAH-MON-YE, his x mark, Whirlwind Dog.
HA-HA-KAH-TAH-MIECH, his x mark, Poor Elk.
WAM-BU-LEE-WAH-KON, his x mark, Medicine Eagle.

CHON-GAH-MA-HE-TO-HANS-KA, his x mark, High Wolf.WAH-SE-CHUN-TA-SHUN-KAH, his x mark, American Horse. MAH-HAH-MAH-HA-MAK-NEAR, his x mark, Man That Walks Under The Ground.
MAH-TO-TOW-PAH, his x mark, Four Bears.
MA-TO-WEE-SHA-KTA, his x mark, One That Kills the Bear.
OH-TAH-KEE-TOKA-WEE-CHAKTA, his x mark, One That Kills In a Hard Place.
TAH-TON-KAH-TA-MIECH, his x mark, The Poor Bull.
OH-HUNS-EE-GA-NON-SKEN, his x mark, Mad Shade.
SHAH-TON-0H-NAH-0M-MINNE-NE-OH-MINNE, his x mark, Whirling Hawk.
MAH-TO-CHUN-KA-0H, his x mark, Bear's Back.
CHE-TON-WEE-KOH, his x mark, Fool Hawk.
WAH-HOH-KE-ZA-AH-HAH, his x mark, One That Has The Lance.
SHON-GAH-MANNI-TOH-TAN-KA-I, his x mark, Big Wolf Foot.
EH-TON-KAH, his x mark, Big Mouth.
MA-PAH-CHE-TAH, his x mark, Bad Hand.
WAH-KE-YUN-SHAH, his x mark, Red Thunder.
WAK-SAH, his x mark, One That Cuts Off.
CHAM-NOM-QUI-YAH, his x mark, One That Presents The Pipe.
WAH-KE-KE-YAN-PUH-TAH, his x mark, Fire Thunder.
MAH-TO-NONK-PAH-ZE, his x mark, Bear With Yellow Ears.
CON-REE-I-KA, his x mark, The Little Crow.
HE-HUP-PAH-TOH, his x mark, The Blue War Club.
SHON-KEE-TOH, his x mark, The Blue Horse.
WAM-BALLA-OH-CONQUO, his x mark, Quick Eagle.
TA-TONKA-SUPPA, his x mark, Black Bull.
MOH-TO-HA-SHE-NA, his x mark, The Bear Hide.
Attest:
S. E. Ward
Jas. C. O'Connor.
J. M. Sherwood.
W. C. Slicer.
Sam Deon.
H. M. Matthews.
Joseph Bissonette, *Interpreter.*
Nicholas Janis, *Interpreter.*
Lefroy Jott, *Interpreter.*
Antoine Janis, *Interpreter.*

Executed on the part of the Minneconjou *[sic]* band of Sioux by the chiefs and headmen whose names are hereto subscribed, they being thereunto duly authorized. At Fort Laramie, D.T., May 26, '68, 13 names.

HEH-WON-GE-GE-CHAT, his x mark, One Horn.
OH-PON-AH-TAH-E-MANNE, his x mark, The Elk That Bellows Walking.

At Fort Laramie, May 25, '68, 2 names.

HEH-HO-LAH-REH-CHA-SKAH, his x mark, Young White Bull.

WAH-CHAH-CHUM-KAH-COH-KEE-PAH, his x mark, One That Is Afraid of Shield.

HE-HON-NE-SHAKTA, his x mark, The Old Owl.

MOC-PE-A-TOH, his x mark, Blue Cloud.

OH-PONG-GE-LE-SKAH, his x mark, Spotted Elk.

TAH-TONK-KA-HON-KE-SCHNE-his x mark, Slow Bull.

SHONK-A-NEE-SHAH-SHAH-A-TAH-PE, his x mark, The Dog Chief.

MA-TO-TAH-TA-TA-Tonk-Ka, his x mark, Bull Bear.

WOM-BEH-LE-TON-KAH, his x mark, The Big Eagle.

MA-TOH-EH-SCHNE-LAH, his x mark, The Lone Bear.

MAH-TOH-KE-SU-YAH, his x mark, The One Who Remembers The Bear.

MA-TOH-OH-HE-TO-KEH, his x mark, The Brave Bear.

EH-CHE-MA-HEH, his x mark, The Runner.

TI-KI-YA, his x mark, The Hard.

HE-MA-ZA, his x mark, Iron Horn.

Attest:

Jas. C. O'Connor.

Wm. H. Brown.

Nicholas Janis, *Interpreter.*

Antoine Janis, *Interpreter.*

Executed on the part of the Yanktonais band of Sioux by the chiefs and headmen whose names are hereto subscribed, they being thereunto duly authorized:

MAH-TO-NON-PAH, his x mark, Two Bears.

MA-TO-HNA-SKIN-YA, his x mark, Mad Bear.

HE-O-PU-ZA, his x mark, Louzy.

AH-KE-CHE-TAH-CHE-CA-DAN, his x mark, Little Soldier.

MAH-TO-E-TAN-CHAN, his x mark, Chief Bear.

CU-WI-H-WIN, his x mark, Rotten Stomach.

SKUN-KA-WE-TKO, his x mark, Fool Dog.

ISH-TA-SAP-PAH, his x mark, The Chief.

I-A-WI-CA-KA, his x mark, The One Who Tells The Truth.

AH-KE-CHE-TAH, his x mark, The Soldier

TA-SHI-NA-GI, his x mark, Yellow Robe.

NAH-PE-TON-KA, his x mark, Big Hand.

CHAN-TEE-WE-KTO, his x mark, Fool Heart.

HOH-GAN-SAH-PA, his x mark, Black Catfish.

MAH-TO-WAH-KAN, his x mark, Medicine Bear.

SHUN-KA-KAN-SHA, his x mark, Red Horse.

WAN-RODE, his x mark, The Eagle.

CAN-HPI-SA-PA, his x mark, Black Tomahawk.

WAR-HE-LE-RE, his x mark, Yellow Eagle.

CHA-TON-CHE-CA, his x mark, Small Hawk, or Long Fare.
SHU-GER-MON-E-TOO-HA-SKA, his x mark, Tall Wolf.
MA-TO-U-TAH-KAH, his x mark, Sitting Bear.
HI-HA-CAH-GE-NA-SKENE, his x mark, Mad Elk.
Arapahos.
LITTLE CHIEF, his x mark.
TALL BEAR, his x mark.
TOP MAN, his x mark.
NEVA, his x mark.
THE WOUNDED BEAR, his x mark.
WHIRLWIND, his x mark.
THE FOX, his x mark.
THE DOG BIG MOUTH, his x mark.
SPOTTED WOLF, his x mark.
SORREL HORSE, his x mark.
BLACK COAL, his x mark.
BIG WOLF, his x mark.
KNOCK-KNEE, his x mark.
BLACK CROW, his x mark.
THE LONE OLD MAN, his x mark.
PAUL, his x mark.
BLACK BULL, his x mark.
BIG TRACK, his x mark.
THE FOOT, his x mark.
BLACK WHITE, his x mark.
YELLOW HAIR, his x mark.
LITTLE SHIELD, his x mark.
BLACK BEAR, his x mark.
WOLF MOCASSIN, his x mark.
BIG ROBE, his x mark.
WOLF CHIEF, his x mark.
Witnesses: Robt. P. McKibbin, *Capt. 4ᵗʰ Inf. Ret. Lt. Col. U.S.A. Comdg. Ft. Laramie.*
Wm. H. Powell, *Bvt. Maj. Capt. 4ᵗʰ Inf.* Henry W. Patterson, *Capt. 4ᵗʰ Infy. [sic].*
Theo. E. True, *2d Lieut. 4ᵗʰ Inf.* W. G. Bullock.
Chas. E. Guern, *Special Indian Interpreter for the Peace Commission.*
Fort Laramie, Wg. T., November 6, 1868.
MAKH-PI-AH-LU-TAH, his x mark, Red Cloud.
WA-KI-AH-WE-CHA-SHAH, his x mark, Thunder Man.
MA-ZAH-ZAH-GEH, his x mark. Iron Cane.
WA-UMBLE-WHY-WA-KA-TUYAH, his x mark, High Eagle.
KO-KE-PAH, his x mark, Man Afraid.
WA-KI-AH-WA-KOU-AH, his x mark, Thunder Flying Running.
*Witnesses:*W. McE. Dye, *Bvt. Col. U.S.A. Comg.*
A. B. Cain, *Capt. 4ᵗʰ Inf. Bt. Maj. U.S.A.*
Robt. P. McKibbin, Capt. 4 Inf. Bvt. Lt. Col. U.S.A.
Jon Miller, *Capt. 4ᵗʰ Inf.*

G. L. Luhn, *1ˢᵗ Inf. Bvt Capt. U.S.A.*
H.C. Sloan, *2d Lt. 4ᵗʰ Inf.*
Whittingham Cox, *1ˢᵗ Lieut. 4ᵗʰ Inf.*
W. VOGUES, *1ˢᵗ Lieut. 4ᵗʰ Inf.*
Butler D. Price, *2ⁿᵈ Lt. 4ᵗʰ Inf.*
Headqrs., Fort Laramie, Novr [*sic*]. 6, '68
Executed by the above on this date.
All of the Indians are Ogallalahs [*sic*] excepting Thunder Man and Thunder Flying Running, who are Brulés.
Wm. McE. Dye, *Maj. 4ᵗʰ Infy. And Bvt. Col. U.S.A. Comg.*
Attest: Jas. C. O'Connor . . .Nicholas Janis, *Interpreter* ... Franc. La Framboise, *Interpreter* ... P. J. De Smet, S. J., *Missionary among the Indians* ... Saml. D. Hinman, B. D., *Missionary.*

Executed on the part of the Uncpapa [*sic*] band of Sioux, by the chiefs and headmen whose names are hereto subscribed, they being thereunto duly authorized:
CO-KAM-I-YA-YA, his x mark, The Man That Goes In The Middle.
MA-TO-CA-WA-WEKSA., his x mark, Bear Rib.
TA-TO-KA-IN-YAN-KE, his x mark, Running Antelope.
KAN-GI-WA-KI-TA, his x mark, Looking Crow.
A-KI-CI-TA-HAN-SKA, his x mark, Long Soldier.
WA-KU-TE-MA-NI, has x mark, The One Who Shoots Walking.
UN-KCA-KI-KA, his x mark, The Magpie.
KAN-GI-O-TA, his x mark, Plenty Crow.
HE-MA-ZA, his x mark, Iron Horn.
SHUN-KA-I-NA-PIN, his x mark, Wolf Necklace.
I-WE-HI-YU, his x mark, The Man Who Bleeds From The Mouth.
HE-HA-KA-PA, his x mark, Elk Head.
I-ZU-ZA, his x mark, Grind Stone.
SHUN-KA-WE-TKO, his x mark, Fool Dog.
MA-KPI-YA-PO, his x mark, Blue Cloud.
WA-MLN-PI-LU-TA, his x mark, Red Eagle.
MA-TO-CAN-TE, his x mark, Bear's Heart.
A-KI-CI-TA-I-TAU-CAN, his x mark, Chief Soldier.

Attest:
Jas. C. O'Connor.
Nicolas Janis, *Interpreter.*
Franc. La Frambois, *Interpreter.*
P. J. DeSmet, S. J., *Missy. [sic] Among the Indians.*
Saml. D. Hinman, B. D., *Missionary.*

Executed on the part of the Blackfeet band of Sioux by the chiefs by the chiefs and headmen whose names are hereto subscribed, they being thereunto duly authorized.

CAN-TE-PE-TA, his x mark, Fire Heart.
WAN-MDI-KTE, his x mark, The One Who Kills Eagle.
SHO-TA, his x mark, Smoke.
WAN-MDI-MA-NI, his x mark, Walking Eagle.
WA-SHI-CUN-YA-TA-PI, his x mark, Chief White Man.
KAN-GI-I-YO-TAN-KE, his x mark, Sitting Crow.
PE-JI, his x mark, The Grass.
KDA-MA-NI, his x mark, The One That Rattles As He Walks.
WAH-HAN-KA-SA-PA, his x mark, Black Shield.
CAN-TE-NON-PA. hi x mark, Two Hearts.
Attest:
Jas. C. O'Connor.
Nicolas Janis, *Interpreter.*
Franc. La Framboise, *Interpreter.*
P. J. DeSmet, S. J., *Missy. [sic] Among the Indians.*
Saml. D. Hinman, B. D., *Missionary.*

Executed on the part of the Cutheads Band of Sioux by the chiefs and headmen whose names are hereto subscribed, they being thereunto duly authorized.
TO-KA-IN-YAN-KA, his x mark, The One Who Goes Ahead Running.
TA-TAN-KA-WA-KIN-YAN, his x mark, Thunder Bull.
SIN-TO-MIN-SA-PA, his x mark, All Over Black.
CAN-I-CA, his x mark, The One Who Took The Stick.
PA-TAN-KA, his x mark, Big Head.
Attest:
Jas. C. O'Connor.
Nicolas Janis, *Interpreter.*
Franc. La Frambois[e], *Interpreter.*
P. J. DeSmet, S. J., *Missy. [sic] Among the Indians.*
Saml. D. Hinman, B. D., *Missionary.*

Executed on the part of the Two Kettle Band of Sioux by the chiefs and headmen whose names are hereto subscribed, they being thereunto duly authorized.
MA-WA-TAN-NI-HAN-SKA, his x mark, Long Mandan.
CAN-KPE-DU-TA, his x mark, Red War Club.
CAN-KA-GA, his x mark, The Log.
Attest:
Jas. C. O'Connor.
Nicolas Janis, *Interpreter.*
Franc. La Framboise, *Interpreter.*
P. J. DeSmet, S. J., *Missy. [sic] Among the Indians.*
Saml. D. Hinman, *Missionary to the Dakotas.*

Executed on the part of the Sans Arch [*sic*] Band of Sioux by the chiefs and headmen whose names are hereto annexed, they being thereunto duly authorized.

HE-NA-PIN-WA-NI-CA, his x mark, The One That Has Neither Horn.
WA-INLU-PI-LU-TA, his x mark, Red Plume.
CI-TAN-GI, his x mark, Yellow Hawk.
HE-NA-PIN-WA-NI-CA, his x mark, No Horn.
Attest:
Jas. C. O'Connor.
Nicolas Janis, *Interpreter.*
Franc. La Frambois[e], *Interpreter.*
P. J. De Smet, S. J., *Missy. [sic] Among the Indians.*
Saml. D. Hinman, *Missionary to the Dakotas.*

Executed on the part of the Santee band of Sioux by the chiefs and headman whose names are hereto subscribed, they being thereunto duly authorized.
WA-PAH-SHAW, his x mark, Red Ensign.
WAH-KOO-TAY, his x mark, Shooter.
HOO-SHA-SHA, his x mark, Red Legs.
O-WAN-CHA-DU-TA, his x mark, Scarlet All Over.
WAU-MACE-TAN-KA, his x mark, Big Eagle.
CHO-TAN-KA-E-Na-PE, his x mark, Flute Player.
TA-SHUN-KE-MO-ZA, his x mark, His Iron Dog.
Attest:
Saml. D. Hinman, B. D., *Missionary.*
J. N. Chickering, 2d Lt. 22d. Infy., Bvt. Capt. U.S.A.
P.J. De Smet, S. J.
Nicholas Janis, *Interpreter.*
Franc. La Framboise, *Interpreter.*

Appendix C

The Meriam Report of 1928

THE 1928 PUBLICATION of the "Meriam [subcommittee] Report" initiated a paradigm shift in congressional attitudes, understandings, and actions toward American Indian tribes. The full report, submitted to Congress upon conclusion of the committee's three years of field work, can now be viewed on-line: http://www.eric.ed.gov/PDFS/ED08 7573.pdf Meriam, Lewis. 1928 *The Problem of Indian Administration*. Baltimore: John Hopkins Press)]. The following excerpts sample the breadth of the Meriam committee findings:

"From the educational standpoint, the young child does not belong in a boarding school. For normal healthy development, he needs his family and his family needs him. Young children, at least up to the sixth grade, should normally be provided for either in Indian Service day schools or in public schools. Not until they have reached adolescence and finished the local schools should they normally be sent to a boarding school."

"Both the government and the missionaries have often failed to study, understand, and take a sympathetic attitude toward Indian ways, Indian ethics, and Indian religion. The exceptional government worker and the exceptional missionary have demonstrated what can be done by building on what is sound and good in the Indian's own life."

"In recreation and other community activities the existing activities of the Indians should be utilized as the starting point. That some of their dances and other activities have objectionable features is, of course, true. The same thing is true of the recreation and the community activities of almost any people."

"The economic basis of the … Indians has been largely destroyed by the encroachment of white civilization. The Indians can no longer make a living as they did in the past by hunting, fishing, gathering wild products and the extremely limited practice of … agriculture. The social system that evolved from their past economic life is ill-suited to the conditions that now confront them, notably in the matter of the division of labor between the men and the women

They are by no means yet adjusted to the new economic and social conditions that confront them."

"In all these activities the Indian point of view and the Indian interests should be given major consideration. In home design and construction the effort should be made to adapt characteristically Indian things to modern uses. For example, among Indian tribes the outdoor arbor in some form is almost universal and is used for many purposes. Several of the wealthy Osages with elaborate modern houses, the like of which relatively few white men can boast, have erected in addition elaborate adaptations of the arbors. These arbors gave them the chance for self-expression. The Indians will take more interest in their homes and in the improvement of them if the construction appeals to Indian taste and is well adapted to Indian uses. There is no reason at all why the Indians should be urged to have dwellings which are replicas of what white men would build. Some of the Indians' ideas regarding outdoor rooms may be ... [adopted] ... by whites."

"Among the Indians, community activities are probably even more important than among white people because the Indians' social and economic system was and is ... [operated at the tribal community level]. Individualism is almost entirely lacking in their native culture. Thus, work with communities as a whole will follow a natural line and will result in accelerated group progress."

"When the government adopted the policy of individual ownership of the land on the reservations, the expectation was that the Indians would become farmers. Part of the plan was to instruct and aid them in agriculture, but this vital part was not pressed with vigor and intelligence. It almost seems as if the government assumed that some magic in individual ownership of property would in itself prove an educational civilizing factor [i.e., a mechanism toward the conversion of tribal economics to farm-based economies], but unfortunately, this policy has for the most part operated in the opposite direction ... In some instances Indians have not only never lived on their allotments, they have never seen them and have no desire to go to the place where their land is. In such cases the land should, if possible, be sold and the proceeds used to purchase land for the Indian in the neighborhood where he desires to live ..."

"In some jurisdictions the economic resources are apparently insufficient, even if efficiently used, to support the Indian population according to reasonable standards. In some cases, the Indians were given poor lands; in others during the course of years the whites have gained possession of the desirable lands. Nothing permanent is to be achieved by trying to make the Indians wrest a living from lands which will not yield a decent return for the labor expended."

"The health of the Indians as compared with that of the general population is bad. Although accurate mortality and morbidity statistics are commonly lacking, the existing evidence warrants the statement that both the general death rate and the infant mortality rate are high. Tuberculosis is extremely prevalent Trachoma, a communicable disease which produces blindness, is a major problem because of its great prevalence and the danger of its spreading among both the Indians and the whites."

"The policy of individual allotment ... has largely failed in the accomplishment of what was expected of it. It has resulted in much loss of land and an enormous increase in the details of administration without a compensating advance in the economic ... [well-being] ... of the Indians. The difficult problem of inheritance is one of its results ..."

"The government [federal government, in concert with state and local governments] has stimulated the building of modern homes, bungalows, or even more pretentious dwellings, but most of the permanent houses that have replaced ... [traditional]... dwellings are small shacks with few rooms and with inadequate provision for ventilation ... From the standpoint of health, it is probably true that the temporary ... [traditional]... dwellings that were not ... air-tight ... and were frequently abandoned were more sanitary than the permanent homes that have replaced them."

"Water is ordinarily carried considerable distances from natural springs or streams, or occasionally from wells. In many sections the supply is inadequate, although in some jurisdictions, notably in the desert country of the southwest, the government has materially improved the situation, an activity that is appreciated by the Indians..."

Index